DATE DUE

AGING AND THE ECONOMY

AGING
and the Economy

Edited by Harold L. Orbach and Clark Tibbitts

Preface by Wilma Donahue

Michigan, University. Conference on Aging, 1962
...

Ann Arbor

THE UNIVERSITY OF MICHIGAN PRESS

PREFACE

The University of Michigan's 15th Annual Conference on Aging held in Ann Arbor, June 18–20, 1962, was devoted to the topic *Aging and the Economy*. This book incorporates the papers and addresses prepared for the conference along with the two major panel discussions which were held as part of the program.

Since 1948, the University has sought through these annual meetings to focus attention on basic aspects of the circumstances of older people in our society and the manner in which the phenomenon of aging has affected our society through changes in institutional and social structure. Commencing with the exploration of the needs and problems of the aging individual, the conferences over the years, in accordance with both the vastly increased size of our older population and the rising national consciousness of the social and economic impact of an aging population, have turned the center of their attention to the larger societal field within which the individual's needs and problems have found their expression and avenues of resolution.

The interest and activity of this larger social scene have been reflected during these years by the maturation of our national social security system, the rapid growth of private pensions, the greater recognition of the issues involved in an aging population by government at all levels, by business, labor, private and voluntary organizations, and by the introduction of the problems faced by our older citizens into the political arena as a major issue in electoral campaigns.

Within the last few years, as our economic sophistication has increased and as the new revolution occasioned by automation has erupted to change the whole economic pace, greater attention and concern have been given to the state of all aspects of our nation's economy—to our economic growth, our employment problems, our position in world trade and economic development. The economic implications of an aging population loom large in the total economic picture facing the nation. Automation leading to early obsolescence of skills, the trend toward earlier retirement while average life expectancy is being lengthened, the pressures of young people and middle-aged women seeking to enter the work force, and the growing demand for shorter work hours are all serving to heighten interest in the work status of older people and to aggravate concern in some quarters over the capacity of the economy to support millions of older persons in retirement. At the same time, the economic consequences of the diverse institutional structures that have arisen to deal with the question of economic security in old age have come to the fore of public concern in this last decade as they have assumed a permanent and significant role in the national economy.

For example, in 1948 only some 1.5 million or 13 per cent of a total of 11.5 million persons aged 65 and over were receiving retirement income through the Old-Age and Survivors Insurance program. The monthly rate of disbursements to them and to some 800 thousand survivors and dependents under age 65 at the end of the year was $45.9 million. By the end of 1962, OASI payments were being made to 12.5 million persons 65 and over representing 71 per cent of a total older population numbering about 17.4 million persons. The monthly rate of disbursements to them and to some 1.6 million persons between age 62 and 64 and some 4 million younger survivors and dependents was more than $1.1 billion. On a yearly basis OASI payments increased from $524 *million* to $13 *billion* in this 15-year period. At the same time, contributions from national income into the OASI fund rose from $1.7 billion to $12.1 billion per year. In this time period, also, private pension plans increased greatly in scope and coverage—witness alone the growth of reserve assets in these plans from less than $10 billion to over $55 billion by the end of 1961.

In the light of these developments, the 15th Annual Conference devoted itself to an examination of the interrelationship of aging and the economy. In order to place the relevant economic and social factors in perspective with one another so that we could arrive at a means for developing a rational basis for sound national policies the following objectives for the conference were outlined:

To achieve understanding of the relationship of national income and wealth to the capacity to support the expanding older population.

To examine the work roles of older people in the light of the rising population, national security, and trends in productivity.

To evaluate current methods and adequacy of supporting the retired population and to consider probable and desirable trends.

To study expenditure patterns and needs of older people in relation to varying circumstances and styles of life.

In fulfillment of these goals, the University invited the participation of a broad range of social scientists, business and labor leaders, and representatives of government and voluntary organizations. Since many of these subjects have hardly been previously examined, the contributions include a number of original researches which are presented as explorations into this important area.

Joining the University [1] in this undertaking through co-sponsorship and planning [2] of the conference were the United States Department of Commerce, the Department of Health, Education, and Welfare, the Department of Labor, the Housing and Home Finance Agency, and the Federal Council on Aging. Also serving as co-sponsors were seven Michigan state agencies—the departments of Health, Mental Health, Public Instruction, Social Welfare, and the Employment Security Commission, Office of Vocational Rehabilitation, and Commission on Aging—and the Michigan Society of Gerontology. Acting as participating agencies were some 194 national, state and local voluntary, fraternal, labor, business, and governmental organizations representing a full spectrum of interests and concerns with the field of aging and our national economy.

[1] The University groups joining the Division of Gerontology, Extension Service and Summer Session in co-sponsorship were the Department of Economics, Schools of Business Administration, Medicine, Public Health, and Social Work, and the Survey Research Center.

[2] The planning committee representing the co-sponsors consisted of the following persons: Solomon J. Axelrod, M.D., Floyd A. Bond, Hyman Bookbinder, Angus Campbell, Fedele F. Fauri, William Haber, Ronald W. Haughton, George Katona, Harry J. Kelley, William H. Kelly, M.D., Donald P. Kent, George Landsman, James N. Morgan, Charles E. Odell, George S. Odiorne, Jane Potts, Warren T. Roudebush, John T. Simmons, Russell A. Smith, Sidney Spector, Clark Tibbitts, Charles J. Tupper, M.D., and Seymour L. Wolfbein; the University organizers were Wilma Donahue, Woodrow W. Hunter, Helen K. Maurice, and Harold L. Orbach.

Credit is due the two editors of this volume not only for an editorial task well done, but for the searching out of the most cogent of the contemporary problems facing the economic future of old people. The editors have created an invaluable reference book. As director of The University of Michigan annual conferences on aging, I wish, also, to express appreciation for the unfailing support and encouragement which Dr. Everett Soop, director of Extension Service, has given to these conferences and the work of the Division of Gerontology.

Wilma Donahue

CONTENTS

LIST OF CONTRIBUTORS

DAVID S. BLANCHARD
Deputy Director, Washington Branch, International Labor Office, Washington, D.C.

JEAN A. CROCKETT
Associate Professor of Finance, Wharton School of Finance and Commerce, University of Pennsylvania, Philadelphia

JOHN M. CONVERY
Consultant, Industrial Relations Division, National Association of Manufacturers, New York

ALVIN DAVID
Assistant Director, Bureau of Old-Age and Survivors Insurance, Social Security Administration, U.S. Department of Health, Education, and Welfare, Baltimore

LENORE A. EPSTEIN
Assistant Director, Division of Program Research, Social Security Administration, U.S. Department of Health, Education, and Welfare, Washington, D.C.

JANET A. FISHER
Lecturer, Department of Economics, and Project Associate, Social Science Research Institute, The University of Wisconsin, Madison

MARGARET S. GORDON
Associate Director, Institute of Industrial Relations, The University of California, Berkeley

WILLIAM HABER
Chairman, Department of Economics, The University of Michigan

PAUL P. HARBRECHT, S.J.
Research Director, Study of Power, Ownership and Property in Modern Capitalism, The Twentieth Century Fund, Georgetown University Law Center, Washington, D.C.

A. J. JAFFE
Director, Manpower and Population Program, Bureau of Applied Social Research, Columbia University, New York

DONALD P. KENT
Director, Office of Aging, Welfare Administration, U.S. Department of Health, Education, and Welfare, Washington, D.C.

HELEN H. LAMALE
Chief, Branch of Consumption Studies, Division of Prices and Cost of Living, Bureau of Labor Statistics, U.S. Department of Labor, Washington, D.C.

CHARLES A. LININGER
Senior Study Director, Survey Research Center, The University of Michigan

DAVID LIVINGSTON
President, District 65, Retail, Wholesale and Department Store Union, AFL-CIO, New York

ORMOND E. LOOMIS
President, Senior Citizens Services, Inc., Clearwater, Florida

ROBERT J. MYERS

Chief Actuary, Social Security Administration, U.S. Department of Health, Education, and Welfare, Washington, D.C.

HAROLD L. ORBACH

Research Associate, Division of Gerontology, The University of Michigan

ETHEL SHANAS

Associate Professor, Department of Sociology, and Research Associate, Committee on Human Development, The University of Chicago

CHARLES R. SLIGH, JR.

Executive Vice President, National Association of Manufacturers, New York

HERBERT E. STRINER

Director of Program Development, The W. E. Upjohn Institute for Employment Research, Washington, D.C.

CLARK TIBBITTS

Deputy Director, Office of Aging, Welfare Administration, U.S. Department of Health, Education, and Welfare, Washington, D.C.

JACK WEINBERG, M.D.

Clinical Professor, University of Illinois School of Medicine and Attending Man, Psychosomatic and Psychiatric Hospital for Research and Training, Michael Reese Hospital, Chicago

SEYMOUR L. WOLFBEIN

Deputy Assistant Secretary of Labor, U.S. Department of Labor, Washington, D.C.

INTRODUCTION
Harold L. Orbach and Clark Tibbitts

It is little more than twenty-five years since the problem of economic security for the nation's older population was dramatically brought to the center of public concern as a consequence of the spectacular rise of the Townsend movement. Prior to this, while there had been growing concern over the need for economic security in old age, represented by the existence of a number of state old-age pension programs and various federal relief measures, and while a detailed study of the total problem had been undertaken by the President's newly created Committee on Economic Security, the older person's plight had not achieved the status of an urgent major issue in the public arena. Almost overnight, another dramatic issue requiring public action was recognized and made a part of the tremendous reforms in American society which were taking place in the shadow of the mass unemployment of the great depression.

Within the short period of the mid-1930's a fundamental change in approach was evolved and enacted into law, and a vast institutional framework for dealing with the economic problems of the aged was established. The Social Security Act of 1935 stands today as a landmark in our national policy. Yet the economic goals it advanced have yet to be fully realized. The advent of World War II and the period of economic prosperity which followed have resulted in basic modifications in its structure. What began as a form of social insurance for wage-workers was universalized to include almost the entire national labor force. The entire phenomenon of the aging of our population became a matter of new and heightened consciousness as the rapid increase in the number of older persons and the mounting problems accompanying the meeting of a new and distinct set of needs and demands aroused the attention of government, private and voluntary organizations, and the public.

The growth of retirement as a new pattern of social life accompanied a changing orientation in the American people. The character of this change was described by a group of social scientists in 1954:

The new watchword of the American people is *Security*. For a young and vigorous nation this seems surprising. Not that the interest in security is new; it has been one of man's concerns for ages. What is unusual is our preoccupation with the subject. This concern is interpreted in two ways. Some say that it reflects a softening of the rugged self-reliance of the past —an attitude of dependence that ill becomes the American tradition. Others see it as evidence of social maturity—the dawning of a new and better day from which the specter of want will at last be barred.

Whatever the explanation—and this will vary with one's social philosophy—it cannot be denied that the American people are determined to reduce the economic hazards of old age. Regardless of whether this determination springs from fear, humanitarianism, or enlightened self-interest, it is an established fact. Historically, our type of economy and our general cultural pattern have changed so greatly that hard work and thrift by themselves no longer seem to carry the assurance of yesteryear that they will provide security after retirement.[1]

This quest for security in the span of a quarter of a century has brought a new approach to and a new concern for the economic problems of old age. Old-Age and Survivors Insurance, Old-Age Assistance, and the more recent spectacular development of private pensions for industrial and other wage and salaried employees have created a new and continually expanding element in our economy and in the lives of the American citizen. The ramifications of aging upon the economy are far-reaching and complex. The approach to and solution of the problems raised involve fundamental questions of social and cultural values.

As we enter the 1960's, the heritage of the past generation's accomplishments looms large before us. The institutional accompaniments of past policy are becoming firmly embedded in our nation's economic and social structure. In the process of improving and expanding the character of economic security in old age we are confronted with the problem of taking stock of the accomplishments of past and current policies, viewing what they augur for the future and interpreting and understanding their impact on our nation's economy. We are confronted with the necessity of making important decisions as to the character and direction of future efforts in the light of present results and trends, and in order to make these decisions intelligently we must have a broader awareness of the factual and valuational elements which are involved.

For the issues are not simply technical ones of adopting suitable means to achieve certain clear-cut goals on the basis of readily agreed upon facts. And while there is a great need for objective knowledge and understanding of the factual workings and implications of the economic structures that have evolved to deal with security in old age, there is as great a need for clarity concerning the underlying values which we are assuming in the process of meeting these goals. Only then can we freely discuss the suitable means. The purpose of the 15th Annual Michigan Conference on Aging was to contribute toward this process of understanding the relations of aging and the economy in order that we may more intelligently and consciously proceed with the tasks ahead.

THE PRESENT VOLUME

The various papers in this volume have been designed to delineate the issues, both factual and valuational. In contrast with the past decade or two, when the major concern was on finding means of rapidly securing a minimal economic foundation for the widespread hazards of old age, the present decade is and must be concerned with developing a fuller, richer, and more adequate mode of existence for the nation's older people. The initial successes of past policies have led to their general acceptance, and, with this acceptance, a demand for something better. This demand comes during a period in our nation's history when we have experienced and have recognized the contribution of changing technology and automation to a generally rising level of national and personal income. We have witnessed a steady growth in individual purchasing power along with large increases in the production of goods and services in the economy. More technological advance, more production, higher incomes, greater purchasing power for the employed have been the pattern. But what of the retired living on fixed incomes set to earlier standards? How are they to share in the fruits of modern production?

ECONOMIC CAPACITY OF THE NATION

This raises the question of our national capacity to provide a better economic basis for the lives of our older people. What level of support can our economy provide, and how shall we go about organizing and securing it? In his paper, Dr. Herbert Striner gives a clear and unequivocal answer to this question. He calls for a greater measure of economic security and argues that we are well able to afford it within the framework of our public system of social security without in any way endangering the economic growth of our nation. He argues that we have been diverted from the original goals and aims of the Social Security Act and in allowing ourselves to be diverted, we have failed to provide the necessary level of economic support which we *can, have been able to,* and *should* provide for our older generation.

But what of the opportunities for work? Does economic security in old age have to rest on the basis of pensions for retired workers? What are the trends and prospects for the aging worker in the labor market? Don't we need the manpower of the older population in order to meet the challenges and demands of the times? Dr. A. J. Jaffe again provides a clear answer. We do not need the work of our older population to meet our present or anticipated production requirements, given the nature of our population structure and industrial capacity. To meet the needs adequately and carry forward a healthy economic growth and development, we *can* do without their manpower, although this does not mean or imply that we should.

In point of fact, we are continually beset with an economic problem of a different nature—the problem of assuring full employment for workers of *all ages* in the face of a productive capacity that constantly runs ahead of our ability to organize rationally the consumption of its products. Whatever economic loss the departure of older workers past retirement age would create would easily be taken up by the full employment of other workers at all ages now unable to secure regular employment. The issue here seems to be more one of social values and social consequences than economic requirements. Must men work in paid employment to maintain self-dignity and economic independence?

CHANGING EMPLOYMENT OPPORTUNITIES

Our economy has undergone and is continuously undergoing vast changes in its technology and in consequence in its occupational structure. Old occupations and jobs are being replaced by new ones in a continually changing process of growth and development. New industries arise and old ones disappear. New skills are required and old ones become redundant. What is the character of this occupational transformation? How has it and how will it affect the employment prospects of the aging worker? Dr. Margaret Gordon traces the recent history of these occupational changes and assays the future prospects. For the older worker of today they are not especially encouraging, although far from being entirely negative. And as Dr. Seymour Wolfbein points out, the problem of the aging worker is not unique. A similar problem faces vast numbers of the huge generation of youth now approaching working age. The older worker's situation is the extreme case of the general problem facing those most lacking in education, skills, and unique capabilities. The tempo of industrial and technological growth is predicated on changes in the character of production signaled by the advent of automation. The problem is that of learning new skills, those required in the contemporary economy. The need is for training, retraining, and continuing education and training to keep pace with our changing times. Dr. Wolfbein reports that the first steps in this direction seem promising, but greater effort is required to meet the challenges ahead.

Here we face a problem of utmost importance. Many of today's older workers cannot, because of lack of past educational and technical background, successfully compete for the better new jobs becoming available. For many the choice of continued work in place of retirement means the choice between socially and economically less satisfying and rewarding work and the economic prospects offered by retirement. Within the confines of retirement, what is the present economic status of the aged? How sufficient are today's retirement incomes? How well off are the older and retired people today? How can we determine the adequacy of retirement incomes? What other financial assets do the aged have which must be considered in order to determine this question? What are the future prospects for those approaching retirement age?

INCOME AND RESOURCES OF THE AGED

The contributions by Charles A. Lininger, Lenore A. Epstein, Janet A. Fisher, and Alvin M. David are addressed to the issues raised by these questions. From them we can discern a general measure of agreement concerning the present economic condition of the older population, one that has been consistently reinforced over the past decade by numerous and diverse scientific researches.[2]

By any current standards the aged are economically disadvantaged in contrast with younger segments of the population. That they are not more disadvantaged is primarily the consequence of the vast improvements that the various forms of income security instituted since the late 1930's have brought about, improvements which have had a generally healthy and prosperous economic climate as a background to their development.

The continuous progress along these lines is traced in Alvin M. David's paper which also emphasizes the basic role that the Social Security System has played. At the same time the great disparities in income level among different segments of the aged population are noted as presenting a problem which requires further effort in the future to ensure the provision of an adequate income for all older persons.

In Chapters V and VI the results of some recent studies and analyses of data on the income and general economic position of the aged are presented to help provide an adequate picture of the current situation. Unlike many previous contributions to this topic, these attempt to place the questions of income and financial position in a more meaningful context by detailed and specific consideration of the contrast between the position of distinct groups of older persons and their counterparts in the rest of the population.

Charles A. Lininger contrasts the population 65 and over with younger age groups in the life-cycle to illustrate the differences in economic position and the possible pattern of changes over the course of the adult years. Lenore A. Epstein shows in detail the income differences between comparable categories of persons 65 and over with those under 65 and analyzes the variations in income position of households headed by persons 65 and over as they relate to the employment of older persons and of other family members and with the economic status of family units with whom older persons reside.

The results of these analyses serve to underline the special situations which arise for large numbers of older persons who have distinct and specific problems of income security related to their past life history and present circumstances, such as older women whose husbands were not covered by social security or private pensions and who had no labor force participation of their own. At the same time, they seem to draw attention to the fact that while the prospects for many of tomorrow's older persons are much brighter as a consequence of social security, private pensions and a relatively long period of general prosperity, still many others are not so well endowed. The proportion of the labor force today covered by both social security and supplementary retirement pensions is around 40 per cent—but how many of the persons in the over-45 age group are so covered? And how many of the 40 per cent will actually secure a private pension of any magnitude?

With the continuous and relentless pressure toward a greater retirement of persons over 60, and the sharp differences in the income position of the older retired person as contrasted to the older working person, what sort of standards of adequacy can we determine for retirement income? Janet A. Fisher's study adds another dimension to this problem by focusing in part on the problem of distribution of income and financial assets within the older population. Her findings of greater income and asset inequality within the older population than within other age groups pointedly demonstrates the need for close examination of the oft-quoted statistics of the high average assets of the aged. When the top 20 per cent of the aged population possess 78 per cent of the group's total liquid assets and the bottom 30 per cent have none at all, of what meaning is the average liquid asset? When this factor is taken in conjunction with the income distribution figures, we are left with a total picture which still emphasizes a very large proportion of the older population with severely limited incomes and little or no assets which are of any value in providing for current living needs.

CONSUMPTION PATTERNS AND BUDGETARY NEEDS

This brings us to the question of determining the budgetary needs of older persons and examining their consumption patterns and habits. In her study of the consumption patterns of older people, Jean A. Crockett shows the existence of areas both of similarity and of difference in the consumer behavior of older and retired persons and that of younger age groups of comparable income and family size. It has been frequently argued that increased income for older and retired persons is almost directly translated into increased expenditures which are beneficial for the economy as a whole, and Professor Crockett's analysis tends to support this at least insofar as low-income groups are concerned. Differences in consumer behavior between older and younger age groups are seen as related to such factors as income, size of assets held, size of family, home ownership, and employment status. One general pattern seems to be that those with greater economic security in terms of income, assets, and employment are more likely to approximate younger age groups of similar status in general expenditure patterns, while those with lesser economic security are more likely to have expenditure patterns at variance with younger groups of similar status.

Questions of expenditures and consumption patterns lead directly to the problem of budgetary standards. The pioneer effort in providing a norm for adequate living standards for retired persons has been the Bureau of Labor Statistics' Retired Couples' Budget. The character and content of the budget is discussed by Helen H. Lamale who presents the rationale and reasoning behind this estimate of the needs of retired persons. The complex character of the budget and its guiding normative concept of "modest but adequate" standards lead her quite rightly to caution against its indiscriminate use in making broad generalizations in the light of changing conditions and diverse circumstances. The fact nevertheless remains that retirement incomes have by and large fallen far short of the standards set, despite their "modest but adequate" character. Whether one takes the budgets as minimal standards or "modest but adequate" ones, they represent an important tool for making comparisons and estimates of the needs and requirements of the retired. As such they should certainly be periodically revised to keep up-to-date and expanded to cover other segments of the retired population.

IMPLICATIONS OF ECONOMIC SECURITY PROGRAMS

The quest for economic security has taken a decidedly new turn since the beginning of the 1950's, with the rapid development and rise to prominence of private pension systems on a previously unprecedented scale. Representing an alternative to an expansion of the Social Security Act, they have arisen as a means of attaining an adequate source of retirement income when added to the basic foundation of social security benefits. In part they also represent a philosophy of sharing the costs of retirement between public and private means, their "private" character deriving from the sense of being funded and controlled outside of government channels although subject to government control and regulation. To the various forms of previously existing private corporate pensions, mainly for the benefit of supervisory and executive personnel, and the state and local government pension systems was added the industrial pension system covering vast numbers of wage earners in industry. The impetus for this huge expansion came through the legitimation by the courts of pension benefits as a subject for collective bargaining under the Taft-Hartley Act. Along with the union-negotiated plans came additional private systems and revision and expansion of public systems for government employees at all levels.

Thus, in the same decade during which social security itself came to maturity and assumed the role of the major source of income for retired persons and indeed for the entire 65 and over population, the private pension funds also became an important component of the income picture of a limited number of older persons approaching retirement. The 1950's might thus be termed the "age of security." While the number of persons currently receiving benefits from private plans (at the end of 1961 about 1½ million compared to over 12 million recipients of social security benefits) has not yet reached anywhere near the levels that the future will bring—when the presently covered labor force approaches retirement age—their very existence has had an immediate and profound impact on the nation's economy. The nature of this impact is the topic discussed by Father Paul P. Harbrecht. Describing the growth and magnitude of the private plans, he delves into their operation and legal status and raises serious questions about their future implications.

For the individuals covered by private pension plans, the prospects for economic security in retirement are far brighter than most would have ever dreamed a generation ago. Representatives of the business world point to them as an example of a nongovernment means of providing for retirement, and very often contrast their security with the supposedly less secure social security system, which is pictured as being subject to political tampering and even extinction with no legal guarantees of property rights to benefits. How accurate are such comparisons? Are private pension systems more secure and tamper-proof than public retirement under social insurance? What sort of legal and property rights do persons covered under private pensions have?

Father Harbrecht delineates important deficiencies in the private pension structure which mitigate their imputed efficacy. Private plans are for the most part noninsured. Their continued existence is subject to the fortunes and hazards of the companies providing them or the funds created to sustain them. If negotiated under union contracts, as the largest number of them in terms of covered workers are, their continuance is subject in addition to the vagaries of union-management relations. The end of a contract-period ends the legal obligation for continued contributions by employers. Where employee rights to a pension are vested and the plans are funded, the individual can at least look forward to the payment of accrued pension rights even when the plan is terminated, or he changes employment, or the company falls upon bad times, as Professor William Haber points out. This means, however, that the guarantee of future retirement income at a given level is not assured, but dependent on numerous other factors of which the general economic situation is most crucial. The recent example of the mine workers' pension fund reducing retirement pensions by one-fourth is a prime example of one type of problem involved for an industry in lesser economic health than others in the nation. There certainly is no more guarantee that a given company or industry will continue life indefinitely and thus be able to fulfill commitments than that the nation as a whole through government will do so. Finally, the nature of the individual's legal and property rights to a pension are far from being clearly settled in law. The individual does not have a clear property title in most cases, and he does not possess any economic power in consequence.

The implication of economic power is seen as the dramatic and far-reaching issue raised by the existence of pension funds. Who "owns" these funds? Who controls them, under what authority, and with what restrictions as to their use? As they continue to increase in size at a voluminous rate, will they represent a new form of economic power and imply a radical change in the structure of our economy and society? Has the process of developing economic security for old age within this structure of the private sector of the economy created an entirely new type of economic relationship which by-passes contemporary concepts of property much as social insurance did with respect to older concepts of private insurance? The answers given by Father Harbrecht are challenging, as are his views concerning the fashion in which these and other funds can be used more intelligently for social and economic purposes consonant with their nature. The commentaries on his remarks by William Haber, Robert J. Myers, and David S. Blanchard serve to remind us of the fact that these issues are not limited to our society alone but are important questions throughout the entire world. The provision of economic security for old age implies dedicated and regulated savings on a social level of a previously unheard of scale. The purposes to which these savings should be applied become a major question of social and economic policy.

SOCIAL POLICIES AND SOCIAL VALUES

The dramatic impact which aging has thus had and continues to have upon the economy in economic terms is matched by the corresponding impact on the political and social structure of society. Questions of economics are rapidly transformed into questions of social policy and underlying these are basic political and social values. What directions should the provision of economic security follow? What is the proper role of government—federal, state and local—in meeting the economic needs and formulating policies for action? What is the function of voluntary and professional organizations? Who should assume major responsibility? Why?

The answers to these questions generally seem to fall into two distinct categories of response. On the one hand, we have the view, ably represented by Charles R. Sligh, Jr., that the role of government, especially the federal government, should be minimized and give way to private means as much as possible. Two types of arguments are advanced in support of this view. First, the problems themselves are minimized and seen as less demanding than the solutions offered. Second, there is general concern over the economic and political implications of extensive government activity involving large expenditures of funds and the creation of governmental organizations to act directly upon problem areas. There is the general attitude that private means are inherently better and more socially conducive to proper solution of these types of problems.

The other approach is a more pragmatic and open one that welcomes and promotes contributions from all levels of government and private sources, but stresses the central role of the federal government in facilitating the meeting and dealing with questions that are of a national character transcending the means and abilities of local communities to cope with them. Drawing upon the experience of the past generation, it views the issues arising from an aging population as national in character and looks upon the past record of successful government actions in this field as proof of both need and value of similar action in newly emerging areas of public concern. That there has been general public approval of action in these areas has hardly been questioned. The issue today is determining exactly what additional forms of action are required. Dr. Donald P. Kent emphasizes this point of view in his review of the shaping contours of government policy for the future.

It is abundantly evident that the most challenging questions concerning aging and the economy now lie in the realm of social values.[3] They constitute not a question of economic ability but of social willingness to assume the responsibility for the provision of adequate levels of income for the aged during retirement. This point emerges forcefully in the panel discussion on "Social Attitudes Toward Retirement and Support of Older People." It is not a question of being able to afford such an assumption of responsibility, but of willingness to take it on. David Livingston has expressed the issue quite aptly in his comment: Are we willing to demand for others the level of economic security we ourselves expect to attain, and, if so, how can we best go about this, immediately, not tomorrow or the day after?

For Mr. Livingston and the members of his union, the answer is clear. They have made the choice and secured their objective through united action. And so have many other groups in our society. But the problem is that not all of us are so situated that we are able as a group, or are our employers alone able, to make such provision. The advantage seems to lie with those fortunate enough to be employed by large and economically well-situated employers, or in large and economically powerful unions that can develop suitable and persuasive means whereby employers can be helped to meet such conditions.

However, there is the question of the rest of us, those not now enjoying such retirement provisions nor likely to come under them in the future; and most directly those retiring today with little more than social security benefits to live on. We are witnessing the creation of a second-class category of retired persons. Persons who fall into this category for no reason of logic or justice, unless not being organized into a persuasive union or choosing the right employer falls into the spheres of logic or justice. Can we endure a situation in which over 60 per cent of the retiring cannot look forward to pension benefits in addition to social security, while 40 per cent can, and still justify large tax exemptions and special benefits for the lucky minority at the expense of the unlucky majority?

Are we willing to assume the burden necessary to make provisions for greater economic security? Dr. Ethel Shanas indicates that we are;

as she puts it, we're not that inhuman to deny older persons a decent standard of living. We may grumble a little about the cost, but we are agreed about the value and rightness of the basic process itself. If this is the case, then the next decade should witness a further revolution in our approach to the economic problems of the aged comparable to those of the 1930's and the 1950's, and the unfinished tasks implicit in the goals set 25 years ago will be attacked with vigor and determination.

NOTES TO INTRODUCTION

The opinions expressed hereinafter are those of the authors and do not necessarily represent those of the University of Michigan or the Department of Health, Education, and Welfare.

[1] Floyd Bond *et al, Our Needy Aged* (New York: Henry Holt, 1954), p. 333.

[2] Cf., among the more important: John J. Corson and John W. McConnell, *Economic Needs of Older People* (New York: The Twentieth Century Fund, 1956); Peter O. Steiner and Robert Dorfman, *The Economic Status of the Aged* (Berkeley: University of California Press, 1957); Ethel Shanas, *Financial Resources of the Aging*, Research Series No. 10 (New York: Health Information Foundation, 1959); Margaret S. Gordon, "Aging and Income Security," in Clark Tibbitts (ed.) *Handbook of Social Gerontology* (Chicago: University of Chicago Press, 1960), pp. 208–60.

[3] See the penetrating analysis of this question by Irving Rosow, "Old Age: One Moral Dilemma of an Affluent Society," *The Gerontologist*, 2 (December, 1962), 182–91.

I. The Economy and the Aged: Supporting the Older Population

CHAPTER 1

THE CAPACITY OF THE ECONOMY
TO SUPPORT OLDER PEOPLE

Herbert E. Striner

When I was first asked to address myself to the topic of whether or not our economy could support additional expenditures for the elderly, the immediate thought which entered my mind was to accept, and then indicate that the entire paper could be summed up in one word—*yes*. My next thought was to the effect that given our present and projected level of economic wealth, how could we afford not to meet the responsibility which a nation owes to those who have helped to provide the economic base of the past upon which we plan to build our future? However, though the economist is not new to this form of analysis concerning the funding of needed programs and social goals, I must admit to the fact that I personally have not specialized in the problems of the elderly.

Perhaps my situation is best illustrated by a joke I hope too many of you have not heard before. A one-hundred-year-old, after joining his ancestors, found himself confronted by Saint Peter at the entrance to Heaven. After soothing the recently deceased and assuring him of his qualifications to enter the promised land, Saint Peter asked if there was one wish which had always gone unfulfilled on earth. The new arrival immediately and vigorously answered in the affirmative. "Never," he said, "as a survivor of the Johnstown Flood, did I have a sufficiently large and attentive audience to hear of my harrowing experiences." Saint Peter nodded his head understandingly and indicated that he would be delighted to provide a large and celestial group which, he was certain, would lend an attentive and sympathetic ear. The conference was arranged and just as Saint Peter was about to introduce the eager speaker, Peter leaned over and whispered: "I'd better warn you, my dear old soul, Noah is in the Audience."

Quite seriously, however, if the proverbial visitor from Mars could eavesdrop on some of our debates over our national ability to finance programs for education, housing, defense and retirement, I am sure he would relegate the United States to the position of one of the more impoverished nations on this planet. We seem to learn little concerning our capacity to do great things from past experience. I recall that just prior to the Korean War a defense budget of $13 billion was viewed as an upper limit, beyond which an excessive burden would be imposed upon our economy. Within three years of that dire prediction, the defense budget had risen from $13 billion to approximately $44 billion. Moreover, this $44 billion for defense in 1954 was more than the 1950 sum of *all* federal expenditures! Our self-imposed limits vanished as we maturely faced our national responsibilities. Neither our economy nor our society collapsed or went bankrupt.

GOALS OF THE SOCIAL SECURITY ACT

I need not consume any time by delineating the growth rate of the elderly population of this country. The size of this population and the meagerness of its financial resources represents increasing grounds for a "bill of complaint" against the society of this nation which demands immediate consideration and action. This is so for several reasons. To begin with, I would submit that the intent of our social security legislation enacted during the mid-1930's has been either forgotten or radically diluted. The Cabinet Committee which reported to President Roosevelt in 1934 stated that a program of economic security "must have as its primary aim the assurance of an adequate income to each human being in childhood, youth, middle age or old age—in sickness or in health. It must provide safeguards against all of the hazards leading to destitution or dependency." The Social Security Program which these recommendations gave birth to shared this philosophy and the language of the original legislation reflects this high sense of purpose.

One need not look beyond the fact that at present, among the more than 17 million people in the 65 and over age group, about 53 per cent had annual incomes of less than $1000, 24 per cent had annual incomes of $1000 to $2000, 10 per cent had annual incomes of $2000 to $3000, and only about 13 per cent had annual incomes of $3000 or more. Of close to 7 million families with the head of the family 65 or over, half had incomes under $2900 per year, and 25 per cent had yearly family incomes of less than $1600.[1] This is the situation, roughly, at present, about a generation after the passage of our basic social security law. We point "with pride" to Old-Age and Survivors Insurance payments of about $12 billion to about 11 million elderly, at the same time that we have a national level of output of goods and services totaling around $550 billion. OASI payments account only for about 2 per cent of our Gross National Product. If we include all types of federal programs, our expenditures for the elderly account for about 3 per cent of our GNP.

It is a pity that these numbers cannot provide a better reflection of what it must mean to an elderly person who has led a productive and dignified life to be forced to face the last decade or so of existence in a younger society on the daily brink of financial disaster and poverty of pride. Surely a nation capable of a Marshall Plan, a continuing foreign-aid program of about $4 billion a year, farm subsidies of several billion a year, and a national security budget of close to $50 billion a year is also capable of providing more than a subsistence level of life for that segment of our population that has gone beyond the age limit where there is adequate economic demand for its services. The tragedy of this situation is that there are indeed numerous avenues by means of which adequate income can be provided for the elderly population without resort to ludicrous or truly unrealistic schemes.

HOW MUCH MONEY IS NEEDED?

To begin with, let us get some idea of the sums of money which we should envision as being needed. To move the average individual, aged 65 or over and living alone, or with younger relatives, from the present level of income—that is on the average of $1000 a year—to one which is held to be a desirable minimum would require about $1500. I arrive at this $1500 figure on the basis of the recent work done by the U.S. Bureau of Labor Statistics on estimated budgets of retired couples in 20 large cities and suburbs. This study, done in late 1959, revealed a range of $2641 to $3366, depending on the city, as being needed to provide "a healthful self-respecting manner of living which allows normal participation in community life." Since this range of annual incomes is for a couple, I have perhaps too arbitrarily reduced it by about $500 in order to arrive at a working figure for an individual retiree living alone. In the case of retired elderly couples, 65 and over, I would propose that the average yearly income be raised to $3500. This is about $100 higher than the upper end of the BLS study range, but I assume this "extra" could be well utilized. I know that historically we have tended to understate needs and budgets of the elderly.

Rather than undertake an analysis of projected future changes in GNP, changes in income distribution by age and sex, and changes in age distribution, I am going to look at the present situation and think out loud about how we could at present have been in a far different situation had we so chosen. I will attempt to indicate the ways and means which could have been utilized during the last several years in order to provide the indicated higher levels of income for the elderly.

HOW CAN THE NECESSARY FUNDS BE OBTAINED?

To begin with, I am going to assume that the needed funds which we must attain would come solely from federal programs. In Tables 1, 2, and 3 we see that a sum of approximately $13.4 billion is needed. There are several ways of obtaining this sum. Allow me to list those which I feel to be of interest:

1. Changes in the OASI tax.
2. Changes in the OASI taxable base.
3. Use of general government revenue instruments to augment OASI funds:
   A. Taxes
   B. Deficit financing
4. Increasing "Permitted Earnings" beyond the present levels.

CALCULATION OF AGGREGATE ANNUAL FUND NEEDED TO IMPROVE ECONOMIC CONDITIONS OF OLDER PERSONS TO MEET REQUIREMENTS OF AN ADEQUATE BUDGET

TABLE 1

Families with Head Age 65 Years and Older
(*Assume $3500 as estimated average budget; 6.2 million total families*)

No. of families (millions)	1960 income	Increment needed per family	Aggregate ($ millions)
.20	Under $ 500	$3250	$ 650
.37	$ 500– 999	2750	1,018
.64	1000– 1499	2250	1,440
.74	1500– 1999	1750	1,295
.72	2000– 2499	1250	900
.55	2500– 2999	750	413
.42	3000– 3499	250	105
Total Fund Needed			$5,821

TABLE 2

Unrelated Individuals Age 65 Years and Older
(*Assume $2500 as estimated average budget; 3.653 million persons*)

No. of persons (millions)	1960 Income	Increment needed per person	Aggregate ($ millions)
.50	Under $ 500	$2250	$1,125
1.24	$ 500– 999	1750	2,170
.78	1000– 1499	1250	975
.38	1500– 1999	750	285
.23	2000– 2499	250	58
Total Fund Needed			$4,613

TABLE 3

Elderly Persons Living with Younger Relatives
(*Approx. 2.3 million persons*)

Estimated at same level of budget need as unrelated "individuals" = 64%
of $4,613,000 = $2,952,320

Summation of Tables
Total of: Table 1 = $ 5,821 million
Table 2 =   4,613
Table 3 =   2,952
Total Aggregate Annual Fund Needed $13,386 million

Let me hasten to interject that these federal government techniques should not be taken to indicate my being averse to the philosophy that private pensions and personal family arrangements are not to figure as important asset sources as well. I look forward to the increasing role of private pension plans in future years. However, for two reasons this source is omitted in my talk today. First, I am here concerned with what the federal government could have done in recent years to change the OASI program in order to attain those glowing objectives of the mid-1930 social security legislation. Second, all available information indicates that meaningful private pension payments usually accrue to those elderly who are in the upper end of the income range. These are —and will probably continue to be for some time—in the great minority. Moreover, this is to be expected since there will be more lower and middle income people than higher income people, and payments into private pension plans with the resultant benefits will reflect this situation. Now, let us return to the "Ways and Means" section.

CHANGES IN THE OASI TAX

At the very outset, the OASI tax was held to be minimal, and the stated plan was to increase the tax gradually in order to build the OASI reserves held to be necessary. Even the present tax level of 3⅛ per cent from the employee and the 3⅛ per cent from the employer does not represent the original program as envisioned in the 1930's. Indeed, a 3 per cent tax level was planned as being achieved by 1948, with both the employee and employer contributing to a 6 per cent total payment. Now 14 years later, we have only achieved the 6¼ per cent total payment. Present plans are to go to a total tax of 6.9 per cent in 1968. This is far too low! If, for example, the OASI tax had been a total of 12 per cent during the last few years, based upon the $4800 taxable base, by 1960 we would have had an OASI Tax Income of $22 billion a year instead of roughly $11 billion. Thus, for the $13.4 billion I earlier estimated we need, we could have obtained far more by a more realistic tax rate.

I hasten to add that proof of the realism of this tax rate for a pension program does not rest on intuition or values which are mine alone. I would remind this audience that the bulk of the civilians who work for the federal government are covered by the Civil Service Retirement Act. This Act calls for an employee contribution of 6.5 per cent of the employee's *Base Pay*. This is, in turn, matched by the employing agency. The total tax is 13 per cent of the total *Base Pay*, not the first $4800. The success of this program should have educational value for groups and legislative bodies concerned with problems of the elderly. A 65-year-old retired civil servant is not noticeably different in his needs, values, or illnesses from his counterpart who has worked in the private sector of our economy. Let me now move to the second "Ways and Means" item.

CHANGES IN THE OASI TAXABLE BASE

As in the case of the tax rate, there is valid reason for moving the taxable base sharply upward. In fact, if we once take price and income changes into account, the present $4800 tax base covers much less real income than was the case in 1939, when the taxable base was $3000. As an economist I find it appalling that we so frequently fail to adjust base figures for price level changes. In the present situation, if we were to use the 1939 set of price relationships, when 94 per cent of all full-time employed males were earning below the 1939 maximum taxable base of $3000, we would automatically have to raise the taxable base to about $10,000.

If we estimate that in 1960 about 31 per cent of the male labor force had incomes between $5000 and $10,000, while 4.4 per cent of the female labor force had incomes in that range, a 12 per cent tax, shared by employer and employee would have yielded an OASI Tax Revenue of about $14 billion a year in the last several years. You will notice that this sum plus that resulting earlier from a 12 per cent tax on incomes up to $4800, would yield a total of $25 billion a year in new OASI income, or almost *twice* that which is needed for our target figure of $13.4 billion.

USE OF GENERAL GOVERNMENT REVENUE INSTRUMENTS TO AUGMENT OASI FUNDS

Under this third point, I would like to discuss the needs which may develop to provide funding for elderly programs which would lie outside of pension needs in the usual sense. I imagine that in the very near future a host of programs which involve geriatric research, housing adapted to special needs of the elderly, and special training and educational programs to upgrade skills and possibly to provide more part-time employment opportunities will call for more revenues than currently are available. There are three major sources for such additional needs.

The first source may be derived from growth in our Gross National Product. As our economy grows, additional tax funds are made available to our state and federal governments; these funds can be used for current programs and their expansion or for new programs. This does not rely on new forms of taxation, but merely from the growing revenues which governments obtain from the larger economic "pie."

This leads to the second source of tax revenues—that which can result from changes in our tax base. We are free at any time to change the rates of taxation, thereby generally affecting—upward or downward—the funds available from wages, salaries, and industry income. Though we tend to believe that taxes move only in an upward direction, in 1954 new federal tax legislation dropped the ratio of average personal income tax to average personal income from 14 per cent to the present level of approximately 10 per cent. During a period of prosperity and high levels of employment—should we have the political fortitude—even if we returned only to the 1953 tax base, sizable funds would be available from this tax source for many of the programs which large numbers of us feel are urgently needed.

The Question of Tax Burden   As a point of interest, I would like to say something about the tax burden in the United States in comparison with the personal income tax burden in other countries. For comparison, let us look at the United Kingdom. Assuming a married couple and two children in 1956 had an income of $5600, after allowable deductions but before personal exemptions, the marginal tax rate in the United States was 20 per cent. In the United Kingdom, the marginal rate was 41 per cent. If we assume the same family of four with an income of $11,200, after allowable deductions but before personal exemptions, the marginal tax rate was 26 per cent in the United States as compared with 65 per cent in the United Kingdom, for the same period. I have used the year 1956 not because of a favorable picture which it lends my argument, but because of easily available data for this paper. Colleagues of mine in the tax field assure me that much the same sort of situation exists presently. It would seem to me that we are a fat economy with a long, long way to go before additional taxes could impair our efficiency or effectiveness during a period of high levels of employment.

The third source of funds emanating from the government sector would be deficit financing. As we know, deficit financing consists of the government issuing bonds as a basis for the printing of currency. Each time the government creates a dollar in this manner, it undertakes a liability of a like amount. At the present time, the federal debt is approximately $297 billion. In 1948, the federal debt was approximately $252 billion. Great concern exists over this amount of increase of our federal debt. I am likewise concerned with the increase in federal debt, since we have to pay interest on it. Additionally, it may, depending on the amount of deficiteering undertaken and when it is undertaken, create an inflationary effect. However, all of these effects taken together must be viewed in the perspective of the rate of growth of the economy.

If one views federal deficits as the liabilities side of a balance sheet, then one must at the same time compare it with the items on the assets side of the balance sheet. To my mind, the Gross National Product of the United States represents the dynamic asset in our national balance sheet. Our history has been one, normally, where our GNP has grown far more rapidly than our national debt or our ability to pay for things has been growing with respect to our national buying on credit. When viewing this comparison, it is difficult to understand how anyone can envision the minuscule absolute increase in national debt as a factor capable of leading to national economic bankruptcy.

The ratio of United States debt to Gross National Product has descended very sharply from .98 in 1949, to .54 at the present time. Indeed, if we were to increase our national debt by $5 billion a year between 1962 and 1965, the ratio of United States debt to Gross National Product would decrease by one percentage point each year if our economy grew merely by the normal 3.5 per cent.

Deficit Financing and Balancing the Budget   In the event that we chose neither to finance needed programs for the elderly by new taxes or by allocating a portion of new tax income resulting from economic growth, then I would not hesitate to run a deficit. On this matter of deficit financing, I believe that a few additional words of clarification are badly needed. The terms, definitions, and concepts of our national budgeting procedures determine to a great degree whether we really have a deficit or not. We are governed by our own "rules of the game," and among modern governments of the present-day world, our rules of the game are the most conservative and border upon being economically debilitating. It is by no accident that ours is an uphill struggle in justifying necessary federal expenditures which involve so-called deficits.

In all modern countries except ours, the budgeted activities of the government are divided between current expenditures and capital expenditures. The latter would include expenditures for such programs as highways, housing, urban renewal, or other similar items where the returns to the society benefit it for a period of a year or longer. Current expenditures are for such items as salaries of employees of most agencies, pay for the armed forces, raw materials purchases, maintenance of facilities, and printing and publishing. A balanced budget for the average European nation consists of yearly government revenues which are at least equal to just the current expenditures. However, in our country a balanced budget is one where the yearly revenues must at least equal *all* government expenditures, current as well as capital.

Now what does this mean? The present estimated capital budget of the United States is between $4 billion and $20 billion a year, depending upon whether such expenditures as those for education, research, and development are included in this estimate. Most fiscal economists calculate that if we are to persist in using our present archaic budgeting procedures, we should be running a current deficit of about 8 to 10 billion in order to provide the needed stimulus to break out of a currently sluggish economy. To make matters even worse, current budget practice also carries, as an expenditure, several billion dollars worth of loans which will be repaid, but omits the multibillion dollar operations of the Social Security and Highway Trust Funds, which could be viewed as current income.

As a result, then, the present damper on vital federal programs (payments for "elderly programs" included), which is turned on whenever we approach a deficit budget, is not only ridiculous and unnecessary, but also operates as a governor on economic growth. As acknowledged in the Employment Act of 1946, an avowed policy of the federal government is to provide for sustained levels of high employment, by various means, including expenditures calculated to increase the demand for goods and services. I would suggest that the elderly group is one which deserves such an expenditure program at least as much as numerous other groups currently entitled to subsidies and favorable tax treatment. Running a deficit—by present definition—is not, I think I have shown, a valid reason for holding back on such a program.

In the light of present indications that 1963 may see a general reduction in taxes in order to stimulate an economy which seems to rest on an uneasy balance between recovery and recession, we must either envision a large deficit or a change in our budgeting practices. I would be in favor of the latter so that we could plan more sensibly for long-term capital programs as contrasted with expenditures for current operations. In this instance, I think we could well learn from the experience of other governments whose present record for economic growth well exceeds the performance of our own. I might also say that the capital budget procedure I have briefly described is the accepted technique of business firms throughout the world. Perhaps if more of the critics of this form of budgeting, who attack its proponents as "academicians who have never met a payroll," applied some of their very own business accounting methods to government budgeting we would impose fewer meaningless but costly restraints on our economy and society.

INCREASING "PERMITTED EARNINGS" BEYOND THE PRESENT LEVELS

With respect to the final item I suggested earlier, we might view as an additional source of funds for the elderly income which can be earned above and beyond OASI payments. I feel quite strongly that the present level is too low. The OASI principle should not seek to punish individual incentive, but rather to provide a basis for leading a constructive life. However, while I feel that this level should be raised, perhaps to $2500 in addition to the OASI payment, I must admit that present and projected forces in our economy do not bode well for many elderly gaining much from employment. All of the forces seem to run counter to growing employment opportunities for those in their sixties and beyond. All the more need for realistic and, I might add, humane levels of retirement benefits.

CONCLUSIONS

In conclusion, I would like to add that the changes I have suggested in the OASI tax and the level of taxable income are quite reasonable and should be undertaken in one jump. Our incomes and economy can sustain it, especially since the resulting increase in payments will incur no withdrawals of income, since the nature of the need for funds by the elderly insures that the increased OASI payments will be spent on consumption needs rather than take the form of savings by the elderly. Hence, there will be no serious threat of deflation.

In addition to these changes, I also suggest that automatic relationships be established between retirement payment levels and changes in the price level. Suggested automatic devices for increasing bond yields in order to offset price inflation is certainly of value to private pension plan investment portfolios. However, the great majority of the elderly are not recipients of large or even meaningful sums from such plans. This may change in the future, of course, but probably only in the distant future, and there should and must be an overwhelming sense of urgency with respect to the here and now.

The automaticity which I have suggested regarding the tieing of retirement benefits to changes in price levels is complicated but necessary. No doubt Congress will oppose losing its prerogative to consult, discuss, and ponder each change in benefits, but this loss is as nothing compared to the deprivation of millions of elderly who have frequently had to watch slim savings slip away and higher prices erode purchasing power. High priorities accorded to defense budgets and election-year antics, of small numbers assuredly, often prevent an otherwise willing Congress from acting speedily enough. In our progressive income tax system we have quite properly built in an automatic mechanism which changes our tax rate as our incomes go up or down. The same concept of equity should govern the relationship of pension payments to prices we must pay, especially during those later years when overtime-work or part-time employment is no longer a realistic opportunity.

As I indicated at the outset of this brief talk, this field is new to me, but now that I have a nodding acquaintance with the problem, the sense of the tragic is compelling. Literally millions who have little recourse to new, challenging, and economically gainful work must depend in a nation of historically unequaled wealth on a relative handful of special pleaders and legislators to provide in reality what is already provided for in legislation and philosophy of government. The general welfare clause of the Constitution preceded by close to 150 years the Social Security Program of the 1930's; however, there are still insecure and nearly destitute millions of elderly. I think that those who could act on this might bear in mind the advice of Marcus Aurelius in his *Meditations:* "Do not act as if thou wert going to live ten thousand years. Death hangs over thee. While thou livest, while it is in thy power, be good."

NOTES

[1] U.S. Bureau of the Census, "Income of Families and Persons in the United States: 1960," *Current Population Reports: Consumer Income,* Series P-60, No. 37 (January 17, 1962).

II: The Economy and the Aged:
Work and Employment Opportunities

CHAPTER 2

POPULATION, NEEDS, PRODUCTION, AND OLDER MANPOWER REQUIREMENTS

A. J. Jaffe

The subject I have been asked to discuss is "Population, Needs, Production, and Older Manpower Requirements." But before we can consider any of these problems, we must settle on the approximate meaning of some of the terms involved. In the correspondence between the conference organizers and myself, such terms were used as: "capacity of economy to support," "legitimate claims," "needs," "older manpower requirements," "population structure," and "population estimates." We have all used these terms, but we all have our own definitions of what they mean, and they can mean many things. I want to emphasize this very strongly: we cannot fruitfully discuss these things, still less decide what ought to be done about them, until we reach some common understanding about what they are.

For most of the really important problems, either the data are lacking, or else they are so fragmentary that only the most tentative and arduous conclusions can be drawn from them. In any case, even if we had the best conceivable data, we could not assume that they would automatically lead to any program of action. Inferences supposedly drawn from statistics, and policies based on statistics, are determined largely by the values and attitudes of our society and those who govern it, and not by the statistics *per se*.

Suppose that we lived in a society which honored its older population and insisted on absolute filial devotion, according to the ideals of some higher Confucianism. Then there would be no need for a conference on this subject. We should all be taking care of our parents and elders without asking any questions about their "needs" or our ability to supply them. As Confucius said, "When a youth is at home let him be filial, when abroad respectful to his elders . . ." (*Analects I, Chapter VI*). But, as it happens, we differ among ourselves about how we ought to feel toward older people, and it may be fruitful to discuss this matter so that we can try to agree on some philosophy and some appropriate action.

SOME BASIC FACTS

Let us begin by examining the available statistics on population and labor force growth for the period 1950 to 1980. Between 1950 and 1962 the United States population grew by 24 per cent—from 150 to 186 millions. Between 1962 and 1970 it will grow between 12 and 15 per cent, and from 1970 to 1980, between 17 and 21 per cent. For the entire period, from 1962 to 1980, the population is expected to grow between 32 and 40 per cent (Table 1). These estimates prepared by the U.S. Census Bureau are the best ones available.

What is the available supply of labor which such population numbers can provide? In order to try to answer this question we must make a number of assumptions regarding the length of the work week, the number of weeks worked per year, and the proportions of each age-sex group which is—or will be—in the labor force. If we want to estimate how much of this labor will be utilized, then we must also assume certain employment and unemployment conditions. I choose to abide by the original meaning of the term "labor force," namely the number of persons who are available for work at a given time and under the employment conditions existing at that time.

Accordingly, then, I am assuming that the supply of labor which will be available in 1970 and 1980 (given the expected total population of the United States) is to be calculated by assuming that the same proportions of each age and sex group in the labor force in April 1962 will continue unchanged to 1970 and 1980. I am assuming further that the length of the work week will remain unchanged and, for the sake of simplicity, that all persons are employed 52 weeks per year. Obviously, under these conditions the total supply of labor will not be utilized by the economy, but I am not at this moment concerned with the demand side; I simply wish to estimate the total available supply. Given these assumptions we see that in 1962 there are about 74 millions of persons available for work; this will increase to 84 millions in 1970 and 99 millions in 1980. The growth in the labor supply is projected to be about 34 per cent between 1962 and 1980. This is about the same as the projected growth of the total population, which we noted will be between about 32 and 40 per cent.

At this point it is necessary to remind ourselves that the purpose of

TABLE 1

Labor Productivity, Labor Supply, and Total Population in the United
States, 1950 to 1980

Year	Productivity [1] (*1962 = 1.00*)	Number in labor force [2] (*millions*)		Available labor supply [3] (*millions*)		Total population [4] (*millions*)	
		Total	*Age 14–64*	*Total*	*Age 14–64*	*II*	*III*
1950	.704	59.6	56.8	42.0	39.8	150.2	150.2
1962	1.000	73.7	70.4	73.7	70.4	185.8	185.8
1970	1.268	84.2	80.4	106.8	101.9	214.2	208.9
1980	1.704	98.8	94.1	168.3	160.3	260.0	245.4
% Change							
1950–62	42	24	24	75	77	24	24
1962–70	27	14	14	45	45	15	12
1970–80	34	17	17	58	57	21	17
1962–80	70	34	34	128	128	40	32

[1] Productivity per man hour in private economy. Basic data from U.S. Bureau of Labor Statistics, *Trends in Output per Man-Hour in the Private Economy, 1909–1958,* BLS Bulletin 1249 (Washington, D.C.: U.S. Government Printing Office, 1959). Indices after 1958 calculated on basis of 3 per cent growth per year.

[2] Data for 1950 from U.S. Bureau of the Census, *1950 Population Census Report P-C1,* Detailed Characteristics, Table 120; for 1962 from U.S. Bureau of Labor Statistics, "Monthly Report on the Labor Force, April, 1962," *Employment and Earnings,* 8 (May 1962); 1970 estimated by applying April 1962 age-sex specific labor force participation rates to age and sex composition as estimated for 1970 in U.S. Bureau of the Census, "Interim Revised Projections of the Population of the United States, by Age and Sex: 1965 and 1970," *Current Population Reports: Population Estimates,* Series P-25, No. 241 (January 17, 1962); 1980 estimated by applying same rates to estimated 1980 population, U.S. Bureau of the Census, "Illustrative Projections of the Population of the United States, by Age and Sex: 1960 to 1980," *Current Population Reports: Population Estimates,* Series P-25, No. 187 (November 10, 1958). (Series II projections were used.)

[3] Obtained by multiplying number in labor force by productivity index.

[4] 1950 and 1962 are Census counts or Census estimates (P-25, No. 241). For 1970 and 1980 two projections are given, series II and series III; see 2 for sources.

labor is to produce goods and services. In this connection the technology available to the worker is of the utmost importance in determining the total amount of goods and services which he will produce. Accordingly, let us examine trends in labor productivity. The increase in productivity per man hour in the private nonfarm economy averaged about 2 per cent per year increase between 1919 and 1949 and 2.8 per cent per year between 1949 and 1958. In the farm sector productivity increased by an estimated 1 to 2 per cent per year until 1949, and then increased at an annual rate of 6.4 per cent between 1949 and 1958 (Table 1). In summary, then, it would appear to be reasonable to assume an average increase for the total economy of some 3 per cent per year in the future.

Given such a rate of productivity increase, then one man hour of labor in 1970 is equal to 1.27 man hours in 1962. In 1980 one man hour of labor will be the equivalent of 1.70 man hours of labor in 1962.

It follows, then, that if we are to estimate the supply of labor available in the future we must take into account these productivity increases. When this is done we find that the estimated 84 millions of persons in the labor force in 1970 are the equivalent of about 107 million "1962 persons." And the projected 99 million in the 1980 labor force are the equivalent of 168 million "1962 persons." Since the total amount of goods and services which can be produced is a function of both the numbers of workers and their productivity, then the total amount of goods and services can increase from the amount produced by 74 millions of workers in 1962 (or would have been produced if all had worked) to the amount which 107 millions could produce in 1970, and to the amount which 168 millions could produce in 1980. In short, total production could increase by 45 per cent between 1962 and 1970, and by 128 per cent between 1962 and 1980.

If all this labor supply were at work how much would per capita product increase? We can estimate that the amount of goods and services available per person would increase by 26 per cent between 1962 and 1970, and by 63 per cent between 1962 and 1980. In terms of average annual per capita rates these percentages signify an average increase of about 2.8 per cent per year between 1962 and 1980. For comparison we may note that per capita real product in the United States (in 1954 dollars) increased by only about 1.5 per cent per year between 1949 and 1959.[1]

In summary, then, it would appear that if the supply of labor were

to remain a constant proportion of the population (i.e., the ag
participation rates were to remain unchanged), and all of this su
were to be utilized to the same extent as in April 1962 (i.e., in te
of hours per week and weeks per year), per capita real product co
increase about twice as rapidly as it has in the last decade, 2.8 per
cent versus 1.5 per cent.[2]

IS THE WORK OF OLDER PERSONS "NEEDED?"

In light of these observations we may ask whether the work of older
persons, say those aged 65 and over, is "needed." My answer is "no"
with the following explanation. If all persons aged 65 and over were
to withdraw from the labor force immediately, per capita production
of goods and services could still increase by a little under 3 per cent
per year—perhaps about 2.5 per cent—between 1962 and 1980. Actually, considering the volume of unemployment and involuntary part-
time work in 1962, per capita output could increase by some 3 per
cent per year even without those aged 65 and over, if all the younger
persons were fully employed.

At this point we may ask: how rapidly can we expect per capita
product to increase? I suspect that most people will agree that the observed rate of 1.5 per cent between 1949 and 1959 was too low. How
high should it be? I suspect that double that rate—3 per cent—is the
most any economy ever attains over a number of decades, except under
very unusual conditions. Historically, during the period 1929 to 1959
inclusive, the United States economy grew at a rate of about 2.6 per
cent per capita annually.[3] This rate can be achieved in the future on
the basis of the labors of those aged 14 to 64, plus 3 per cent increase
annually in labor productivity. Of course, if very unusual conditions
should arise, as during the early 1940's for example, the labor supply
of older persons may be needed. But we are not looking forward to
such unusual conditions.

The labor force participation rates of persons aged 65 and over has
decreased considerably among men, and increased but slightly—if at
all—among women. In 1890 some two-thirds of men in this age group
were in the working force, in 1950 some 46 per cent, and in 1962 only
31 per cent were in the labor force. Among these older women about
10 per cent were in the labor force in 1950 and 1960. These changes
are a result of several conditions, including the availability of pensions,
attractiveness of retirement for some persons, and the inability to ob-

tain employment since the economy did not really "need" their labors. I see no reasons for predicting that increased proportions of older persons will work in future years.

SHOULD THESE OLDER PEOPLE WORK FOR MONEY?

We can speculate on the answer to this question as follows:

1) Some older people have skills "needed" or desired by the economy, such as those of Pablo Casals. These are mainly certain professional and craft groups and constitute but a small proportion of the persons aged 65 and over. Persons with such rare skills have employment now and can continue to have employment as long as they are capable of working and wish to do so.

2) The great majority of the older workers have no special skills "needed" by or "useful" to the economy. These people can have work only as special arrangements are made, such as spreading the work through part-time jobs, or union contracts which keep older workers on the job, or reducing the work week for everyone.

3) Some older persons who wish to work can be used in certain service occupations which are perhaps understaffed at this time. One such occupation, in short supply according to some young parents, is baby-sitting.

4) The main argument advanced by many persons is that these older people need the money which only a job can provide. It is true, according to Census figures, that families in which the head is aged 65 and over, have lower median incomes than do families with younger heads. In 1960 median income for these older family heads was $2897 as compared with $5907 for family heads under age 65. Whether this means poverty or not, I do not know.[4]

It should be noted that the average number of persons per family in which the head was aged 65 and over was 2.45; this provides income of almost $1200 per person. Among families in the United States in which the head was under 65 there was an average of 3.9 persons per family, or a little more than $1500 per person income.

Among unrelated individuals (i.e., persons living alone) median income was $1053 for those aged 65 and over, as compared with $2571 for persons under age 65. For men, who comprised 27.5 per cent of these unrelated individuals 65 and over the figure was $1313 compared to $3371 for men under 65. For women, 72.5 per cent of unrelated individuals 65 and over, median income was $960 compared to $2152 for women under 65.*

These median values distort the picture since they do not show how many, or what proportion, have incomes below some socially acceptable minimum. What that socially acceptable minimum income is I do not know. I simply wish to emphasize that there are too many poor people among all age groups. The older population may be somewhat poorer than the younger; the older population may have more than its "share" of the very poor, but all of the older population is not poverty stricken and all of the younger population is not wealthy. I am not as optimistic about the economic condition of the older population as Davis [5] is, but neither am I as pessimistic as are some others.

WHERE OLDER WORKERS MAY BE NEEDED

Our society carries on—or tries to carry on—a number of activities on a voluntary rather than a paid basis. We talk constantly of the need for people to serve as recreation workers or "pals to juvenile gang members," as Red Cross workers in hospitals, and in other nonprofit-making but presumably humanitarian, educational, or scientific enterprises. In very many instances our society does not look upon these activities as jobs to be paid for in cash; yet our society ascribes high moral value to such work. An outstanding example is that of Dr. Albert Schweitzer, who is lauded but not exactly paid for his great humanitarian work.

Presumably, there is no limit to the amount of such work which could be carried out if people were willing to do it. To the extent that older people may have none or grossly insufficient income, they are forced to ask pay for services performed. However, to the extent that their monetary needs are taken care of, to that extent they can be used for carrying on many of these socially desirable but unpaid functions.

SUMMARY AND IMPLICATIONS

As I understand the term "need," the United States economy does not "need" the labors of older persons, say those aged 65 and over,[6] unless very unusual conditions should arise. The amount of labor offered by those under age 65, if fully utilized, together with an annual

* [Ed. Note: The details of the income distribution can be found in Table 2 of Chapter 6.]

ase of 3 per cent in productivity per worker per hour could pro-
an average annual increase in per capita goods and services of
close to 3 per cent per year. I do not think that our economy will grow
any more rapidly than this; at least it has not done so in the past.

If productivity should increase to over 3 per cent per worker per
hour, as is not at all impossible, even fewer workers would be required
in order to provide a per capita annual increase in goods and services
of 3 per cent. If labor productivity were to increase to 4 per cent, per
capita product could increase about 3.5 per cent per year, on the basis
of the labor supplied by those under age 65. I believe that we can expect increases in worker productivity in the future.

Perhaps we should remind ourselves that one of the characteristics
which differentiates a developed and industrialized society such as ours
from the underdeveloped ones, which we are trying to aid via the
Agency for International Development, is the vastly greater production capacity of our society. In many underdeveloped societies everyone has to work, since the output per worker is so small that nonwork-
ers cannot be fed. In our society the output per worker is so vast that
we are plagued by consumption rather than production problems. We
can produce more food than the Americans can eat, and we can produce more automobiles than there are people to drive them. Clearly
there is no sense in arguing that we must all work or we will starve, as
is the case in primitive societies.

In short, I see no value in work only for the sake of work. Work is
valuable only insofar as it produces goods and services which people
wish to consume, or insofar as it provides psychological satisfactions
to the workers.

Now I suspect that only a few people get great psychological satisfaction from their work; presumably artists do, some craftsmen probably do, and who else? Therefore, I submit that if older people must
have their psychological satisfactions they should obtain them from
sources other than a "job" as we understand the term.

The implication which follows from the preceding is that older people should receive pensions permitting them to live a more satisfactory
life than many of them are now able to live. Many older persons receive such small pensions that a good Confucian must hang his head
in shame. Others who are perhaps better off financially, cannot pay
the extraordinary medical expenses frequently incurred through fail-
ing health in later life. In short, I recommend that we get our economy

going at top speed and produce such a vastly increased output of goods and services with the labor supply offered by those under age 65, so that we can support properly the older population. Remember, the OASI is an insurance program to which we are all paying premiums, and the more rapidly the economy grows the more dividends will result from these premiums.

NOTES

[1] Data on real output per capita in 1954 dollars from U.S. Department of Labor, *The American Workers' Fact Book, 1960* (Washington, D.C.: U.S. Government Printing Office, 1960), p. 85. The average annual rate of growth calculated as b+ mean of Y.

[2] C. D. Stewart estimated gross national product per capita on the assumption of a 37 hour week (and separately on a 30 hour week) and about 3 per cent increase in labor productivity per year. On the basis of a 37 hour week (which is about 3 hours fewer than the amount worked in 1962) gross national product per capita would increase by 2.3 per cent per year between 1960 and 1970; on the basis of a 30 hour week it would increase 1.1 per cent during this decade. Apparently, even with a 25 per cent reduction in the length of the work week the United States economy could still increase per capita goods and services. Papers and Proceedings of the 68th Annual Meeting of the American Economic Association, "Economic Growth VII: The Shortening Work Week as a Component of Economic Growth. The Alternatives," *American Economic Review*, XLVI (May, 1956), 211–17.

[3] See footnote 1 for source of data and method of computation.

[4] These income statistics from U.S. Bureau of the Census, "Income of Families and Persons in the United States: 1960," *Current Population Reports: Consumer Income*, Series P-60, No. 37 (January 17, 1962). For other information on the economic position of older persons see the excellent study by Ethel Shanas, *Meeting Medical Costs Among the Aging*, Research Series 17 (New York: Health Information Foundation, 1960). [Ed. Note: On this point, cf. Chapter 6 by Lenore Epstein which discusses this disparity and analyzes the differences in income in greater detail.]

[5] Joseph S. Davis, "The Plight of the Aged?" (notes for talk to the Fellowship Forum, Palo Alto, February 27, 1962, mimeo.). On the other hand, George Meany wrote, "We must face the fact that poverty is the great affliction of the aging." U.S. Department of Health, Education and Welfare, *Aging With a Future*, Reports and Guidelines from the White House Conference on Aging (Washington, D.C.: U.S. Government Printing Office, 1961), p. 50.

[6] The median age of these people in 1960, was 72.1 years.

CHAPTER 3

PROJECTING EMPLOYMENT OPPORTUNITIES FOR MIDDLE-AGED AND OLDER WORKERS

Margaret S. Gordon

Throughout the 1950's, there was a great deal of concern in the United States about the employment problems of older workers. Older persons were looked upon as a disadvantaged group in the labor force, along with minority groups and, at least in certain types of work, women. There were numerous studies of the problem of age discrimination in hiring, and a number of states enacted legislation aimed at combatting such discrimination.

As we move into the 1960's, concern over the employment problems of older persons continues, but the upward drift in the unemployment rate since about 1953, along with the sharp rise in the number of young persons entering the labor force, has given rise to a broader concern over the general problem of unemployment, including its impact on youth.

In this paper, I shall be concerned primarily with the manner in which labor market changes are affecting the employment opportunities of middle-aged and older workers, with particular emphasis on the extent to which recent developments may suggest the need for modification of predictions that might have been generally accepted five or ten years ago. I shall have very little to say about the problem of age discrimination in hiring, since most of the useful things that can be said on that subject have long since been said. And, although my topic is "projecting employment opportunities of middle-aged and older workers," I shall not engage primarily in forecasting. Forecasting is a hazardous business and, to the extent that it is at all successful, it depends on a thorough understanding of past changes, and particularly on an ability to distinguish between long-term trends and short-term fluctuations.

Since the most important factors influencing the employment opportunities of older workers in recent years have been the upward drift

in the unemployment rate and the changes in the occupational structure that have been associated with automation and other technological and structural changes, we need to consider these background
factors first.

UNEMPLOYMENT RATES AND OCCUPATIONAL CHANGES

By now, most Americans are familiar with the general dimensions
of the unemployment problem that has been facing us in recent years.
During the 1950's and early 1960's, the unemployment rate has displayed a disturbing upward trend, although it has fluctuated over the
course of the business cycle. In each of the completed business upswings during this period, the average unemployment rate has been
somewhat higher than in the preceding upswing—3.8 per cent in
1949–53, 4.4 per cent in 1954–57, and 5.8 per cent in 1958–60 (on
a seasonally adjusted basis). In recessions, as well, the unemployment
rate has displayed an upward trend—averaging 4.7 per cent in
1953–54, 5.6 per cent in 1957–58, and 6.2 per cent in 1960–61.[1]
Currently, the unemployment rate is 5.5 per cent, and, unless the rate
of economic expansion can be stepped up appreciably, it may not fall
much below this level during the present upswing.

There has been considerable debate among economists as to whether
the unemployment problem is primarily aggregative (reflecting a general slowing down in the rate of growth of the economy because of a
deficiency of aggregate demand) or structural (reflecting the impact
of technological and structural changes that are creating unusually
severe adjustment problems). Although my own view is that the
problem is predominantly aggregative, I am quite prepared to con-
cede that, even if the economy were expanding at a more rapid rate,
the types of occupational shifts required as a result of automation and
other related developments might be difficult to achieve even with the
greatly increased emphasis on retraining which we are now beginning
to see. This is because, on the whole, the most rapidly expanding
types of employment have been those requiring professional or technical training, and displaced blue-collar workers lack the necessary
educational background for these types of employment.

Recent occupational changes have largely been consistent with
long-run trends, but with certain exceptions. During the first half of
this century, occupations requiring a substantial amount of education,
skill, or specialized training gained ground, in general, at the expense

of farming and unskilled occupations (see Table 1). However, two occupation groups that did not require a great deal of skill—the operatives or semi-skilled group and service workers (other than private household)—also represented an increasing proportion of the total labor force. But between 1950 and 1960, although for the most part these same general trends continued, the proportion of operatives declined somewhat as a percentage of the labor force. Meanwhile,

TABLE 1

Persons in the Economically Active Civilian Population, by Major Occupation Group, United States, Selected Years, 1900 to 1960

Major occupation group	1900	1920	1940	1950	1960
Both sexes					
Total	100.0	100.0	100.0	100.0	100.0
White-collar workers	17.6	24.9	31.1	36.6	42.2
Professional, technical, and kindred workers	4.3	5.4	7.5	8.6	11.4
Managers, officials, and proprietors, exc. farm	5.8	6.6	7.3	8.7	8.5
Clerical and kindred workers	3.0	8.0	9.6	12.3	15.0
Sales workers	4.5	4.9	6.7	7.0	7.4
Manual and service workers	44.9	48.1	51.5	51.6	51.5
Craftsmen, foremen, and kindred workers	10.5	13.0	12.0	14.1	14.3
Operatives and kindred workers	12.8	15.6	18.4	20.4	19.9
Private household workers	5.4	3.3	4.7	2.6	2.8
Service workers, exc. private household	3.6	4.5	7.1	7.9	9.0
Laborers, exc. farm and mine	12.5	11.6	9.4	6.6	5.5
Farm workers	37.5	27.0	17.4	11.8	6.3
Farmers and farm managers	19.9	15.3	10.4	7.4	3.9
Farm laborers and foremen	17.7	11.7	7.0	4.4	2.4

SOURCES: U.S. Bureau of the Census, *Occupational Trends in the United States, 1900–1950* (Washington, D.C.: The Bureau, 1958), p. 7; and U.S. Bureau of the Census, *Tables Relating to the Labor Force,* prepared for a session on unemployment at the Conference of Business Economists, May 10, 1962 (Washington, D.C.: The Bureau, 1962).

the proportion of professional and technical workers increased at an accelerated rate.

A thorough analysis of occupational changes in the 1950's cannot be made until detailed data from the 1960 Census are available, but in recent years the Department of Labor has been publishing data from the Monthly Labor Force Survey on 31 occupational classes, thus making possible certain additional observations.

Between 1950 and 1960, employment increased sharply for medical and other health workers, teachers, "other professional workers," salaried managerial workers, self-employed businessmen and women, semi-skilled workers in durable goods manufacturing, foremen, "waiters, cooks, and bartenders," female clerical workers, female sales workers other than in retail trade, and all female service categories. Employment increased more slowly for most types of skilled craftsmen, semi-skilled workers in nondurable goods manufacturing, most types of male service workers, and certain types of sales workers. Occupation groups which were characterized by declining employment between 1950 and 1960 were male sales workers in retail trade, carpenters, other construction workers, male private household workers, farmers and farm laborers, laborers, and female craftsmen.

However, as those who have been following recent labor market trends are well aware, the gains in a good many of these occupations were made in the early 1950's and have been followed by declines in more recent years. Between 1957 and the spring of 1962, employment declined for male sales workers in retail trade, most skilled craft categories, a number of the semi-skilled categories, farmers and farm laborers, and nonagricultural laborers. Employment showed impressive gains for medical and other health workers, teachers (especially male teachers), "other professional workers," salaried managerial workers, female clerical workers, private household workers, and "other service workers." More modest gains in employment were made by male clerical workers and some of the sales categories.

It is important to recognize that these observations are dependent on the particular classification scheme involved. When more detailed comparisons can be made, we shall undoubtedly find that particularly sharp increases occurred during the 1950's in certain specific occupations, such as electronic technicians. Furthermore, the trend in employment in some of the occupation groups in the last five years is not entirely clear, since the 1957 data are on an annual average basis and are not directly comparable with data for the early part of 1962.

On the whole, however, it is clear that employment opportunities have recently been particularly favorable for persons who can qualify for professional, technical, and salaried managerial positions. For those with a lower level of education, employment opportunities have been reasonably favorable in sales work and in many of the service occupations, and it seems likely that a good many displaced blue-collar workers have been moving into service jobs. Employment of women in clerical work continues to increase fairly steadily from year to year, and there is little evidence as yet that "automation in the office" is impairing the over-all expansion of office employment, although some groups of office workers have had to face various types of adjustment problems.[2]

It is the decline in employment in most blue-collar occupations other than service work in recent years that has, of course, been attracting particular attention and giving rise to special concern. If current trends continue, they may require some modification of Department of Labor projections of occupational changes from 1960–70. The prediction of a sharp increase in the number of professional and technical workers and fairly pronounced increases in other white-collar groups and service occupations appear consistent with recent trends, but the estimates of increases of over 20 per cent in the number of skilled workers and of slightly less than 20 per cent in the number of semi-skilled workers may turn out to be overly optimistic in the light of recent developments.[3]

How have older workers been affected by all these changes? When permanent layoffs occur, because of automation and other developments, older workers are less likely to be affected than younger workers, since they tend to have higher seniority, and, even if there is no formal seniority system, employers often hesitate to lay off long-service employees. However, seniority does not necessarily protect the older worker if an entire department is discontinued, a plant is closed down, or operations are shifted to another location. A good many older workers have lost their jobs in recent years in such situations.

Thus, it is of considerable interest to analyze the data relating to the impact of recent labor market changes on older workers. Since the impact on older men and women has been significantly different,

I propose to deal with the two sexes separately in much of my discussion.

OLDER MEN IN THE LABOR MARKET

Unemployment   Interestingly enough, analysis of unemployment data indicates that the percentage of older men who are out of work has not increased disproportionately in recent years. Unemployment rates for older men have fluctuated upward and downward with the general unemployment rate, but there has been a tendency for comparative unemployment rates for older men to decline somewhat in relation to those for younger men.

Among the various age groups in the male population, those aged 35 to 44 almost invariably experience the lowest unemployment rate, while youths who have just entered the labor force have the highest rates. Men in the 45 and older age brackets tend to have somewhat higher unemployment rates than the 35–44 age group, but the difference has been narrowing since the middle 1950's, at least for those aged 55 and over. The unemployment rate for men aged 55 to 59 was only 19 per cent above that for men in the favored 35–44 age bracket in the first quarter of 1962, as compared with 32 per cent in the year 1955 (see Tables 2 and 3). The drop was even sharper for those aged 60 to 64—from 65 per cent above the rate for the 35–44 year olds in 1955 to only 6 per cent in the first quarter of 1962—and, as we shall see at a later point, this decline may have been associated with a tendency for men in this age group to drop out of the labor force. Similarly, there has been a decline in the relative severity of unemployment among men aged 65 and over, and here again the change may have been associated with a substantial decline in the labor force participation rate of these elderly men.

However, analysis of unemployment rates tells only part of the story. The duration of unemployment is also very significant in any analysis of the impact of unemployment. In recent years, there has been some tendency for the long-term unemployment rate—the percentage of unemployed workers who are out of work 15 weeks or more—to rise, but it has fluctuated over the business cycle and has tended to be particularly high in the late stages of recessions and the early phases of recovery periods.[4] As has invariably been true, moreover, the long-term unemployment rate has been higher for older men than for younger men and boys. In the year 1955, for example, the

TABLE 2

Unemployment Rates, for the Civilian Labor Force and Older Workers, by Age and Sex, United States, Annual Averages, Selected Years, 1950–60, and First Quarter, 1960 and 1962

	Men					Women				
	Annual average			*1st quarter*		*Annual average*			*1st quarter*	
Age	1950	1955	1960	1960	1962	1950	1955	1960	1960	1962
Total, 14 years and over	4.6	3.9	5.4	6.1	6.4	5.3	4.3	5.6	5.8	6.5
35–44	3.3	2.8	3.8	4.4	4.9	4.0	3.6	4.8	5.1	5.8
45–54	3.9	3.0	4.1	4.8	5.0	4.2	3.1	4.2	4.2	4.8
55–64	4.7	4.1	4.6	5.5	5.6	3.9	3.3	3.4	3.8	3.9
55–59		3.7	4.4	5.7	5.8		3.6	3.3	3.8	4.1
60–64		4.6	4.8	5.2	5.2		3.0	3.5	3.9	3.5
65 and over	4.6	3.7	4.2	5.2	5.3	3.4	1.8	2.8	3.7	3.5

SOURCES: U.S. Bureau of the Census, *Annual Report on the Labor Force,* Series P-50, Nos. 31 and 67 (Washington, D.C.: U.S. Government Printing Office, 1951 and 1956); U.S. Bureau of Labor Statistics, *Special Labor Force Report,* No. 14 (Washington, D.C.: U.S. Government Printing Office, 1961); and *Employment and Earnings,* February to April issues, 1960 and 1962. The quarterly unemployment rates for 1960 and 1962 are unweighted averages of monthly rates.

long-term unemployment rate was only 15 per cent for youths aged 14 to 17, but rose more or less steadily with advancing age to 39 per cent for men in the 65 and older bracket. Since 1955, however, there has been a tendency for this difference to narrow, at least if we confine our attention to men under 65 years of age. During the first quarter of 1962, the long-term unemployment rate was 28 per cent for boys aged 14 to 17 and rose somewhat irregularly to 38 per cent for men aged 45 to 64. Thus, the rate for men aged 45 to 64 scarcely differed from that which prevailed in 1955, whereas the rates for younger men were substantially higher. Men in the 65 and older bracket occupied, however, an even more disadvantageous position than in 1955, with a long-term unemployment rate of 46 per cent.

TABLE 3

Ratio of Unemployment Rates for Men in Older Age Groups to the Rate for Men Aged 35 to 44, and for Women in Older Age Groups to the Rate for All Women, Aged 14 and Over, United States, Annual Averages, Selected Years, 1950–60, and First Quarter, 1960 and 1962

	Men					*Women*				
	Annual average			*1st quarter*		*Annual average*			*1st quarter*	
Age	1950	1955	1960	1960	1962	1950	1955	1960	1960	1962
35–44	1.00	1.00	1.00	1.00	1.00	.75	.84	.86	.88	.89
45–54	1.08	1.07	1.08	1.09	1.02	.79	.72	.75	.72	.74
55–64	1.43	1.46	1.21	1.25	1.14	.74	.77	.61	.66	.60
55–59		1.32	1.16	1.29	1.19		.84	.59	.66	.63
60–64		1.65	1.26	1.18	1.06		.70	.62	.67	.54
65 and over	1.39	1.32	1.11	1.18	1.08	.64	.42	.50	.64	.54

SOURCE: Computed from data in Table 2.

Case studies of groups of displaced workers that have been conducted in recent years, such as those of Wilcock and Franke, invariably show that older workers have greater difficulty in obtaining re-employment than younger men and that they also may have difficulty in qualifying for retraining programs.[5] Thus the problem of long-term unemployment among older men is a matter of considerable concern. In emphasizing the narrowing of the differences between long-term unemployment rates of younger and older men, I do not mean to minimize the difficulties faced by many older workers.

Labor Force Participation It is likely that unemployment rates would be considerably higher for men aged 60 and older than they are at present were it not for the fact that these men have been dropping out of the labor force at an accelerated rate. The long-run decline in the labor force participation rate of men aged 65 and older is, of course, familiar, as is the fact that the decline has been occurring unusually rapidly since about 1950. Between 1950 and the first quarter of 1962 the proportion of men in this age bracket in the labor force fell from 46 to 31 per cent (see Table 4). In the 60 to 64 age group, however, any long-run tendency toward decline in the labor force participation rate has been very slight, and thus the substantial drop that has taken place during the last eight years or so is noteworthy.[6] In 1954 (the first year in which data for five-year age groups were regularly published), 84 per cent of all men aged 60 to 64 were in the labor force, but by the first quarter of 1962 the rate was down to 80 per cent.

The decline in the labor force participation rate of elderly men in recent years does not appear to have been systematically related to changes in the unemployment rate, either on a year-to-year or a quarter-to-quarter basis. And yet it seems highly likely that the upward trend in the unemployment rate has played a role in encouraging elderly men to drop out of the labor force, even though the response of labor force participation rates to changes in the unemployment rate may have been somewhat sluggish. In the past, the decade-to-decade decline in the proportion of elderly men in the labor force has been particularly pronounced in decades characterized by heavy unemployment.[7]

During the last year, men aged 62 to 64 have been encouraged to retire as a result of the provision for payment of actuarially reduced OASI benefits under the 1961 amendments to the Social Security Act. But it is interesting to note that the proportion of men aged 60 to 64 in the labor force was almost as low in the third quarter of 1960 as in the first quarter of 1962, though it was somewhat higher in intervening quarters. Thus, the liberalized social security provision has not as yet had the effect of bringing the labor force participation rate of men in this age group to an unprecedentedly low level, even though there has been a noticeable decline since the provision went into effect.

Another factor which may have encouraged early departure from the labor force in the last few years is a trend toward more generous provisions for early retirement in negotiated pension plans. Some of the provisions apply only to voluntary early retirement, whereas others are designed to apply to situations in which elderly workers are permanently laid off as a result of automation or other changes.

Probably the most widely publicized arrangement of this sort was the early retirement feature of the 1960 "mechanization fund" agreement in the West Coast longshore industry.[8] A report on changes in

Per Cent of All Persons Aged 14 and Over, and of Older Persons, in the Labor Force, by Age and Sex, United States, Annual Averages, Selected Years, 1950–60, and First Quarter, 1960–62

Age	Annual average									First quarter		
	1950	1953	1954	1955	1956	1957	1958	1959	1960	1960	1961	1962
Men												
Total, 14 years and over	84.4	84.4	83.9	83.6	83.7	82.7	82.1	80.5	80.1	79.8	79.7	78.4
35–44	97.6	98.2	98.1	98.1	98.0	97.9	98.0	96.6	96.5	97.5	97.6	97.4
45–54	95.8	96.6	96.5	96.5	96.6	96.4	96.3	94.6	94.5	95.3	95.7	95.1
55–64	87.0	87.9	88.7	87.9	88.5	87.5	87.8	85.9	85.4	86.2	87.7	86.6
55–59			92.4	92.5	92.5	91.5	91.8	91.3	91.6	90.5	91.9	91.8
60–64			84.3	82.5	83.8	82.9	83.2	82.8	81.2	81.1	82.5	80.4
65 and over	45.8	41.6	40.5	39.6	40.0	37.5	35.6	33.4	32.3	32.7	32.8	30.7
Women												
Total, 14 years and over	33.1	33.6	33.7	34.8	35.9	35.9	36.0	35.8	36.4	35.0	36.5	35.9
35–44	39.1	41.3	41.3	41.6	43.1	43.3	43.4	43.1	43.2	42.5	44.1	43.3
45–54	38.0	40.4	41.2	43.8	45.5	46.5	47.9	48.6	49.4	48.4	49.5	50.2
55–64	27.0	29.1	30.1	32.5	34.9	34.5	35.2	36.2	36.8	35.9	38.4	37.9
55–59			32.6	35.6	37.9	38.2	39.5	41.1	42.2	40.4	44.6	43.9
60–64			27.0	29.0	31.4	30.3	30.4	31.4	31.4	30.7	31.4	31.0
65 and over	9.7	10.0	9.3	10.6	10.9	10.5	10.3	9.9	10.5	9.9	11.4	10.4

SOURCES: U.S. Bureau of the Census, *Annual Report on the Labor Force* (Washington, D.C.: U.S. Government Printi 1950 and 1953 to 1958); U.S. Bureau of Labor Statistics, *Special Labor Force Reports*, Nos. 4 and 14 (Washington, I Government Printing Office, 1960 and 1961); and *Employment and Earnings*, February to April issues, 1960 to 1962. terly data for 1960 to 1962 are unweighted averages of monthly labor force participation rates.

100 negotiated pension plans between 1957–58 and the spring of 1961 indicated that special early retirement provisions were added to 12 plans—5 negotiated by the Automobile Workers, 6 by the Steelworkers, and one by a group of craft unions with American Radiator and Standard Sanitary Corporation.[9] Under these provisions early retirement benefits, substantially exceeding those available for regular early retirement at the employee's option, are provided for workers compelled to retire early or retiring under "mutually satisfactory" conditions. The UAW plans provide double the normal benefit at age 60 with 10 years' service until age 65 (62 for women), when the normal benefit is payable. The Steelworkers' plan is somewhat similar, but special early retirement benefits are available to any employee aged 55 or more whose age and years of service add up to at least 75, or to those with at least 15 years of service, whose age and years of service add to 80. The 1962 agreement also added the so-called "carrot stick" provision, under which special "retirement credits" would be available for steelworkers retiring at age 65, but would be reduced by 10 per cent for every three months worked after age 65.[10] This arrangement was clearly designed to induce retirement, under an agreement with no mandatory retirement age.

So far as older men below age 60 are concerned, there has been no clearcut downward trend in labor-force participation rates in recent years, although there have been some year-to-year fluctuations. The evidence suggests that men aged 45 to 59 have not elected to leave the labor force in appreciable numbers even though a good many of them have experienced substantial spells of long-term unemployment.

Part-Time Work   To what extent have displaced older workers turned to part-time or intermittent work? The fact that a sizable proportion of older workers is to be found in part-time or intermittent employment is well known, as is the fact that the proportion increases with advancing age. Furthermore, some of the recent changes in the occupational and industrial structure, particularly the comparatively rapid growth of the trade and service industries, have encouraged an increase in the relative number of part-time and intermittent workers in the labor force.

Has there been an increasing tendency for older men to be employed in part-time or intermittent work in the last decade? The answer appears to be yes, but the changes have been very slight, except in the case of the 65 and older group, for whom there has been a marked increase in the proportion working part time or irregularly among those remaining in the labor force. In 1953—the first year in which data from the annual work experience survey were presented for five-year age groups—19 per cent of all men aged 65 to 69 who worked at all during the year were employed on a part-time basis, while 24 per cent worked full time for only part of the year. By 1960, 30 per cent were working part time, and 27 per cent worked full time during part of the year. Similar changes occurred among those 70 and over.[11] Among men in the age brackets from 45 to 64, however, such changes as occurred were very moderate and did not necessarily indicate a long-run trend. The available data reveal a clear tendency, as we would expect, for the proportion of part-time workers in all age groups to rise in recessions and decline in business upswings.

Occupational Changes   If employment patterns of men aged 45 to 59 have been somewhat more stable in recent years than might have been expected, part of the explanation seems to lie in changes that are occurring in the occupational distribution of men in this age group. So far as nonagricultural employment is concerned, older men have always tended to be disproportionately represented in managerial positions, in which relatively little unemployment is experienced, and in the skilled manual occupation group, in which the unemployment rate tends to be lower than in semi-skilled or unskilled manual work. Men aged 55 or older are also disproportionately represented in service work. Between 1950 and 1960, the most pronounced change that occurred was an increase in the proportion employed in managerial positions—from 17 to 19 per cent of nonagricultural workers aged 45 to 54 and from 17 to 21 per cent of those aged 55 to 64 (separate data are not available for the 55 to 59 age group, at least for 1960). There has also apparently been a slight increase in the proportion engaged in professional and technical work, although the percentage of men aged 45 to 64 in this occupation group continues to be appreciably smaller than among men aged 25 to 44. Thus, employed older men, along with most of the remainder of the adult male population, are more likely to be engaged in relatively high-level white-collar work than was the case a decade ago, and this

TABLE 5

Occupational Distribution of Men Employed in Nonagricultural Jobs, United States, 1950 and 1960

Year and major occupation group	Total 14 years and over	14 to 19 years	20 to 24 years	25 to 34 years	35 to 44 years	45 to 54 years	55 to 64 years	65 and over
1950								
Total	100.0	100.0	100.0	100.0	100.0	100.0	100.0	100.0
Professional, technical, and kindred workers	8.8	2.0	6.5	10.6	9.7	8.4	7.5	9.0
Managers, officials, and proprietors, exc. farm	12.8	1.4	4.1	9.5	15.0	17.5	16.8	17.4
Clerical and kindred workers	7.7	10.4	11.2	8.3	6.7	6.7	6.8	6.5
Sales workers	7.7	16.1	8.2	8.0	6.9	6.7	6.6	8.1
Craftsmen, foremen, and kindred workers	22.2	8.5	17.6	22.4	23.6	24.3	24.3	20.6
Operatives and kindred workers	24.0	30.5	33.3	27.1	23.9	20.1	18.3	13.6
Private household workers	—¹	0.4	0.1	0.1	0.2	0.3	0.3	0.5
Service workers, exc. private household	7.0	11.0	5.4	5.0	5.8	6.6	9.9	14.1
Laborers	9.7	19.7	13.6	9.0	8.3	8.5	9.5	10.3
1960								
Total	100.0	100.0	100.0	100.0	100.0	100.0	100.0	100.0
Professional, technical, and kindred workers	11.9	2.2	10.7	16.5	13.0	10.3	9.3	11.8
Managers, officials, and proprietors, exc. farm	14.9	0.9	4.5	10.8	17.1	19.3	21.0	22.8
Clerical and kindred workers	7.9	9.8	11.7	8.6	7.1	6.7	6.6	7.7
Sales workers	6.8	15.7	6.4	6.8	6.1	5.4	5.9	8.8
Craftsmen, foremen, and kindred workers	20.8	6.3	16.2	20.2	23.5	23.9	22.5	16.1
Operatives and kindred workers	21.6	27.1	30.8	23.5	21.0	20.0	17.2	10.2
Private household workers	0.1	0.8	0.1	—¹	—¹	—¹	0.1	0.4
Service workers, exc. private household	7.2	13.1	6.3	5.5	5.3	6.8	9.8	14.2
Laborers	8.9	24.0	13.4	7.9	6.9	7.5	7.6	8.0

trend seems likely to continue, since it is in line with long-run changes in the occupational structure. However, before commenting any further about probable future changes, let us turn to an analysis of the impact of labor market changes on older women.

OLDER WOMEN IN THE LABOR FORCE

One of the most spectacular, and by now thoroughly familiar, labor market developments of the 1950's was the sharp rise in the labor force participation of middle-aged and older women. Thus, in discussing employment opportunities of mature women, it is virtually imperative that we start with an analysis of changes in their labor force participation rates.

Although the over-all rise in the proportion of women in the labor force between 1950 and 1960—a matter of about three percentage points—was not unprecedented, the rate of increase was relatively high for the 45 and older group. Among those aged 45 to 54, the increase was from 38 per cent in 1950 to 49 per cent in 1960, and for those aged 55 to 64, from 27 per cent in 1950 to 37 per cent ten years later (see Table 4). Within the latter group, however, the increase was more pronounced for those under 60 than for those aged 60 to 64.

To a considerable extent, the sharp increase in the labor force participation of older women reflected a continuation of a tendency that had first become pronounced in the 1940's. Before 1940, the proportion of women in their forties and fifties in the labor force had gradually increased, but at a much slower rate, whereas sharper increases had taken place in the labor force participation rates of women in their twenties and thirties. The accelerated movement of older women into the labor force in the last two decades has apparently been influenced by a combination of factors—more favorable social attitudes toward working wives, generally favorable employ-

SOURCES: U.S. Bureau of the Census, *Census of Population: 1950*, Vol. II, Part 1 (Washington, D.C.: U.S. Government Printing Office, 1953), Table 127; and U.S. Bureau of Labor Statistics, *Special Labor Force Report*, No. 14 (Washington, D.C.: U.S. Government Printing Office, 1961), Table C-8. It should be noted that the data for 1950 and 1960 are not strictly comparable, since the 1950 data are based on the decennial census, while, for 1960, we have used annual average data based on the Monthly Labor Force Survey. However, occupational data by age based on the 1960 Census are not yet available.

[1] Less than 0.05 per cent.

opportunities for women, a scarcity of youthful entrants into the
an labor force in the early 1950's because of the low birth rates
e 1930's and because of military service in the Korean conflict,
finally, earlier marriages and the higher birth rates of the 1940's
and 1950's had the effect of keeping large numbers of young married
women out of the labor force and, indirectly, of improving job opportunities for older women.

The fact that employment opportunities have been particularly
favorable for women in recent decades is attributable to a considerable
extent to the broad changes occurring in the occupational structure
which have already been discussed. The relatively rapid increases in
the employment of clerical workers and in certain professional occupations in which women have traditionally been employed, such as
teaching and nursing, have been especially important.

However, the increase in the labor force participation of women in
general, and of older women, has not occurred at a steady rate from
year to year. There has been some tendency for the proportion of
women in the labor force to increase particularly rapidly in periods
when total employment was rising sharply and more moderately at
other times. Moreover, there was no net increase in the over-all labor
force participation rate of women from 1956 to the first quarter of
1962, although there were some slight fluctuations in the interim (see
Table 4). It seems reasonable to suppose that less favorable employment opportunities associated with the upward drift in the unemployment rate have been at least partly responsible for this leveling off
in the labor force participation of women, even though, as in the case
of declining participation of elderly men, there does not seem to have
been a systematic relationship between changes in labor force participation rates and unemployment rates on a year-to-year or quarter-
to-quarter basis.

If the labor force participation rate of women has leveled off in
recent years, this has not, however, been true for those in the 45 to
54 and 55 to 59 age brackets, although the net increase since 1956
or 1957 has been somewhat more moderate than earlier. But for
women aged 60 to 64, the rate has shown no tendency to increase
in recent years. Probably, the availability of social security benefits
for women aged 62 to 64 since the enactment of the 1956 amendments
has influenced this development. As for women aged 65 or more,
their labor force participation rate has displayed slight year-to-year

fluctuations but no clear trend since 1950, having hovered around ten per cent throughout the period.

What is the explanation of the continued increase in labor force participation rates of women aged 45 to 54 at a time when the increase for women as a whole has leveled off? In seeking an answer to this question, let us consider the unemployment experience of older women and any changes which may have been occurring in their occupational distribution.

Unemployment The unemployment rate for women tends to be slightly higher than for men in relatively prosperous years, probably because women are more likely to move into and out of the labor force and to be employed on an intermittent basis. This difference, however, tends to disappear in recessions, since relatively more men work in industries characterized by wide cyclical fluctuations in employment. Moreover, age variations in unemployment rates tend to differ somewhat for men and women. Young girls have the highest unemployment rates, but the rate shows a tendency to fall off more or less steadily with increasing age, and thus the lowest rates are found in the oldest female age brackets. This probably reflects some tendency for unemployed older women to drop out of the labor force.

In analyzing recent changes in comparative unemployment rates for women of various ages it seems more appropriate, because of the differing pattern of age variation, to compare the rates for older women with that for all women rather than with those aged 35 to 44, as we did in the case of men. Among women aged 35 to 44 the unemployment rate has shown some tendency to rise relative to that for all women, but the reverse has generally been true for the age groups who are 45 or older (see Tables 2 and 3).

As for the duration of unemployment, women are somewhat less likely to experience long-term unemployment than men, but the long-term unemployment rate tends to rise with advancing age, just as it does in the case of men. Moreover, in the first quarter of 1962, long-term unemployment rates for older women were appreciably higher than they had been in 1955 and were very close to those for older men. Long-term unemployment rates for young women have also risen substantially, and age differences in this respect have narrowed, as we found in the case of men.

Part-Time and Intermittent Work   Part-time and intermittent work patterns are much more common among women than among men, and their prevalence tends to increase in the older age brackets. Moreover, the proportion of part-time and intermittent workers in the female work force tended to increase between 1953 and 1960. This was probably associated chiefly with the rising proportion of married women in the labor force, since it is primarily married women who have part-time or intermittent work patterns. In 1960, 72 per cent of the women aged 45 to 54 who had any work experience during the year worked full time, but only 47 per cent worked full time the year round. 28 per cent of the women in this age group worked on a part-time basis—many of them for only part of the year. Among women aged 55 and older, the proportion of part-time workers increased steadily with advancing age, while the percentage working full time the year round fell somewhat irregularly.

Occupational Changes   In 1950 older women were somewhat more likely to be engaged in professional and managerial work than younger women and were also more likely to be employed in private household and other service jobs. On the other hand, the proportion engaged in clerical work was considerably smaller than among younger women (see Table 6).

Between 1950 and 1960, the most significant change in the occupational distribution of older women was an increase in the proportion engaged in clerical work. Among women aged 35 to 44, for example, 30 per cent were engaged in clerical work in 1960, as compared with 24 per cent in 1950. Similar changes occurred in the age groups who were 45 or older, although the percentages of clerical workers continued to decline with advancing age. On the other hand, among women under 25 years of age, the increase in the proportion engaged in clerical work in the ten-year period was less pronounced. In large part, these changes probably reflect the influence of long-run changes in the occupational structure. Women moving into the older age brackets today are more likely to have been employed previously in clerical work than was the case in earlier decades, and indeed in many cases may well have been employed in a steady clerical job for some time. Analysis of changes in the numbers in the various cohorts suggests that this may be the major explanation of the increase in the number and proportion of older clerical workers, although there

TABLE 6

Occupational Distribution of Women Employed in Nonagricultural Jobs, United States, 1950 and 1960

Year and major occupation group	Total 14 years and over	14 to 19 years	20 to 24 years	25 to 34 years	35 to 44 years	45 to 54 years	55 to 64 years	65 and over
1950								
Total	100.0	100.0	100.0	100.0	100.0	100.0	100.0	100.0
Professional, technical, and kindred workers	13.0	5.5	13.0	12.7	14.0	14.9	14.4	13.7
Managers, officials, and proprietors, exc. farm	4.6	0.5	1.3	3.2	6.0	7.2	7.7	9.0
Clerical and kindred workers	28.9	38.4	46.0	32.3	24.0	21.4	15.5	10.3
Sales workers	8.9	14.8	7.0	7.4	9.2	9.7	9.5	8.3
Craftsmen, foremen, and kindred workers	1.6	0.7	1.0	1.6	1.9	1.9	1.9	1.7
Operatives and kindred workers	20.3	14.8	17.0	23.0	22.8	20.1	19.2	15.8
Private household workers	9.0	11.2	4.7	6.9	8.6	10.4	13.8	21.7
Service workers, exc. private household	12.9	13.2	9.3	12.1	12.9	13.6	17.4	18.4
Laborers	0.9	0.9	0.7	0.9	0.9	0.8	0.8	0.8
1960								
Total	100.0	100.0	100.0	100.0	100.0	100.0	100.0	100.0
Professional, technical, and kindred workers	12.8	3.5	16.2	15.3	11.6	13.9	13.7	11.1
Managers, officials, and proprietors, exc. farm	5.2	0.4	1.2	2.7	5.6	7.8	8.3	11.3
Clerical and kindred workers	31.3	38.8	49.1	37.4	29.9	25.3	20.1	15.6
Sales workers	8.0	12.0	4.2	5.9	7.9	9.3	9.0	8.6
Craftsmen, foremen, and kindred workers	1.1	—[1]	0.7	0.9	1.2	1.2	1.2	1.0
Operatives and kindred workers	15.7	7.4	11.4	17.1	20.1	17.3	14.5	10.3
Private household workers	10.2	23.1	5.4	7.0	7.1	8.7	14.2	23.4
Service workers, exc. private household	15.4	14.5	11.4	13.5	16.2	16.0	18.4	18.1
Laborers	0.4	0.4	0.3	0.3	0.4	0.5	0.4	0.5

SOURCES: See Table 5.

[1] Less than 0.05 per cent.

57

may also have been some tendency for employers to modify their well-known reluctance to hire older women for clerical jobs.

During the 1950's there was also a slight increase in the proportion of older women engaged in service work, an appreciable decline in the percentage employed as "operatives and kindred workers," and a slight decline in the proportion engaged in professional work. All in all, however, the percentage of women employed in white-collar jobs increased significantly in all the older age brackets. This was also true for younger female workers except for teen-age girls.

On the whole, our analysis of unemployment and occupational changes for women does not provide a clearcut explanation of the continued increase in labor force participation of older women in a period when the rise in labor force participation of women as a whole has slowed to a halt. Unemployment rates have increased less for older women than for younger women, but, within the unemployed group, the proportion experiencing long-term unemployment has increased. Most older women are employed in occupation groups that have been expanding, but so are most younger women. Probably the chief explanation is that the strength of the long-run forces making for increased labor force participation of older women is considerably greater than for younger women—in fact, there has been a decline for certain young, female age groups—and the relatively unfavorable labor market situation of recent years has merely slowed down but has not halted the movement of older women into the labor market.

Whether this will continue to be true, however, is, at the moment uncertain. Not only has there been a retardation in the rate of increase for older women, but in the last few years the labor force as a whole has been increasing somewhat less rapidly than Department of Labor projections predicted.[12] These developments will bear watching and careful study in the next few years.

CONCLUSIONS

I now come to the point at which I can no longer ignore the word "projections" in the topic assigned to me. On the whole, I find it easier to make certain comments about probable long-run trends than about the shorter-run outlook for the next four or five years.

If the unemployment rate continues its upward drift or merely maintains approximately its average level of recent years, it seems clear that we shall see continued pressure to encourage, or in some industries to compel, the early retirement of older men from their regular jobs. The labor force participation of middle-aged and older women, moreover, will probably increase at a slower rate than in the early 1950's. Displaced older workers will continue to encounter difficulty in obtaining re-employment and are likely to fail to qualify for some of the retraining programs that will be developed. I hope that, in the formulation of policies and regulations under the Manpower Development and Training Act of 1962, some attention will be given to retraining displaced older workers for service occupations in those cases in which they cannot qualify for programs aimed at preparing displaced workers for skilled jobs. I believe, also, that we need to take a critical look at the adequacy of our income-maintenance policies as they apply to displaced or disabled older workers, particularly those who have not yet reached the age of 62. This is a subject that has many ramifications, and I shall merely stress what I have increasingly come to regard as an appalling deficiency in our social security program—the fact that in many parts of the United States public assistance is either unavailable to an unemployed worker who has exhausted his right to unemployment insurance benefits or is available only on the most meager, restrictive, and humiliating terms. In this respect, we are clinging to Elizabethan attitudes toward poor relief that have long since been discarded in most other advanced industrial nations.

On the other hand, if we succeed, through a skillful combination of national economic policies, in reducing the unemployment rate substantially below the average levels of recent years, the outlook for older workers will be much more promising. Some older workers will continue to be displaced as a result of automation and other technological or structural changes in the economy, but the problem of assisting them in obtaining re-employment will be far more manageable. In fact, I believe that under these conditions the problem of ensuring adequate employment opportunities for young persons who do not complete a program of higher education or receive appropriate specialized training before entering the labor market may well be considerably more difficult than the problem of displaced older workers.

From a long-run point of view, the gradual occupational upgrading of the older labor force that appears to be taking place is distinctly encouraging. There is every indication that the proportion of

white-collar workers in general, and of professional workers in particular, in the older labor force will continue to rise in the future, as
the large numbers of younger people now engaged in these types of
work move on into the older age groups. This will probably mean
somewhat enhanced job security for older workers, although it may
well mean, also, that a growing proportion will be subject to compulsory retirement at a fixed age, since salaried white-collar workers
are particularly likely to be subject to mandatory retirement policies.

As time goes on, moreover, the educational gap between younger
and older workers will probably narrow. As Clarence Long has
pointed out, the gap tended to widen between 1910 and 1950,[13] but
this trend is likely to be reversed in the near future. In 1950 the
median number of years of school completed by persons in the 35
to 39 age group was 20 per cent higher than in the 45 to 49 age
group, but the 25 to 29 age group had only a 13 per cent advantage
over those ten years older.[14] The reversal of the earlier trend will
chiefly reflect two influences—the sharp drop in immigration after
the beginning of World War I and the fact that the increase in high-
school enrollment between 1920 and 1930 was more pronounced than
in earlier or later decades.

However, rapid technological changes will undoubtedly continue
to confront the older workers of the future with the threat of occupational and educational obsolescence. Their higher average educational
attainment and the fact that they will be more likely to be engaged
in white-collar work may not protect them from the impact of these
changes unless employers and community agencies place more emphasis on continuing retraining and education through the adult years
than has been the case in the past.

NOTES

[1] Averages were computed from data in U.S. Bureau of Labor Statistics,
Employment and Earnings Statistics for the United States, 1909–60 (Washington, D.C.: U.S. Government Printing Office, 1961), p. 535. The business cycle

turning points used were those that have been identified by the National Bureau of Economic Research.

² Cf. Ida R. Hoos, *Automation in the Office* (Washington, D.C.: Public Affairs Press, 1961).

³ See U.S. Department of Labor, *Manpower: Challenge of the 1960's* (Washington, D.C.: U.S. Government Printing Office, 1960), p. 11.

⁴ See Jane L. Meredith, "Long-Term Unemployment in the United States," *Monthly Labor Review*, 84 (June, 1961), 601–10.

⁵ See Richard C. Wilcock and Walter H. Franke, *Unwanted Workers: Permanent Layoffs and Long-Term Unemployment* (New York: The Free Press of Glencoe, Inc., 1963).

⁶ For labor force participation by age and sex from 1890 to 1955, see Gertrude Bancroft, *The American Labor Force* (New York: John Wiley & Sons, 1958), p. 207. It should be noted that the decennial census data presented by Bancroft are not precisely comparable with the monthly labor force data presented in Table 4. For a discussion of the differences, see *ibid.*, pp. 157–74.

⁷ Cf. Clarence D. Long, *The Labor Force Under Changing Income and Employment* (Princeton, N.J.: Princeton University Press, 1958), Chapters 1 and 9. For further discussion of these relationships, see my chapter entitled "Work and Patterns of Retirement," in Robert W. Kleemeier (ed.), *Aging and Leisure* (New York: Oxford University Press, 1961), pp. 15–53.

⁸ See Max D. Kossoris, "Working Rules in West Coast Longshoring," *Monthly Labor Review*, 84 (January, 1961), 1–10.

⁹ "Recent Changes in Negotiated Pension Plans," *Monthly Labor Review*, 85 (May, 1962), 528–32; and U.S. Bureau of Labor Statistics, *Digest of One-Hundred Pension Plans Under Collective Bargaining, Spring 1961*, BLS Bulletin No. 1307 (Washington D.C.: U.S. Government Printing Office, 1962).

¹⁰ For further details, see *Daily Labor Report*, No. 64, April 2, 1962, pp. D2 to D4, and No. 70, April 10, 1962, Supplement. For a discussion of experience under UAW early retirement provisions, see Harold L. Orbach, "Normative Aspects of Retirement," in Clark Tibbitts and Wilma Donahue (eds.), *Social and Psychological Aspects of Aging* (New York and London: Columbia University Press, 1962), pp. 53–63.

¹¹ U.S. Bureau of the Census, *Current Population Reports: Labor Force*, Series P-50, No. 54 (Washington, D.C.: U.S. Government Printing Office, 1954), p. 5; and U.S. Bureau of Labor Statistics, *Special Labor Force Report*, No. 19 (Washington, D.C.: U.S. Government Printing Office, 1962), p. A-6.

¹² Since this paper was given, the Department of Labor has published interim revised projections which are somewhat lower than the earlier projections. See Sophia Cooper, "Interim Revised Projections of U.S. Labor Force, 1965–75," *Monthly Labor Review*, 85 (October, 1962), 1089–99.

¹³ Clarence D. Long, *op. cit.*, p. 14.

¹⁴ U.S. Bureau of the Census, *Historical Statistics of the United States: Colonial Times to 1957* (Washington, D.C.: U.S. Government Printing Office, 1960), p. 214.

CHAPTER 4

MEASURES TO IMPROVE EMPLOYABILITY AND INCREASE WORK OPPORTUNITIES

Seymour L. Wolfbein

I think that, as Dr. Margaret Gordon has pointed out (Chapter 3), no matter how we assess the present general economic situation, and the employment and unemployment situation in particular, we really can't escape the fact that we have had for a considerable period of time an economic climate which has left us with a rate and level of joblessness which are both too high.

It is now the 55th consecutive month in the United States where the seasonally adjusted unemployment rate has remained above 5 per cent. As Dr. Gordon indicated, there is a lot of argument among economists as to whether the unemployment problem is generated by a lack of over-all economic growth, or whether it can be traced to basic structural changes in our economy. I, too, would prefer not to engage in that controversy. To attempt to pursue this dichotomy is, I think, rather fruitless, because in an economy as complex as ours, our current problems almost certainly are generated by both factors. Programs and policies, therefore, should take both into account.

But just for the record, Dr. Gordon did say that she suspected that when all is said and done, if she had to vote she would go on the aggregate economic growth side. You will be delighted to hear that if I had to vote, I would vote on the structural unemployment side. This should confirm your suspicions that economists have almost a natural proclivity to disagree.

It seems to me that the primary point that stands out, when one reads the returns that come in every month on the employment and unemployment side, is that we keep on reporting month after month record levels of employment. Since I have the dubious honor of announcing these figures, I stand before a press conference and announce each month that we have achieved another new record level of employment. As a matter of fact, I announced in May 1962 that over 62,800,000 people had nonfarm jobs and that was a record for any month in history. But, then, we also have to turn around and say we are also getting some pretty high records on the *unemployment* side as well.

THE PROBLEM OF PERSISTENT UNEMPLOYMENT

In other words, while we have been increasing employment in the United States at a record rate, we have not made a corresponding dent on unemployment. So we still have more than a million and a quarter people who are long-term unemployed and the way we count unemployed, you've really got to be long-term to fall into our category. Only one hour of work during the census week classifies a person as employed, even if he seeks work actively the rest of the week. Yet, month after month, we are showing well over a million people whom we classify as long-term unemployed—that is, people without even an hour of work in any given week and actively seeking a job for a period of 4 months or more.

Now when we ask ourselves, "Why is this going on, why do we keep making all these employment records, yet not achieve any corresponding diminution on the unemployment side?" we think that as we read the returns one very important answer emerges, one that is particularly relevant to the group that we are discussing at present. We think that the common denominator that brings this group together in a very meaningful way is their lack of skill. Lacking skill they are unable to move into the employment opportunities developing in this country. This is why we place so much emphasis on what can be done to posture these unemployed, to endow them, if you wish, with the ability, through the acquisition of new skills, to get back to the job market in a meaningful way which will enable them to get some of the jobs. This is why there has been so much emphasis on the training and retraining aspect of this particular problem.

TRAINING FOR OLDER WORKERS

I would now like to present what I consider to be five important propositions concerning the training and retraining of the older person, viewed in the context of what I consider to be the head-on collision that we are getting and will continue to get between automation and technological change on the one hand and our manpower posture on the other. First, we may expect a continued and, I think, an accelerated increase in automation and technological change. Juxtaposed against this is the sheer manpower posture of this country where, despite dramatic declines in labor market participation among older men, our expectations are still for an almost 20 per cent increase in the number of older workers (defined as 45 years of age and over) in the American labor force during this decade.

I submit these propositions to you with all humility. I emphasize that they are only hypotheses and that we hope to have experimental evidence which will help us assess them as we go along in our training and retraining program. But these hypotheses, these postulates are not only items which require documentary evidence for their assessment. If I may say so, they also involve attitudes, if you wish, a way of thinking, which I would also like to submit to you at the same time.

Proposition *Number One* that we are operating on, and I state these in rather stark, perhaps exaggerated, fashion for the sake of brevity and emphasis, is that *everyone can be trained*. No matter what the person's previous condition of servitude was, or how long he was unemployed, or whether he is functionally literate or not, or whether he had extensive education or not, or whether he was unskilled, skilled, or even a high-class professional-technical person or not, *everyone* can be trained.

Now I say it this way because the little bit of evidence we have been able to accumulate so far, operating under the Area Redevelopment Act of 1961, seems to me to lead very definitely to this hypothesis. We, in the Labor Department, have been charged under the Area Redevelopment Act to train and retrain people in what have come to be called "redevelopment areas." ("Depressed areas" is perhaps the more familiar term.) These are areas, by definition, of substantial and persistent unemployment. Yet the Act says: "You go out and see what you can do about training and retraining unemployed workers *in those areas only.*" And training time is limited to a maximum of 16 weeks. I'm delighted to be able to report to you that *it can be done*. Almost 15 per cent of the people now taking training under the Area Redevelopment Act have had only a grade school education. I'm also glad to report to you that one out of every 3 of our trainees is 35 years of age and over, one out of every 10 is 45 years of age and over, and we're training them and placing them in depressed areas. They take off from the vantage point of all sorts of educational attainments and all sorts of previous work experience, and they are getting jobs in these depressed areas, not only in the white-collar sector, but in the industrial, blue-collar sector as well. And, I repeat, this is occurring in areas which by definition are areas of substantial and persistent unemployment.

It has been a real eye-opener for us to see that when you do a custom-tailored job of training, when you have the resources to do this, you can do a lot in approaching this postulate that everyone can be trained.

Proposition *Number 2* is that *everyone needs to be trained.* I don't think the "older worker" is a particularly unique case in this respect; it pertains to the entire age spectrum. If you read the unemployment returns in detail, the way Dr. Gordon expressed them to you, something stands out very clearly: Unemployed "older workers" are those who are unskilled and whose skills are obsolescent. Only 5 per cent of the American labor force today, as you know, is in the unskilled category. But 18 per cent of the long-term unemployed are unskilled. They make a fabulously disproportionate contribution to the long-term unemployment problem for a very good reason. If anything is apparently in the offing, it is the fact that change and accelerated change has upended and is upending the occupational and industrial structure. *Change* is the key word, and it is obsolescing skills constantly.

Whether one refers to "Detroit automation," where you link assembly lines in a synchronized manner through transfer stations, or whether you talk about numerical control of machine tools, where you pre-program the operation of complex tools and series of tools, or, if you simply refer to sheer technological change of a more simple kind, the impact is on the skills of the labor force. As you may have heard me state so many times before, we can no longer assume that we can very carefully guide, counsel, and train young people and have them enter into an occupation and then get older and gracefully retire from it. Change requires all of us to train and retrain, to remain responsive to changing technology.

Now the *third proposition* I would like to place before you, because you do come from so many different places, is that *every place needs training.* We've come to realize more and more now that no section of the nation is immune to what we have just said. As a matter of fact, areas of economic development are simply predicated more and more on what they do with the training of their personnel. Where are the jobs in the United States? One out of every six jobs in the United States is located in just three states. Can you name them? They are California, Texas, Florida. It wasn't that way a short time ago. People are moving, and the sheer geography of employment opportunities is moving, too. And in their wake they leave the kind of problems we have been talking about—such as depressed areas. This is why every area must also be responsive to change in terms of the manpower resources it offers.

The *fourth proposition* I would like to submit to you, again in relation to the so-called "older worker," is that *we must do much better, in the whole field of the training of these people, in the curriculum that we have for them, and the responsiveness of those curricula in the training programs to the real life of the working world.* And we're not doing so well in that, either.

More and more we will be called on as the training and retraining programs get going, to ask ourselves: "How much better can we do in making the training programs themselves really responsive to what's needed in the changing world of work?"

The *fifth proposition,* and I say this with all respect and humility to those of you who are teachers and trainers, is that *we've got to do a little better, too, in terms of the qualities of trainers themselves.* They must be as responsive to the new world of work as we're asking the trainees to be.

I hope that you who are practitioners in the gerontological field will reflect on these five propositions in terms of the implications they have for all of us. The reason why I say this with such feeling is that, as you must have heard, the Congress has passed the Manpower Development and Training Act and has told us to go ahead with an extensive program of training and retraining. To all intents and purposes they have said: "Here you are. See what you can do in training or retraining people so that they can move into the jobs which are in the offing."

Now, the thing I have always liked about the University of Michigan's Conferences on Aging is that Dr. Wilma Donahue has always insisted that, whenever I make a presentation, I always be sure to offer something on the action side, and it's really a sheer delight to be able to follow her advice, as I finish this afternoon. Because, in the context of philosophy under which we are going to try to operate this program (expressed in the preceeding five propositions), there is an action program in which all of you can participate.

Under the provisions of the Manpower Development Training Act, there is a stipulation for us to encourage the establishment of local committees which are expected to take a look at programs of training and retraining and see if they're really viable programs. Are there jobs in sight? Are we selecting and referring the right kind of unemployed? Are we giving them a needed, responsible kind of training? Are we doing a good placement job? The Manpower Development Training Act specifically raises those questions. And it encourages the establishment of local committees to work with the employment service and with vocational education people in getting viable programs going.

I hereby invite you officially to help establish and serve on those local committees. Please don't let me hear it said at the next conference I come to, as I've often heard said before: "Well, what can I do in terms of action?" You've got an excellent pathway for action now. You can play a very, very active role in this, together with our employment service and vocational education and other education people in the formulation of these programs and their subsequent operations. I am particularly interested in your joining us in this effort because, again, no matter how you move in this, a large group of people whom we want to try to train and retrain and place back into employment are going to be exactly those who are the subject of your discipline, the so-called "older workers."

III. The Economic Status of the Aged:
Income and Resources

CHAPTER 5

SOME ASPECTS OF THE ECONOMIC SITUATION OF THE AGED: RECENT SURVEY FINDINGS

Charles A. Lininger

THE ECONOMIC POSITION OF THE AGED

Consumers are regularly queried by the Survey Research Center about their economic position and their attitudes. Each year since 1946 one major survey has been devoted to the general financial position of American consumers. Special attention has also been directed from time to time to particular facets of consumer attitudes and conditions. From these studies, selected information has been brought together here to form a description of the financial position and the attitudes of those spending units and families whose heads are 65 years of age or over.[1] For comparative purposes parallel information is also presented for the younger age groups. Data are presented on the economic position of the aged, retirement plans of the nonretired, and attitudes toward responsibility for the needy aged.

It is appropriate at this point to define the *spending unit* clearly, for it is the actual unit of analysis. A spending unit is defined as a group of persons residing together who are related by blood, marriage, or adoption and who pool their incomes. Husband and wife and children under 18 living at home are always considered to be members of the same spending unit. For married couples living together, the husband is designated as the head. It may be comprised of one person, or many. After World War II many families were doubled up in housing due to shortages of dwellings. Much undoubling has taken place since then, and today only about 6 per cent of American families are made up of two or more spending units. There are also 2 per cent of all spending units who are roomers, servants, or other unrelated persons who share a dwelling.

Housing   The majority of American families are living in homes that they own. Although only one in 10 of those spending units whose head is 18–24 years old own their own home, the proportion increases to 4 in 10 for those whose head is 25–34, and levels off somewhat above 6 in 10 for all older age groups. The proportion who own their home mortgage-free increases steadily with each older age group, and 53 per cent of all spending units whose head is 65 or over own a mortgage-free home. (Table 1). This represents more than 80 per cent of aged home-owning spending units.

TABLE 1

Housing Status and Number of Persons within Age of Head of Spending Unit, 1960
(*percentage distribution*)

Housing status	All spending units	18–24	25–34	35–44	45–54	55–64	65+
Own home	55	10	41	62	67	61	63
Have no mortgage	23	2	6	13	26	40	53
Mortgage under $5000	12	2	8	14	20	11	8
Mortgage $5000–9999	12	2	16	21	15	8	1
Mortgage $10,000+	8	4	11	14	6	2	1
Rent	34	45	48	31	26	30	26
Other [1]	11	45	11	7	7	9	11
Total	100	100	100	100	100	100	100

Age of spending unit head spans columns 18–24 through 65+.

SOURCE: *1960 Survey of Consumer Finances.*
[1] Includes trailer owners and spending units who neither own nor rent e.g., receive housing as part of their compensation or as a gift.

Number of Persons   The average number of persons per spending unit is lowest for the aged, and lower for units headed by a female for every age group. The proportion of units with a male head declines at the older ages, so that only two-thirds of the units aged 65 or over have a male head (Table 2). The average number of children per spending unit and the percentage of units with children is very low among the older units. Differences in the average number of persons per unit by age groups result largely from variations in the number of children.

TABLE 2

Number of Persons and Children in Spending Unit with Male and Female Head within Age of Spending Unit Head, 1960

	All spending units	Age of spending unit head 18–24	25–34	35–44	45–54	55–64	65+
Per cent of spending units in age group	100	8	21	22	21	14	14
Average number of persons per S.U.:	3.0	2.1	3.7	4.0	3.2	2.1	1.8
Male head	3.3	2.3	3.8	4.3	3.4	2.4	2.1
Female head	1.7	1.4	2.5	2.6	1.8	1.4	1.2
Average number of children per S.U.:							
Male head	1.4	0.6	1.9	2.3	1.3	0.3	0.2
Female head	0.5	0.4	1.4	1.3	0.4	0.1	0.1
Per cent with children:							
Male head	57	39	78	84	61	22	7
Female head	22	21	46	50	18	10	4
Per cent of S.U.'s with male head	81	76	89	85	85	76	67

SOURCE: *1960 Survey of Consumer Finances.*

Income The proportion of spending units with incomes under $3000 doubles from the 45–54 to the 55–64 year age groups, and almost doubles again for those 65 and over. Considering incomes under $2000, the proportions also double from the age groups 45–54 to 55–64, and double again for the age group 65 or over. Only one in 6 (16 per cent) of those spending units whose head is age 65 or over have an income of $5000 or more (Table 3). More than twice that number (33 per cent) of the aged spending units have some wage and salary income, but only about one-fourth of the total income of the aged spending units was from earnings (Table 4). Almost half of their income is transfer income. About three-quarters of the aged spending unit heads either consider themselves retired or were unable to find gainful employment during the previous twelve months; 5 per cent report that they are actively engaged in farming, another 5

TABLE 3

Total Income within Age of Head of Spending Unit, 1960
(*percentage distribution*)

Spending unit money income	All spending units	Age of spending unit head					
		18–24	*25–34*	*35–44*	*45–54*	*55–64*	*65+*
Under $2000	16	26	5	6	10	24	47
$2000–2999	10	15	8	5	8	12	18
$3000–4999	22	35	33	18	20	21	19
$5000–7499	28	13	40	35	26	24	12
$7500–9999	13	10	16	18	14	11	2
$10,000+	11	1	8	18	22	8	2
Total	100	100	100	100	100	100	100

SOURCE: *1961 Survey of Consumer Finances.*

per cent are self-employed, and the remainder (16 per cent) are in the labor force and had gainful employment during the previous year (Table 5). Since more spending unit heads aged 65 or over reported earnings in 1960 than reported being in the labor force early in 1961, many of those who reported earnings in Table 4 were reporting either pre-retirement income or occasional earnings which they did not feel contradicted their retired status.

Assets and Debts   The asset and debt position shows that the aged either refrain from incurring much debt, or are not frequently granted credit, for 84 per cent of the spending units report that they have no installment debt (Table 6). From other studies it is known that older persons think much less favorably about the use of credit than do younger persons. Furthermore, studies over the past 15 years indicate that it is their *generation,* with its related values and experiences, rather than their *present age* which is primarily responsible for their more conservative attitude toward credit. The older people have somewhat less medical debt, as reported in a 1957 Survey, although the decline is most striking between the ages 45–54 and 55–64. A study in 1961 indicated a slightly smaller incidence of "large medical expenses" [2] during the year among the 65 and over, 24 per cent, compared with 28 per cent for those 55–64, although their exposure,

TABLE **4**

Sources of Income within Age of Head of Spending Unit, 1960

Sources of money income	All spending units	Age of spending unit head					
		18–24	*25–34*	*35–44*	*45–54*	*55–64*	*65+*
Mean total income	$5830	$3830	$6150	$7090	$7530	$5130	$2930
Per cent due to:							
Wage and salary income [1]	79	95	90	81	81	80	26
Farming, unincorporated business income [2]	8	1	6	12	10	6	8
Capital income	5	—	1	3	6	8	21
Transfer income [3]	8	4	3	4	3	6	45
Total	100	100	100	100	100	100	100
Per cent of spending units in group with specified type of income:							
Wage and salary income [1]	81	96	94	90	91	82	33
Farming, unincorporated business income [2]	13	4	10	18	17	11	13
Capital income	29	9	23	28	33	35	43
Transfer income [3]	30	19	19	23	18	30	84

SOURCE: *1961 Survey of Consumer Finances.*

[1] Includes income from salaries, wages, professional practice, trade, or other self-employment.

[2] Includes income from farming (of farmers and nonfarmers), roomers and boarders, and unincorporated business.

[3] Includes public transfer payments and private payments if regularly made.

as measured by the average number of persons in the unit, was also less.

One in 5 of all spending units headed by persons aged 65 or over has few or no assets (less than $1000), a figure not substantially different from the next youngest age groups. The proportion who has

TABLE 5

Employment Experience and Extent of Employment within Age of Head of Spending Unit, 1960
(*percentage distribution*)

Employment status of spending unit head	All spending units	Age of spending unit head					
		18–24	*25–34*	*35–44*	*45–54*	*55–64*	*65+*
Employee S.U.'s [1]	71	93	89	81	78	64	16
Employed:							
50–52 weeks	52	55	67	62	58	45	10
40–49 weeks	7	13	9	8	7	6	2
39 weeks or less	11	23	11	10	12	12	3
Not ascertained	1	2	2	1	1	1	1
Farmers	5	3	3	5	6	6	5
Other self-employed	9	2	7	12	12	12	5
Retired	13	—	—	—	1	18	74
Miscellaneous [2]	2	2	1	2	3	—	—
Total	100	100	100	100	100	100	100

SOURCE: *1960 Survey of Consumer Finances.*

[1] Employee spending units include those professional and technical workers, managers, officials, clerical and sales workers, skilled, semi-skilled, and unskilled workers who work for someone else.

[2] Housewives, members of the armed services, students, etc. Housewives 55 years and over who do not generally work for pay and who are the head of a spending unit are classified as retired.

TABLE 6

Personal Debt and Assets within Age of Head of Spending Unit, 1960
(*percentage distribution*)

Item	All spending units	Age of spending unit head					
		18–24	*25–34*	*35–44*	*45–54*	*55–64*	*65+*
Installment debt							
None	52	46	37	41	50	69	84
$1–199	12	15	14	12	14	10	7
$200–999	22	23	29	27	23	14	7
$1000+	14	16	20	20	13	7	2
Total	100	100	100	100	100	100	100

76

Item	All spending units	Age of spending unit head					
		18–24	25–34	35–44	45–54	55–64	65+
Debt owed to doctors, dentists or hospitals [1]							
Per cent who owe	21	20	30	25	22	13	12
Average amount owed	$110	$80	$130	$90	$130	$90	$130
Value of all assets [2]							
None	14	30	16	13	10	14	13
Very limited (Less than $1000)	18	50	29	14	11	10	8
Limited ($1000–4999)	16	14	22	17	15	11	15
Moderate ($5000–9999)	20	2	17	24	23	21	22
Substantial ($10,000–24,999)	19	1	10	20	27	25	23
Very substantial ($25,000 or more)	11	2	4	10	13	17	18
Not ascertained	2	1	2	2	1	2	2
Total	100	100	100	100	100	100	100
Liquid assets [3]							
None	24	34	24	20	20	24	30
$1–999	40	53	54	45	36	30	19
$1000–4999	25	13	19	26	30	27	29
$5000 or more	11	—	3	9	14	19	22
Total	100	100	100	100	100	100	100

SOURCE: *1960 Survey of Consumer Finances,* unless otherwise noted.

[1] Data from *1957 Survey of Consumer Finances.*

[2] Includes equity in home, liquid assets, corporate stock, and value of other real estate owned and share of unincorporated business. For further detail see *1960 Survey of Consumer Finances,* technical appendix to Chapter 7, pp. 119–21.

[3] Includes savings bonds, checking accounts, and savings accounts in banks, savings and loan associations, and credit unions.

no liquid assets increases among the aged, however, indicating the greater difficulty for them of drawing on their accumulated reserves. Low income and low assets tend to be associated among the aged, and about 40 per cent of the aged with incomes below $2000 have very limited assets.

RETIREMENT PLANS OF THE NONRETIRED

Most workers eventually retire, either because they plan to, because of involuntary retirement programs, or because of inability to work.[3] The financial plans and expectations of the nonretired concerning their retirement provide interesting information on the manner in which they approach this very probable event.

Data on retirement plans and attitudes of the nonretired were collected from a national cross-section of spending unit heads early in 1960. All nonretired spending unit heads aged 30 or over were asked about the age at which they plan to retire, their eligibility for social security and private pension programs, and how well they felt they would be able to manage financially during their retirement. These spending unit heads also were asked about any specific plans for what they will do when they retire. These plans and prospects, and data on the present financial and personal circumstances of the nonretired spending unit heads, were analyzed in order to answer two important questions: (1) what are the plans and expectations of the nonretired for their own retirement, and (2) how realistic are these plans?

Most nonretired spending unit heads aged 30 and over plan to retire before they are 70 years old. Only 12 per cent reported that they did not know when they would retire or had not thought about it. However, 25 per cent reported that they did not plan to retire. Indefinite postponement of retirement is viewed as generally unrealistic.

Definite plans for retirement seem to be closely associated with education, occupation, and race. Spending unit heads with college educations plan to retire earlier than those who have not completed high school. White farmers report significantly fewer plans to retire than do others in the sample. Lack of plans may stem from farmers' self-employment status, their general exclusion from compulsory retirement programs, and their irregular hours of work. Nearly half of the nonwhite spending unit heads reported either that they did not plan to retire or that they did not know when they would retire. This may be due to the low economic position of nonwhites and the general instability of their employment.

Those who express plans to retire are much more likely to say that they will be able to get along financially during the retirement years than are those who say that they are uncertain or will never retire. Four of every 5 of those who plan to retire before age 65 expect that they would be able to get along financially during retirement. Those who plan to retire between ages 65 and 70 are only slightly less optimistic. Among those who do not plan to retire or are uncertain about when they will retire, 56 per cent feel they could manage financially.

This finding is emphasized by the experience of persons who have already retired. Spending unit heads who have already retired report

TABLE 7

Amount of Dissaving Since Retirement within Whether Spending Unit Head's Retirement Was Planned
(*percentage distribution*)

Amount of dissaving since time of head's retirement	Head's retirement		All retired spending unit heads [1]
	Planned	Not planned	
Had savings at time of retirement; have used:			
Less than one-fourth	14	6	9
One-fourth to one-half	4	8	7
One-half to three-fourths	3	6	4
More than three-fourths	6	20	15
Amount not ascertained	9	6	7
Have not dissaved; had no savings when retired, have none now	51	37	42
Have saved since retirement	13	17	16
Total	100	100	100
Number of spending unit heads	104	177	304
Per cent of spending unit heads	35	57	100

SOURCE: 1960 "Patterns of Family Change" study.
[1] Includes 8 per cent for whom planning was not ascertained.

much greater dissaving since retirement if their retirement was not planned than if they had planned to retire (Table 7). Included among those who did not plan to retire are some spending unit heads who became disabled and were forced to leave the labor force. For these persons the problem of discontinued earnings may have been accentuated by unusual medical expenses.

Two-thirds of the nonretired spending unit heads aged 30 and older

TABLE 8

Retirement Plans within General Retirement Outlook of Nonretired Spending Unit Heads 30 and Older, 1960
(*percentage distribution*)

	General retirement outlook			All non-retired spending unit heads 30 and older
Retirement plans	Things will be all right	Things will be difficult	Depends, do not know, not ascertained	
Get another job	5	9	5	5
Start business or farm	4	4	1	4
Work on hobbies; other unpaid work	4	3	4	4
Travel	8	0	3	6
Move to another location	4	4	1	4
Other plans	6	4	3	5
No plans	67	74	64	67
Not ascertained	2	2	19	5
Total	100	100	100	100
Number of spending unit heads	1276	270	421	1967
Per cent of nonretired spending unit heads aged 30 or more	66	13	21	100

SOURCE: 1960 "Patterns of Family Change" study.

expect that things will be all right during retirement (Table 8). Non-retired spending unit heads who report that times will be difficult mention plans to take a part-time job after retirement more frequently than heads who feel they will be able to get along. The latter group mention more plans to travel. Differences in plans suggest a considerable variation in the amount of retirement income available to those who will get along and those for whom retirement will be difficult. However, two-thirds of all nonretired spending unit heads 30 years and older mentioned no plans for what they will do during retirement.

As would be expected, the financial resources available for retirement affect retirement outlook. Most of those eligible for social security benefits report that things will be all right during retirement. Less than one-fourth of those who are not eligible for any old-age pensions express optimistic retirement outlooks (Table 9).

TABLE 9

General Retirement Outlook within Eligibility for Pensions of Spending Unit Heads 30 and Older, Not Retired, 1960
(*percentage distribution*)

General retirement outlook	*Eligibility for pensions*			*All spending unit heads 30 and older not retired* [1]
	No pensions	*Only social security*	*Social security and private pensions*	
Things will be all right	22	63	76	66
Things will be difficult	17	16	8	13
Depends	2	6	5	5
Not ascertained	59	15	11	16
Total	100	100	100	100
Number of spending unit heads	136	1098	710	1967
Per cent of nonretired spending unit heads aged 30 or more	6	54	39	100

SOURCE: 1960 "Patterns of Family Change" study.
[1] Includes 23 spending unit heads who will receive only private pensions.

Savings have a similar effect on the retirement outlook of spending unit heads. The larger the liquid assets held by the spending unit, the more likely the head is to expect good times during retirement. The expectation of financial problems during old age increases with the age of the spending unit head: 9 per cent of spending unit heads between the ages of 30 and 45 foresee financial difficulty during retirement; 16 per cent of spending unit heads aged 45 and older foresee economic difficulties after they retire.

In summary, there are many families who approach retirement with vague notions about their retirement income and with indefinite plans about the age at which they will retire. The most concrete plans for retirement include participation in social security and private pension plans which will supply the bulk of retirement income for most families. In a majority of cases participation in these programs is not voluntary. Nearly all families are covered by social security and two-fifths are covered by private pensions. Those persons who are not covered under either public or private pension plans are clearly the worst prepared for retirement. They are unlikely to have savings, substantial equity in a home, or protection against medical expenses. It would appear that many in this group will become dependent on others when their present earnings cease. For this reason, it is useful to examine the attitudes of both the retired and the non-retired toward the responsibility for support of the dependent aged.

ATTITUDES TOWARD RESPONSIBILITY FOR THE NEEDY AGED

Attitudes toward responsibility for old people were ascertained from the following question, asked of all spending unit heads in the sample: "If the older people don't have enough money, do you think their relatives should support them, or should the government take care of them, or what? Why do you say so?" 59 per cent of the spending unit heads felt that relatives should be solely or primarily responsible for older people who are in need (Table 10). Of course, most families are already covered by public or private income maintenance programs, and it is assumed that the responses implied need in addition to support already provided by programs like social security.

A majority of the spending unit heads who feel that relatives should be responsible for older people gave moral or normative reasons for their attitude. One who felt that relatives should be solely responsible said: "It's their duty, just like it was the parents' duty to take care of the kids." Many who gave moral reasons reiterated this idea of a debt to the parents.

TABLE 10

Reasons for Attitude Toward Responsibility for the Aged within Attitude of Spending Unit Heads, 1960
(*percentage distribution*)

		Attitude toward responsibility for the aged				
	Relatives should have:		Relatives and government should share responsibility	Government should have:		All spending unit heads[2]
Reason for attitude toward responsibility for the aged[1]	sole responsibility	primary responsibility		primary responsibility	sole responsibility	
Relatives should have responsibility because:						
Government pensions are too low	1	1	6	5	0	1
Government expenses are too high	11	9	3	1	0	6
Families should care for their own	75	44	29	14	0	38
Older people prefer help from relatives	6	5	2	2	0	3
Other reasons	4	2	6	1	0	2
Who should have responsibility depends on:						
Finances	11	44	27	23	0	20
Other things	2	4	4	10	0	3
Government should have responsibility because:						
Government pensions are adequate	0	2	8	11	13	5
Relatives cannot afford to support them	0	6	16	15	33	11
This is the government's job	0	11	33	45	49	19

TABLE 10 (*continued*)

(*percentage distribution*)

Reason for attitude toward responsibility for the aged [1]	Relatives should have: sole responsibility	Relatives should have: primary responsibility	Relatives and government should share responsibility	Government should have: primary responsibility	Government should have: sole responsibility	All spending unit heads [2]
Older people prefer government help	0	0	1	4	5	2
Other reasons	0	4	6	6	8	4
Number of cases	836	831	266	182	681	2997
Per cent of all spending unit heads	29	30	9	6	21	100

SOURCE: 1960 "Patterns of Family Change" study.

[1] Does not add to 100 per cent because some spending unit heads gave more than one reason and some gave no reasons. Note that people can give contradictory reasons.

[2] Includes 5 per cent of the sample for whom feeling about responsibility for the aged was not ascertained.

Some think that relatives should be responsible because the government already has too many responsibilities or too many expenses. "There is too much feeling nowadays that the government is responsible for all of an individual's problems, rather than the individual himself." "The government can't afford to support everybody," said one, and some thought that "taxes are too high as it is."

Some persons believe that older people themselves would prefer help from their own families rather than from the government: "The old folks have their dignity, they don't want to panhandle from the government;" and "It's bad enough to be getting from their children, but that's better than being on the government."

About one-fifth of the spending unit heads feel that responsibility depended upon whether the old people had children, or whether the children were financially able to help them.

Those who believe that the primary responsibility belongs to the government spoke mostly of the responsibility in terms of the government's role and its obligations. Many people felt that "old folks have been paying taxes all their lives, they should get some of it back." Some mentioned that "the government should start using taxes for our problems rather than for foreign problems." The idea that old people should get some kind of payment in return for their taxes was the most prominent reason given by those who feel that the government should be responsible for older people.

The next most important reason for government responsibility is that relatives could not afford to support anyone outside their immediate families. "Most people can barely take care of themselves," said several; "most folks around here do all they can just to make ends meet."

In order to measure the extent to which attitudes toward relative responsibility reflect local laws, local culture, and local experiences of the aged, the attitude toward relative responsibility was examined with two local area variables. The per cent of the aged in the state who receive either social security benefits or Old-Age Assistance was used to test the hypothesis that, if a substantial fraction of the aged in a state are getting OASI or OAA benefits, then the people in the state might be more likely to see the government as responsible for the aged. Although it is difficult to determine the direction of the causation, the proportion of the aged getting some kind of government assistance seems to be only slightly correlated with attitudes toward responsibility (Table 11). Where less than 70 per cent of the aged receive either OAA or OASI a slightly larger proportion feel that relatives should be responsible; in the few states where 80 per cent or more of the aged get benefits, spending unit heads are strikingly more in favor of government responsibility.

The amount of money per inhabitant paid out in Old-Age Assistance is also weakly related to attitudes about responsibility. Only for the small group where benefits are the largest is there a noticeable relation between payment size and attitudes (Table 12).

In order to determine what causes the differences in opinion among spending unit heads, a multivariate analysis was carried out relating demographic and social characteristics of the spending unit heads, their financial position, and local area factors to their attitudes about financial responsibility for the aged. The most important effects are a positive relation between the indicators of economic status and

TABLE 11

Attitude of Spending Unit Heads Toward Responsibility for the Aged, within Per Cent of Aged in State Who Receive OAA or OASI, 1960
(*percentage distribution*)

Attitude toward responsibility for the aged	*Per cent of aged in state who receive OAA or OASI*				*All spending unit heads*
	Under 70	*70–74.9*	*75–79.9*	*80 or more*	
Relatives only	26	30	30	16	29
Relatives primarily	37	30	27	24	30
Relatives and government	8	10	8	8	9
Government primarily	6	6	7	8	6
Government only	18	20	23	38	21
Other	1	0	1	0	1
Not ascertained	4	4	4	6	4
Total	100	100	100	100	100
Per cent of sample	16	39	42	3	100

SOURCE: 1960 "Patterns of Family Change" study.

family responsibility. Those with higher economic status, measured by the spending unit's income and the earning potential of the spending unit head, more often felt that the family should be responsible. Next most important was a variable describing the composition of the unit which was expected to serve as an index of demands on income and housing space. The relation discovered was that single persons were most in favor of relative responsibility and that childless married couples most favored government responsibility. Personal characteristics, such as political affiliation and the head's attitude toward hard work and lucky breaks, also affect the attitude toward responsibility for the aged to some extent.

A perusal of Tables 13 and 14 reveals that for each age group separately, reliance on government responsibility declines in each higher education group, and similarly, reliance on relative responsibility rises in each education group. There is a similar but less precise relationship for each age group in that reliance on relative responsibility tends to increase for higher income groups.

TABLE 12

Attitude of Spending Unit Heads toward Responsibility for the Aged within Amount of Old-Age Assistance Per Inhabitant of States, 1960
(*percentage distribution*)

Attitude toward responsibility for the aged	*Amount of Old-Age Assistance per inhabitant of states*						*All spending unit heads*
	Under $5	*$5– 7.49*	*$7.50– 9.99*	*$10– 14.99*	*$15– 20.99*	*$21 and over*	
Relatives should have:							
Sole responsibility	33	29	30	29	26	24	29
Primary responsibility	32	30	29	27	31	24	30
Relatives and government should share responsibility	7	10	10	9	10	7	9
Government should have:							
Primary responsibility	4	6	6	6	8	4	6
Sole responsibility	19	21	21	22	21	39	21
Other	1	0	1	1	1	0	1
Not ascertained	4	4	3	6	3	2	4
Total	100	100	100	100	100	100	100
Per cent of spending units	15	24	21	18	20	2	100

SOURCE: 1960 "Patterns of Family Change" study.

TABLE 13

Attitudes of Spending Unit Heads Toward Responsibility for the Aged, within Age and Education of Spending Unit Heads, 1960
(*percentage distribution*)

Attitude toward responsibility for the aged	Education and age of spending unit heads												All spending unit heads
	Less than 12 grades				High school or more				Some college, college degree				
	18–34	35–54	55–64	65+	18–34	35–54	55–64	65+	18–34	35–54	55–64	65+	
Relatives should have:													
Sole responsibility	22	25	17	17	34	38	30	32	41	41	37	40	29
Primary responsibility	28	30	33	27	24	33	29	21	27	33	36	28	30
Total relative responsibility	50	55	50	44	58	71	59	53	68	74	73	68	59
Relatives and government should share responsibility equally	14	8	8	3	14	8	7	10	10	11	13	4	9
Government should have:													
Primary responsibility	24	27	32	36	17	13	19	15	10	9	9	22	21
Sole responsibility	9	6	6	4	9	6	7	7	9	3	2	2	6
Total government responsibility	33	33	38	40	26	19	26	22	19	12	11	24	27
Not ascertained	3	4	4	13	2	2	8	15	3	3	3	4	5
Total	100	100	100	100	100	100	100	100	100	100	100	100	100
Per cent of spending unit heads	11	21	10	11	9	12	2	2	8	9	3	2	100

Attitude of Spending Unit Heads Toward Responsibility for the Aged, within Age of Heads and Gross Disposable Income of Spending Units, 1960 (*percentage distribution*)

Attitude toward responsibility for the aged	Spending unit gross disposable incomes and age of heads																All spending unit heads
	Less than $3000				*$3000–4999*				*$5000–7499*				*$7500 and more*				
	18–34	35–54	55–64	65+	18–34	35–54	55–64	65+	18–34	35–54	55–64	65+	18–34	35–54	55–64	65+	
Relatives should have:																	
Sole responsibility	21	16	15	18	28	27	28	24	37	37	25	30	45	40	27	38	29
Primary responsibility	32	34	41	28	25	37	32	28	26	27	23	14	21	31	34	25	30
Total relative responsibility	53	50	55	46	53	64	60	52	63	64	48	44	65	71	61	63	59
Relatives and government should share responsibility equally	9	6	4	3	16	6	9	4	13	9	10	5	12	10	13	5	9
Government should have:																	
Primary responsibility	25	33	27	34	17	21	19	29	15	17	30	35	12	13	23	18	21
Sole responsibility	9	5	8	4	11	4	5	5	7	8	7	5	8	4	1	0	6
Total government responsibility	34	38	35	38	28	25	24	34	22	25	37	40	20	17	24	18	27
Not ascertained	4	6	5	13	3	5	7	10	2	2	5	11	2	2	2	14	5
Total	100	100	100	100	100	100	100	100	100	100	100	100	100	100	100	100	100
Per cent of spending unit heads	7	8	9	4	7	9	12	14	5	3	4	4	9	3	1	1	100

SOURCE: 1960 "Patterns of Family Change" study.

89

NOTES

[1] Much of the data presented herein has not previously been published; these data, however, are from surveys initially reported in earlier works. Reports of the recent surveys in the annual financial surveys of consumers dating from 1946 are contained in George Katona, Charles A. Lininger, James N. Morgan, and Eva Mueller, *1961 Survey of Consumer Finances* (Ann Arbor: Survey Research Center, 1962) and Economic Behavior Program, Survey Research Center, *1960 Survey of Consumer Finances* (Ann Arbor: Survey Research Center, 1961). The report on the 1962 survey will contain new information on medical debt and expenses, medical insurance, and net worth of consumers. The special survey in 1960 called "Patterns of Family Change" was extensively analyzed and reported in James N. Morgan, Martin David, Wilbur J. Cohen, and Harvey N. Brazer, *Income and Welfare in the United States* (New York: McGraw-Hill Book Company, 1962). Both consumer financial surveys and periodic attitude surveys are referred to in George Katona, *The Powerful Consumer* (New York: McGraw-Hill Book Company, 1960).

[2] Each respondent replied according to his own definition of "large."

[3] See Wilma Donahue, Harold L. Orbach, and Otto Pollock, "Retirement: The Emerging Social Pattern," in *Handbook of Social Gerontology*, edited by Clark Tibbitts (Chicago: University of Chicago Press, 1960), pp. 356 ff.

CHAPTER 6

THE INCOME POSITION OF THE AGED

Lenore A. Epstein

The average annual income, shown in reports by the Bureau of the Census, is substantially less for families with heads 65 years or older than for those headed by persons under 65. Similarly, the yearly income received by older persons who live alone or with nonrelatives is significantly less on the average than the income of younger persons in this category. Such disparity in income reflects, of course, differences in the social and economic structure of these two age groups.

For 1960, for the first time, the Bureau of the Census has tabulated the annual income survey data for older people by major social and economic characteristics.[1] For 1958 the Bureau of the Census has prepared special tabulations which permit joint analysis of personal and family income and the family situation of the aged.[2] These two sets of tabulations supplement and give additional meaning to the annual statistics on the money income of aged persons and of families with head 65 and over.

Most revealing, perhaps, are the income figures for families cross-classified by size and by age of head. It is obviously more meaningful to compare income data for the families of a given size than to compare income per family member for families of all sizes combined. More important, however, is the fact that the distribution by size of family is very different for the two age groups: Of all families with head 65 and over, almost three-fourths were two-person families, as compared with only about one-fourth of families with head under 65 (Table 1). Since two-person families make up the bulk of so-called aged families, it is logical to emphasize their income position when comparing old and young. The median income in 1960 for the two-person family was less than half as large when the head was 65 or older as when he was under 65—$2,530 as compared to $5,314.

Almost one-fourth of all persons 65 and over live alone or with non-

TABLE 1

Money Income of Families with Head Aged 65 and Over and Head Under 65, by Size of Family, 1960
(Noninstitutional population of the United States)

| Money income class | Families having specified number of members | | | | | | | | | |
| | All families | | Two | | Three | | Four | | Five or more | |
	Head 65 & over	Head under 65	Head 65 & over	Head under 65	Head 65 & over	Head under 65	Head 65 & over	Head under 65	Head 65 & over	Head under 65
Total	100.0	100.0	100.0	100.0	100.0	100.0	100.0	100.0	100.0	100.0
Under $2,000	*31.4*	*10.2*	*35.7*	*16.0*	*20.3*	*9.0*	*17.6*	*6.5*	*17.9*	*8.9*
Under $1,000	9.2	4.4	10.0	7.0	8.0	3.7	7.2	2.8	3.6	3.9
$1,000–$1,499	10.3	2.8	11.5	4.4	6.8	2.3	5.2	1.8	9.4	2.4
$1,500–$1,999	11.9	3.0	14.2	4.6	5.5	3.0	5.2	1.9	4.9	2.6
$2,000–$3,999	*32.4*	*16.5*	*35.5*	*18.8*	*28.2*	*16.6*	*15.7*	*14.5*	*20.0*	*15.8*
$2,000–$2,499	11.6	3.5	13.7	4.1	5.9	3.5	7.1	3.1	4.0	3.2
$2,500–$2,999	8.8	3.5	9.8	4.2	6.6	3.7	2.9	2.6	8.0	3.4
$3,000–$3,999	12.0	9.5	12.0	10.5	15.7	9.4	5.7	8.8	8.0	9.2
$4,000 and over	*36.1*	*73.3*	*28.8*	*65.1*	*51.6*	*74.6*	*66.6*	*79.1*	*62.0*	*75.3*
$4,000–$4,999	8.4	10.8	7.9	11.2	12.2	11.5	8.6	10.5	4.9	10.3
$5,000–$6,999	11.3	25.4	9.4	22.8	15.9	25.3	16.6	27.6	19.2	26.2
$7,000–$9,999	8.5	21.8	5.9	18.7	14.8	22.5	18.6	24.5	17.4	21.8
$10,000 and over	7.9	15.3	5.6	12.4	8.7	15.3	22.8	16.5	20.5	17.0
Median income	$2,897	$5,905	$2,530	$5,314	$4,122	$5,930	$6,100	$6,300	$5,727	$6,074
Mean size	2.5	3.9	2.0	2.0	3.0	3.0	4.0	4.0	6.4	6.2
Per cent distribution	100.0	100.0	72.9	26.4	16.4	21.6	5.1	22.9	5.6	29.1

SOURCE: U.S. Bureau of the Census, "Income of Families and Persons in the United States: 1960," *Current Population Reports: Consumer Income*, Series P-60, No. 37 (January 17, 1962), and related unpublished data.

92

relatives (the Census Bureau refers to them as unrelated individuals). Again, there is a substantial difference in the incomes received by older and younger unrelated individuals. The median income is less than half as large for those 65 and over as for those younger, namely $1,050 and $2,570 (Table 2). This is because only about one-fourth of the former had any earnings in 1960 compared with more than five-sixths of the younger persons living alone or with nonrelatives.

TABLE 2

Money Income of Persons Aged 65 and Over and Under 65 Living Alone or with Nonrelatives, by Sex, 1960
(*Noninstitutional population of the United States*)

Money income class	Total		Male		Female	
	65 and over	*Under 65*	*65 and over*	*Under 65*	*65 and over*	*Under 65*
Total	100.0	100.0	100.0	100.0	100.0	100.0
Under $1,000	47.7	26.2	34.6	20.3	52.9	31.0
$1,000–$1,499	21.3	9.3	24.6	8.4	20.0	9.9
$1,500–$1,999	10.4	5.7	13.5	4.7	9.1	6.4
$2,000–$2,499	6.2	7.8	9.5	6.3	4.9	9.0
$2,500–$2,999	3.2	6.6	3.9	6.0	3.0	7.0
$3,000–$3,999	4.7	13.0	4.0	11.6	5.0	14.0
$4,000–$4,999	2.4	12.8	3.8	14.8	1.9	11.2
$5,000 and over	4.0	18.6	6.0	27.9	3.1	11.5
Median income	$1,053	$2,571	$1,313	$3,371	$960	$2,152
Per cent distribution	100.0	100.0	27.5	44.0	72.5	56.0

SOURCE: U.S. Bureau of the Census, "Income of Families and Persons in the United States: 1960," *Current Population Reports: Consumer Income*, Series P-60, No. 37 (January 17, 1962), and related unpublished data.

The disparity in income for two-person families doubtless reflects the relatively large proportion of older couples and other two-person families in which neither member worked during 1960. For three-person families, more likely to have at least one member working, the median income for the older group was about 70 per cent of that for younger families. For even larger families, there was no significant difference in the average income, presumably because the older families contained several adults who might work, and the majority of the younger families contained no members of working age except the head and his wife. For each size of family, however, the proportion with less than $2,000 in 1960 was at least twice as large when the family head was aged 65 or over as when younger.

Persons other than the head typically make a relatively large contribution to the income of the older families.[3] For example, the median personal income reported by men aged 65 and over who were family heads was about $1,900 in 1960 (Table 3). By contrast, the median total income of the families they headed was about $2,900, or 50 per

TABLE 3

Money Income of Family Members Aged 65 and Over, by Marital and Family Status and Sex, 1960
(*Noninstitutional population of the United States*)

| | Family Head | | | | Other relatives of head | |
| | Male | | | | | |
Money income class	Married wife present	Other marital status	Female	Wife of head	Male	Female
Total	100.0	100.0	100.0	100.0	100.0	100.0
Under $1,000	*20.9*	*28.9*	*65.2*	*87.9*	*53.8*	*82.8*
Zero	1.6	4.0	15.2	36.6	17.5	32.4
$1–$999	19.3	24.9	50.0	51.3	36.3	50.4
$1,000–$1,999	*31.0*	*36.5*	*22.0*	*8.1*	*27.6*	*12.1*
$1,000–$1,499	18.7	25.7	13.9	5.4	19.7	7.6
$1,500–$1,999	12.3	10.8	8.1	2.7	7.9	4.5
$2,000–$2,499	12.4	7.9	3.3	1.1	6.3	1.7
$2,500–$2,999	7.4	7.4	2.0	.8	2.6	.9
$3,000–$3,999	8.3	7.0	3.8	.7	2.7	.9
$4,000–$4,999	5.4	1.7	1.3	.6	3.7	.6
$5,000 and over	14.6	10.6	2.5	.9	3.3	.9
Median income, all persons	$1,923	$1,411	$696	$262	$895	$350
Income recipients	$1,955	$1,449	$896	$671	$1,126	$742

SOURCE: U.S. Bureau of the Census, "Income of Families and Persons in the United States: 1960," *Current Population Reports: Consumer Income,* Series P-60, No. 37 (January 17, 1962), and related unpublished data.

cent larger. The corresponding excess of total family income over that of male heads was only about 20 per cent when the head was under age 65. Even more striking is the fact that the median income of families headed by a woman aged 65 or over was $3,100, although less than 8 per cent of all aged female family heads had personal income of $3,000 or more. Indeed, for older families with a woman as head, the median family income was about three times as large as the median income of the women who were income recipients.

The low incomes of aged families and individuals living alone clearly stem in large measure from the fact that so few work. In 1960, only one-sixth of the men 65 and over worked full-time for 50 weeks or more, and only 43 per cent worked at all during the year. Of the aged women, only 16 per cent in all had any work experience in 1960. The median income of the aged men who did not work at all in 1960 was only $1,360, or one-third that of men who had full-time jobs all year ($4,120), and roughly half that of men who worked at full-time jobs for 49 weeks or less.[4]

When classified by source of income rather than work experience, it appears that men with no earnings had not much more than half as much income, on the average, as those with earnings and other income, and one-third as much as aged men whose income was entirely from earnings (Table 4).

For families with head 65 or older, median incomes ranged between $1,920 for the large group (36 per cent) with no earnings to $4,570 for the 10 per cent with all their income from earnings (Table 5). Those with some earnings and some other income (more than half of all aged families) had somewhat smaller incomes, on the average, than those with earnings only. Many of the former group were retired and working only part-time to supplement their retirement income. Some, of course, had substantial income from investments. An important factor, however, was the number of family members with employment. The median income of aged families with one earner was less than two-thirds that of families with two or more earners ($3,420 as compared to $5,520), and the proportion reporting less than $2,000 was nearly twice as large. The additional earners in such families are ordinarily adult children or other younger persons.

Of the older persons living apart from relatives, as has been mentioned, less than one-fourth had any earnings. The median income of this favored group was roughly twice as high as that of the other aged

TABLE 4

Money Income of Persons Aged 65 and Over with Income, by Source of that Income, by Sex, 1960
(*Noninstitutional population of the United States*)

Money income class	Men				Women			
			Some earnings				Some earnings	
	Total	Nonearned income only	And other income	No other income	Total	Nonearned income only	And other income	No other income
Total	100.0	100.0	100.0	100.0	100.0	100.0	100.0	100.0
$1 to $999 or less	24.3	32.2	12.9	20.6	65.7	72.8	31.5	41.7
$1,000–$1,499	20.8	27.5	14.5	6.2	14.7	14.2	20.1	6.7
$1,500–$1,999	12.3	15.1	10.7	2.8	7.3	5.8	16.7	6.7
$2,000–$2,499	11.5	12.1	12.3	5.1	3.4	2.0	9.6	10.3
$2,500–$2,999	6.5	4.4	9.7	7.0	2.1	1.4	4.8	6.7
$3,000–$3,999	7.2	4.4	10.3	12.3	3.1	1.9	7.0	15.3
$4,000–$4,999	5.0	1.9	7.1	14.7	1.3	0.5	4.3	5.8
$5,000 and over	12.2	2.4	22.4	31.3	2.3	1.5	6.1	6.7
Median income	$1,698	$1,324	$2,482	$3,604	$821	$767	$1,460	$1,617
Per cent distribution	100.0	53.1	33.4	9.9	100.0	62.2	10.5	3.7

SOURCE: U.S. Bureau of the Census, "Income of Families and Persons in the United States: 1960," *Current Population Reports: Consumer Income*, Series P-60, No. 37 (January 17, 1962), and related unpublished data.

TABLE 5

Money Income of Families with Head Aged 65 and Over, by Source
of Income and Number of Earners, 1960
(*Noninstitutional population of the United States*)

Money income class	Total	No earnings [1]	*Some earnings*			
			And other income	*No other income*	*1 earner*	*2 or more earners*
Total	100.0	100.0	100.0	100.0	100.0	100.0
Under $2,000	*31.4*	*53.6*	*19.8*	*18.7*	*23.3*	*13.1*
Under $1,000	9.2	15.4	5.0	10.9	7.2	3.5
$1,000–$1,499	10.3	16.4	7.3	5.6	8.0	5.5
$1,500–$1,999	11.9	21.8	7.5	2.2	8.1	4.1
$2,000–$3,999	*32.4*	*37.0*	*31.1*	*24.8*	*34.6*	*22.6*
$2,000–$2,499	11.6	18.8	8.5	4.9	10.1	4.0
$2,500–$2,999	8.8	9.4	9.0	5.3	9.4	7.1
$3,000–$3,999	12.0	8.8	13.6	14.6	15.1	11.5
$4,000 and over	*36.1*	*9.3*	*49.2*	*56.6*	*42.1*	*64.2*
$4,000–$4,999	8.4	3.8	10.8	10.9	11.5	9.8
$5,000–$6,999	11.3	2.6	16.0	15.6	15.6	16.7
$7,000–$9,999	8.5	1.4	11.4	17.0	8.6	19.0
$10,000 and over	7.9	1.5	11.0	13.1	6.4	18.7
Median income	$2,897	$1,916	$3,925	$4,571	$3,423	$5,519
Per cent distribution	100.0	35.8	54.4	9.9	40.9	23.4

SOURCE: U.S. Bureau of the Census, "Income of Families and Persons in the
United States: 1960," *Current Population Reports: Consumer Income*, Series
P-60, No. 37 (January 17, 1962), and related unpublished data.
[1] Includes a small group with no income.

persons living alone or lodging—those without any earned income
(Table 6).

The economic well-being of elderly persons is related not only to
their own personal income, but also to the income of the entire family.
The special analytic tabulations of data from the March 1959 Current Population Survey permit joint analysis of personal and family
characteristics of persons aged 65 and over, relating the personal
money income of individual family members to the money income of

TABLE 6

Money Income of Persons Aged 65 and Over and Under 65, Living Alone or with Nonrelatives, by Source of Income, 1960

(Noninstitutional population of the United States)

Money income class	Aged 65 and over		Some earnings		Aged 14–64		Some earnings	
	Total [1]	Non-earned income only	And other income	No other income	Total [1]	Non-earned income only	And other income	No other income
Total	100.0	100.0	100.0	100.0	100.0	100.0	100.0	100.0
Under $1,000	47.7	52.0	24.4	37.9	26.2	48.6	12.6	19.1
$1,000–$1,499	21.3	25.5	15.9	7.9	9.3	24.2	8.7	8.5
$1,500–$1,999	10.4	9.8	16.2	3.9	5.7	8.4	5.8	6.0
$2,000–$2,499	6.2	4.3	14.0	7.8	7.8	4.0	7.8	9.4
$2,500–$2,999	3.2	2.3	6.1	7.2	6.6	4.2	7.5	7.4
$3,000–$3,999	4.7	3.1	7.9	15.0	13.0	5.7	13.8	15.5
$4,000–$4,999	2.4	1.3	4.7	9.2	12.8	3.2	14.0	15.4
$5,000 and over	4.0	1.8	10.8	11.1	18.6	1.7	29.7	18.6
Median income	$1,053	$976	$1,800	$2,021	$2,571	$1,028	$3,538	$2,972
Per cent distribution	100.0	70.1	19.4	6.1	100.0	9.2	25.4	56.5

SOURCE: U.S. Bureau of the Census, "Income of Families and Persons in the United States: 1960," Current Population Reports: Consumer Income, Series P-60, No. 37 (January 17, 1962), and related unpublished data.

[1] Includes individuals reporting no money income, not shown separately.

the entire family. They show that about two-thirds of all family members aged 65 and over are married and living with husband or wife (Table 7). Of these married persons, more than one-fourth have children or other relatives in the home.

Of all aged persons living in families, three-fifths share a home with a spouse only or with one other relative. About one-fifth live with two

TABLE 7

Distribution of Family Members Aged 65 and Over by Marital and Family Status, and Size of Family, March 1959
(*Noninstitutional population of the United States*)

		Marital and family status of member				
		Head				
		Male				
Size of family	*Total*	*Married wife present*	*Other marital status*	*Female*	*Wife of head*	*Other relative of head*
Total	100.0	40.8	3.5	8.9	25.3	21.5
Two-persons	61.2	29.3	2.1	5.5	19.6	4.7
Three-persons	18.7	6.6	.7	1.7	3.5	6.2
Four-persons	8.1	2.3	.4	.7	1.2	3.5
Five-persons	5.3	1.2	.2	.3	.5	3.1
Six-persons	2.9	.6	.1	.2	.2	1.8
Seven-persons	3.8	.8	.1	.4	.3	2.2

SOURCE: U.S. Bureau of the Census, "Family Characteristics of Persons: March 1959," *Current Population Reports: Population Characteristics,* Series P-20, No. 112 (December 29, 1961). Derived from Table 1.

relatives, and the other fifth are members of families containing 4 or more members.

Of the persons 65 and over living in the home of relatives, one-fifth were in families of 6 or more members, one-half in families of 4 or more (Table 8). Two-fifths of all such older persons were in the home of married couples likely to have dependent children.

The great majority of those who live in the home of relatives have little or no income of their own: more than half the men and four-fifths of the women in this situation had less than $1,000 cash income

TABLE 8

Distribution of Persons Aged 65 and Over Who Live in the Home of Relatives, by Age and Sex of Family Head, and Size of Family, March 1959
(*Noninstitutional population of the United States*)

					Age and family status of head				
		Under 65				*65 and over*			
		Male				*Male*			
Size of family	*Total*	*Total*	*Married spouse present*	*Other marital status*	*Fe-male*	*Total*	*Married spouse present*	*Other marital status*	*Fe-male*
Total	100.0	81.6	56.2	9.7	15.7	18.3	5.5	4.3	8.5
Two-persons	21.7	13.4	—	6.0	7.4	8.2	—	2.9	5.3
Three-persons	28.8	21.8	15.4	2.0	4.4	7.0	3.7	.9	2.4
Four-persons	16.5	14.3	11.8	.7	1.8	2.2	1.2	.5	.5
Five-persons	14.4	14.0	12.4	.5	1.1	.5	.3	*	.2
Six-persons	8.5	8.4	7.2	.5	.7	.1	.1	*	*
Seven or more persons	10.1	9.8	9.4	.1	.3	.3	.3	*	*

SOURCE: U.S. Bureau of the Census, "Family Characteristics of Persons: March 1959," *Current Population Reports: Population Characteristics,* Series P-20, No. 112 (December 29, 1961). Derived from Table 1.
* Less than 0.05.

in 1960 (Table 3). Roughly one-third of those with less than $1,000 income of their own in 1958 were in families with total money incomes below $3,000 in that year, and half were in families with less than $5,000 (Table 9).

These two sets of data made available by the Bureau of the Census at the beginning of 1962 round out the statistics which the Bureau compiles annually. The data on income by family size and by source and those on income of aged persons in relation to family incomes have given more meaning to the regular series on the size distribution of money income for aged persons and for families headed by persons 65 years and over.

It would be very desirable if such tabulations were made yearly. Together with data regularly available from the Survey Research Center on asset holdings and occasional more intensive studies, they would

TABLE 9

Family Members 65 Years Old and Over Who Live in the Home of Relatives by Own Income and Family Income in 1958, by Sex
(*Noninstitutional population of the United States*)

Sex and own income	Distribution by own income	Total	Distribution by family income			
			Under $3,000	$3,000– $4,999	$5,000– $6,999	$7,000 & over
Men	100.0	100.0	24.7	17.0	19.7	38.6
Zero income	14.6	100.0	*	*	*	*
$1–$999 or loss	42.8	100.0	35.4	22.4	17.4	24.8
$1,000 and over	42.6	100.0	8.1	8.8	24.4	58.8
Women	100.0	100.0	27.0	18.9	19.6	34.5
Zero income	35.0	100.0	26.0	16.6	18.3	39.0
$1–$999 or loss	51.3	100.0	31.7	20.2	21.5	26.6
$1,000 and over	13.7	100.0	11.7	19.8	16.0	52.5

SOURCE: U.S. Bureau of the Census, "Family Characteristics of Persons: March 1959," *Current Population Reports: Population Characteristics*, Series P-20, No. 112 (December 29, 1961). Derived from Table 8.
* Per cent not shown where base is less than 200,000.

serve to maintain an up-to-date picture of the financial position of older persons. Clearly, further research is required to determine how disparities in financial position relate to the economic requirements of older and younger families. Such information will play a fundamental role in defining the social and economic issues that affect older persons and in shaping policies to resolve them.

TECHNICAL NOTES

Money income is defined by the Census Bureau to include: (1) Money wages or salary; (2) net income from nonfarm self-employment; (3) net income from farm self-employment; (4) Social Security, veterans' payments, or other government or private pensions; (5) interest (on bonds or savings), dividends, and income from annuities, estates, or trusts; (6) net income from boarders or lodgers, or from renting property to others; (7) all other sources such as unemployment benefits, public assistance, alimony, etc. The amounts are gross before deduction for personal taxes, etc. Excluded are capital gains and losses and lump sum inheritances.

Source and reliability of estimates. Bureau of the Census estimates are based on data obtained in the Current Population Survey. Data on income were collected from approximately 26,000 representative households. Data on family status in March 1959 were collected from approximately 35,000 households.

All estimates are subject to sampling error and also to errors of response and nonreporting. Tables of the standard errors applicable to the data from the Bureau of the Census are included in the reports cited, e.g., P-60, No. 37 and P-20, No. 112.

In most cases, reports on income are based on memory rather than records and this probably produces underestimates because of a tendency to forget minor or irregular sources.

NOTES

[1] U.S. Bureau of the Census, "Income of Families and Persons in the United States: 1960," *Current Population Reports: Consumer Income,* Series P-60, No. 37 (January 17, 1962). Certain unpublished data underlying the summary data published for the aged were generously made available to the Social Security Administration.

[2] U.S. Bureau of the Census, "Family Characteristics of Persons: March 1959," *Current Population Reports: Population Characteristics,* Series P-20, No. 112 (December 29, 1961).

[3] Series P-60, No. 37, p. 8.

[4] *Ibid.,* Table G.

CHAPTER 7

MEASURING THE ADEQUACY OF RETIREMENT INCOMES *

Janet A. Fisher

There are two reasons why I shall not apply the traditional approach to measuring the adequacy of retirement incomes in this paper. First, those seeking results of recent and refined applications of such an approach may find them ably presented elsewhere.[1] Second, the opportunity to advance arguments for an altered approach to the problem is tempting. Income adequacy, in the final analysis, can only be measured at the individual family or spending unit level. It requires the estimation of unit resources, unit needs, and it also involves some assessment of the abilities of the unit member or members to allocate such resources to meet those needs. The tools of survey research have been developed to the point where such an altered approach might be feasible. That it would be difficult could also be interpreted as a challenge.[2]

In the meantime, there are certain materials relevant to the question of income adequacy of older people, all of which have not been fully exploited in the literature alluded to above. Some of them may improve our assessment of retirement incomes, of the ways in which they have been changing, and of the ways in which they are likely to change. These materials include characteristics of the annual incomes and financial resources both for the group in or past the age which our society now almost prescribes for retirement and also for those actually retired. The examination of these questions is made in terms of developments during most of the period since World War II.

During this period, a number of developments have taken place which vitally affect the economic position of persons aged 65 and over.

* The author wishes to thank the Survey Research Center, the University of Michigan and the Federal Reserve Board for making survey data available and to acknowledge computation facilities provided by the Social Systems Research Institute, the University of Wisconsin. She thanks Martin David and John G. Myers for their helpful comments.

Not only have the number and proportion of this group in the population increased, but also its composition has changed dramatically. Between 1947 and 1961, its proportion of farmers declined from 16 per cent to 3 per cent. In the same interval, its proportion of retired rose from 30 to 60 per cent; its proportion of widows not in the labor force increased from about 10 to 20 per cent. The last of these changes is reflected in the increase in single individuals from one-third to two-fifths of this age group.

Whether we examine Census figures, records of the Social Security Administration, special studies or sample surveys, we find much the same story. The figures just cited, however, as well as most of those to follow are from the annual Surveys of Consumer Finances conducted by the Survey Research Center at The University of Michigan. Based upon samples of the spending unit population, they refer not to all individuals belonging to specific age groups but to the separate units of one, two, or more persons headed by persons in these age groups. Responses to a question asked in the 1961 survey indicated that 84 per cent of the units containing one or more persons 65 and over were headed by a person in that age group.

The surveys in the late 1940's provided one of the first comprehensive sets of material for studying the economic status and behavior of people in the age group which more and more closely has become identified with retirement (and/or widowhood).[3] Subsequent surveys provide one of many sources now available to trace developments since then.

POSTWAR INCOME OF AGED SPENDING UNITS

The annual mean income of spending units in the 65 and over age group has averaged about 55 per cent of the annual mean income of all spending units during the postwar period.[4] True, this income mean ratio has varied around its average, rising as high as 66 and falling as low as 50 (Table 1). It has not, however, varied over time in such a fashion as to indicate any clear trend. There is some indication of a counter-cyclical pattern. (Some of this variation undoubtedly reflects fluctuations related to the use of samples rather than complete populations for the derivation of these figures, and some to changes in methods of measuring income.) While the mean income of all units has risen, the mean for those 65 and over has tended to stay at least 40 per cent below the mean for all age groups. In other words, increases in incomes of the units in this age group have apparently only just kept pace with the increased numbers in it and with the over-all rise in personal incomes.

This inference requires some qualification. With the rapid population growth in this country, the average number of people per spending unit has increased in those age groups up to 45, remained about the same in the groups aged 45 to 64, and declined in the group 65 and over. There is no completely satisfactory method yet known for adjusting income figures to reflect the differences or these changes in unit size. Economies of scale rule out simple per capita adjustments as such

TABLE 1

Income Mean Ratios of Spending Units Headed by Persons Aged 65 and Over

Year	Income mean ratio	Year	Income mean ratio
1946	57	1955	50
1950	54	1956	52
1951	66	1957	58
1952	64	1958	55
1953	56	1959	53
1954	54	1960	50

SOURCE: Annual Survey of Consumer Finances, Survey Research Center, The University of Michigan.

a method. However, if we use the unadjusted income mean ratio figures given above as a lower limit, and figures adjusted on a per capita basis as an upper limit, we can establish the range within which the desired measures must lie.

Assuming a constant income mean ratio of 55 for the 65 and over age group and adjusting this to a per capita basis, we get an upper limit of 77 for 1946 and 94 for 1960. If instead we use the actual income mean ratios of 57 and 50 for these two years, we get a per capita adjusted figure of 80 for the former and 85 for the latter period (Table 2).

Two qualifications of our earlier conclusions about the incomes of older people emerge from consideration of these adjusted figures. First, the income mean ratio for a given year with no allowance for unit size does exaggerate somewhat the difference between average incomes of the oldest and average incomes of all other age groups. Second, the inference that there has been no change in relative incomes of the aged ignores whatever improvement that can be associated with the relative and absolute decline in average spending unit size. Just how this improvement has been shared among the members of the older age group, we have not been able to determine. We have only some evidence for an informed guess.

In his work on "low incomes," Lampman investigated the position of single individuals and of families classified by age of head for the years 1947 and 1957. According to his estimates, both single indi-

TABLE 2

Unadjusted and Adjusted Income Mean Ratios of Spending Units Headed by Persons 65 and Over, Selected Years *

Year	Unadjusted income mean ratio	Per capita adjusted actual income mean ratio	Per capita adjusted constant income mean ratio
1946	57	80	77
1956	52	80	89
1960	50	85	94

* In columns 3 and 4 the spending unit income mean ratio is adjusted to a per capita income basis. The first set of adjusted figures is based on the unadjusted figures given in column 2; the second set is based on an assumed constant unadjusted mean ratio of 55.

viduals and families in the 65 and over category had the highest incidence of low incomes in both years. Over the decade, improvement was fairly substantial for families and even for single individuals under 65. It was relatively meager for both groups above that age. For the older families, the estimated proportions with low incomes declined from 53 to 50 per cent, while the numbers rose from 2.3 to 2.9 millions. For single individuals aged 65 and over the comparable proportions were 90 in 1947 and 88 in 1957, with the numbers increasing from 2.1 to 3.0 millions.[5]

The continued very high incidence of low incomes among single individuals suggests that the greater part of any improvement in mean incomes over the longer period 1946 to 1960, as well as within the decade bracketed by Lampman's study, was probably enjoyed by multi-person units. Unfortunately, incomparabilities in the data prevent any conclusive statement on this point.

INCOME DISTRIBUTION WITHIN THE AGED POPULATION

We do know more about certain other aspects of the distributions of income within age groups. For example, in the late 1940's the degree of concentration in income distributions was found to rise progressively with age: the older the age group, the greater was the inequality of income distribution within the group.[6] Among those spending units headed by persons 65 and over, the 10 per cent with the highest incomes received about 40 per cent of the total age group income. The top 20 per cent received nearly 60 per cent of the total age group income. Comparable figures were just about the same in 1956 and 1957. Likewise, the degree of concentration of income in each age group except the very youngest was apparently no different in 1956 and 1957 than in 1948. Inequality in the distribution of incomes was still highest among the group 65 and over. In other words, in that age group with a disproportionately small share of total income, that small share was less equally distributed than was the relatively larger share in other age groups.

From the estimated concentration figures for 1948, 1956, and 1957, we get the strong impression of a persistent age-specific pattern for all but the youngest. However, income figures for 1959 and 1960 weaken this impression. In these two years, the survey estimates indicate a gradual diminution of the inequality in incomes of spending units in the oldest age group, accompanied by no comparable change in the middle age groups. Still, even for these years, the 20 per cent of the spending units with the highest incomes (which ranged upwards from $4300 in 1960) accounted for at least one-half of the income received by the oldest age group (see Table 3). The remaining 80 per cent shared the other half of this age group's income. It would be interesting to know whether or not this indicated decline in income inequality among the aged is one which reflects some real improvement in the relative position of the lower income receiving units that may be explicable in terms of changing Social Security provisions and other arrangements which now affect such a large proportion of the older population.

What can we infer from these descriptive survey measures of incomes during the period considered? The first rough implication is that as a group, the older people are relatively no worse off in terms of annual income than were the older people soon after World War II. The top 10 per cent whose incomes were $5800 or more in 1960 may have been quite well off. A substantial proportion of the 70 per cent with incomes below $3300, and certainly most of the 50 per cent with incomes below $2200 in 1960 probably experienced more than a little financial difficulty, especially if they were primarily dependent upon their incomes to meet current expenditures.

TABLE 3

Proportion of Age Group Income Received within Income Deciles of Spending Units Headed by Persons 65 and Over, Selected Years

Income decile	Year		
	1948	1956	1960
Highest	41	44	31
Second	16	16	18
Third	13	10	13
Fourth	8	8	10
Fifth	7	6	8
Sixth	5	5	6
Seventh	4	4	5
Eighth	3	3	4
Ninth	2	3	3
Lowest	1	1	2
Total	100	100	100

SOURCE: Annual Survey of Consumer Finances, Survey Research Center, The University of Michigan.

Comparable figures for just those units whose heads were retired have been below those for the group aged 65 and over in each of the years since 1955 for which we have this information. For example, while the top 10 per cent of the age group 65 and over received incomes of $5800 or more in 1960, the top 10 per cent of the retired group had incomes of $5100 or more in 1960. This contrasts more sharply still with incomes of the rest of the spending units. Among those not retired the top 10 per cent received at least $11,000 in 1960. One way to view the various income characteristics of the aged is to inquire to what extent they may be described as either age-specific or cohort-specific (or neither). The evidence we have to date suggests that the relative mean incomes of the oldest group may be age-specific, and if our survey estimates had stopped with 1957, we would have had the same impression about the degree of income concentration among the oldest. Yet even had all the evidence supported an age-specific characterization of these income measures, we would still be tempted to examine a number of underlying forces which affect income size in order to evaluate the evidence and to assess future prospects. For example, the sharp decline in labor force participation among those 65 and older has been accompanied by a well-known change in the source of their incomes. Since World War II, Social Security and other retirement programs have been so expanded that, by the late 1950's, they had supplanted earnings as the principal source of incomes for the vast majority of this age group. Changes in the levels of benefits and permissible earnings under Social Security laws now have a far wider impact than they had in the early 1950's. This may explain why in the distributions of income by size, we find more of a shift from the very lowest income levels into the middle brackets ($2000–$5000) for the oldest group than for other age groups. Another aspect of these changes is the failure of the proportion with $7500 and greater incomes to increase among the aged as it has among each of the other age groups.

Properly to interpret these income changes, we must recognize that the spending unit population in this age group is determined by a complex of selection factors. Rising incomes and the increased availability of separate housing facilities have encouraged a substantial amount of undoubling during the postwar period. Other things equal, we might have expected this development to have lowered the average spending unit income and increased the degree of income inequality among the aged. Expanded institutional facilities for the aged provide a way for them to disappear from the spending unit population, and this also may affect not only their numbers, but the survey measures of income as well.

LIQUID ASSETS DISTRIBUTION

In the literature of recent years exploring the many-faceted problems of people aged 65 and over, few if any questions relevant to assessing the adequacy of their incomes have gone unmentioned. The one upon which I should like to focus next is that of financial assets, in particular those assets commonly denoted "liquid." In the Surveys of Consumer Finances, assets measured under this heading include money in checking accounts, all forms of savings accounts, and certain U.S. Government bonds.

Early in 1947, the mean liquid asset holdings of units aged 65 and over was estimated to be 111 per cent of the mean for all spending units. Ten years later, this figure had risen to 170, and by early 1960, the estimated mean ratio of liquid assets for this age group was 175. There seems little reason to believe that the relative proportion of total liquid assets held by the elderly has been age specific throughout these years. In fact, the sharp increase in relative holdings of the cohort now 65 and over is what we had expected to find. A substantial proportion of this group experienced their peak earnings during the war when the social pressures to save increased at least as much as the alternatives to saving declined. By the end of World War II, people in this cohort were already past the life cycle stage in which expenditures tend to be greatest.[7]

Still more interesting is to see how the increase in the liquid asset mean ratio of spending units in the oldest group has been shared among them. We find that it was accounted for primarily by an increase in the proportion with $2000 or more. That proportion rose from 20 per cent in 1947 to 36 per cent in 1957 and to 40 per cent in 1960. Yet throughout the same period the proportion of this age group with *no* liquid assets failed to decline. That proportion was 32 per cent in 1947, 32 per cent in 1957 and—the difference is not statistically significant—30 per cent in 1960. On a simple cohort basis, we might, indeed, have anticipated a decline. Nearly 80 per cent of the cohort, survivors of which entered the oldest age group by 1960 held some liquid assets in the late 1940's.

Even more so than annual incomes, liquid asset holdings are highly concentrated within the 65 and over age group—as, in fact they are within each of the other age groups. When ranked by asset size, the top 10 per cent of all spending units 65 and over held almost three-fifths of the liquid resources owned by this age group at the beginning of 1960. The top 20 per cent then held nearly 80 per cent of this group's liquid resources (Table 4).

Liquid assets and annual incomes are, of course, not perfectly correlated. Less than full year employment, part-time work, shifts to less

skilled jobs as well as retirement, all of these experiences of older people might be expected to affect the relation between past savings and
current income. On the other hand, these income reducing experiences
might also be related to the recent use of past savings.[8]

As noted earlier, in 1956 and 1957, the top 20 per cent of income
receivers among spending units in the 65 and over group accounted
for about 60 per cent of that group's total income. This same top 20
per cent of the income receivers also held close to one-half of the

TABLE 4

Proportion of Age Group Liquid Assets Held by Deciles of Spending Units Headed by Persons 65 and Over, 1960

Liquid asset decile	Per cent of assets held
Highest	59
Second	19
Third	11
Fourth	6
Fifth	4
Sixth	1
Seventh	*
Eighth	—
Ninth	—
Lowest	—
Total	100

SOURCE: 1960 Survey of Consumer Finances.
* Less than 0.5 per cent.

liquid assets owned by units in their age group. Similar relationships
again seem to characterize the retired, and comparable figures from the
1960 Survey of Consumer Finances indicate the same relationship of
liquid asset holdings at the beginning of that year to 1959 income size
for the aged and the retired.

Examination of these financial assets then does little to alter the
general picture that the vast majority of older people still have limited
resources. To include other financial assets such as stocks and municipal bond holdings would only sharpen the outlines of inequality in the
distribution of such resources among the aged. Still, omitted from this
picture, are a variety of other matters relevant to the assessment of

income adequacy. Home ownership, and especially mortgage free ownership is, as Lininger shows in his paper,[9] one of the most important. However, as many are aware, the importance of home ownership can be overestimated. For example, those who would adjust money income to include the value of services currently received from living in an owned home, should also remember that this nonmoney income is not subject to the same optimal allocation on a current basis as is money income. Homes owned by those 65 and older are primarily homes purchased at a much earlier date. Such homes no longer suit the needs of many of their occupants. The value of property investment will in some instances be declining, while potential returns from alternative investments are foregone.

Finally, let us turn from the specific questions of asset ownership to a more general one about economic behavior. Earlier research on current savings by consumer units in different age groups has indicated a relationship that may be helpful in shedding light upon adequate income levels.[10] A high income elasticity of savings among the oldest group—that is relatively little variation of total expenditures with income—suggests that for this group more than any other, there may be some level of income which we might infer to be adequate. And this inference could be based on the spending behavior of people in this age group.

There are, however, a number of problems to be resolved before pursuing this approach. First it must be emphasized that this relationship refers to all spending units with heads aged 65 and over in this country, and not just to the retired. Lydall, who studied the same question in Great Britain for the year 1952, also found a tendency for the income elasticity of savings to increase with age, but only up to age 65.[11] In Britain at that time, a much higher proportion of the oldest group was retired than was the case in this country. Lydall argued that the high income elasticity of savings in the 45–64 age group was associated with the importance of entrepreneurial income in that age group. Given this argument, the importance of entrepreneurial income may also have been the basis for the high income elasticity of savings among those 65 and over in this country at the end of the 1940's. With the sharp decline in importance of such income for the oldest group since then, it would certainly be worth investigating the current income elasticity of saving in this age group in the United States.

How can we find out if the variation of total expenditures with income size still is less for the aged? In recent years, there has been only one study I know of that could give us an answer. That is the 1961 expenditure survey conducted by the Bureau of Labor Statistics. Whatever analyses are made of these data, I do hope that they will be used for this purpose as well.

NOTES

[1] For a few of many recent examples, see Lenore A. Epstein, "Money Income of Aged Persons, A 10 Year Review, 1948–1958," *Social Security Bulletin,* 22 (June, 1959), 3–11; Margaret S. Gordon, "The Income Status of Older Persons and the Adequacy of Retirement Income Provisions," in U.S. Senate Special Committee on Aging, *Retirement Income of the Aging*—Hearings before the Sub-committee on Retirement Income, 87th Congress, 1st Session, July 12–13, 1961 (Washington, D.C.: U.S. Government Printing Office, 1961), pp. 180–87; and James N. Morgan and Martin David, "The Aged and Their Economic Position—Some Highlights of a Survey Taken Early in 1960," *idem,* pp. 188–99.

[2] A retirement study currently being conducted by the School of Commerce and the Survey Research Laboratory at the University of Wisconsin include some questions quite pertinent to this approach.

[3] Although by early 1961, nearly 85 per cent of the spending units in this age group were headed by retired persons or widows not in the labor force, we should be careful to note that a substantial proportion of units headed by the retired and widowed were not in this age group. At this same time, nearly 20 per cent of the retired heads of spending units were younger, as were a still higher proportion of the widows.

[4] The author expresses her thanks to Albert M. Marckwardt of the Survey Research Center for the income mean ratio figures of different age groups from the 1951 through the 1961 Survey of Consumer Finances.

[5] Robert J. Lampman, *The Low Income Population and Economic Growth,* U.S. Congress Joint Economic Committee, Study of Employment and Price Levels, Study No. 12 (Washington, D.C.: U.S. Government Printing Office, 1959), see especially Table 11, p. 17.

[6] Janet A. Fisher, "Income, Spending and Saving Patterns of Consumer Units in Different Age Groups," in *Studies in Income and Wealth,* 15 (New York: National Bureau of Economic Research, 1952), 77–102.

[7] *Ibid.,* and Janet A. Fisher, "Postwar Changes in Income and Saving Among Consumers in Different Age Groups," *Econometrica,* 20 (January, 1952), 47–70.

[8] The extent to which this happens has been documented by Morgan and David, *op. cit.*

[9] Chapter 5.

[10] Janet A. Fisher, "Income, Spending and Saving Patterns of Consumer Units in Different Age Groups."

[11] Harold Lydall, "The Life Cycle in Income, Saving, and Asset Ownership," *Econometrica,* 23 (April, 1955), 131–50.

CHAPTER 8

TRENDS AND PROBABILITIES IN SOURCES OF RETIREMENT INCOME

Alvin M. David

In 1959, in a paper given to the Twelfth Annual Conference on Aging at Ann Arbor on income maintenance for the aged, I said that the aged are among the groups most likely to be left behind as the community makes social and economic progress, and I suggested some measures that could be adopted to improve their relative position.

At that time I noted that since we cannot count on the possibility of productive work as a way of life for any great proportion of our older people, we must expect that most people past so-called "retirement age" will really be retired. And, since more and more people will be living well into the period of retirement, most people will spend a substantial period of time in retired status.

What changes have there been in the sources of retirement income for these older people who can no longer depend on work for their income? What has brought about the changes that have occurred? Are there any new trends? Can the same trends be expected to continue in the future? These are some of the questions the present paper will attempt to answer. A partial answer to some of them can be found by comparing some figures from my 1959 paper with the figures for today.*

Now, as in 1959, old-age and survivors insurance benefits are the principal source of retirement income. At the end of June 1962 about 77 per cent of the aged—as compared with 70 per cent in 1959—were drawing benefits under the old-age, survivors, and disability insurance program or would have been able to draw them when they were no longer supported by substantial earnings from work. In addition, at the beginning of 1962 about 1.7 million people over age 65 were getting

---

* Ed. note: The figures in Mr. David's paper are the latest available as this volume is sent to press in November 1962.

benefits under the public retirement programs for government employees and railroad workers.

In the future these programs will provide retirement income for virtually everyone. The old-age, survivors, and disability insurance program will continue to provide the bulk of the protection. More than 90 per cent of the working population is covered under this program, and most of the rest are covered by the programs for civilian government employees and employees of the railroads. The only working people not covered are self-employed doctors of medicine and those household and farm workers and self-employed people who do not have the minimum earnings or employment required for their particular type of work to be covered. Most of the people who fail to meet these coverage requirements at a given time will over their lifetimes have enough work that is covered so that they will be able to qualify for social security benefits when they retire.

There have been no significant increases in coverage since 1959, but the extensions of coverage adopted earlier in the 1950's and liberalizations in eligibility requirements that enabled newly covered people to qualify for benefits within a reasonably short time are paying off in increased eligibility for benefits. Every year a larger proportion of the people reaching age 65 is eligible for retirement benefits. 87 per cent of those reaching 65 in 1962 are eligible under the social security program as compared with 85 per cent in 1959, and this percentage will rise in the future to 95 per cent or more.

It is worth noting, I think, that the proportion of women eligible for old-age and survivors insurance benefits based on their own earnings records has been rising as a result of their increasing participation in the labor force. At the beginning of 1950 some 306,000 women over 65 years of age—5 per cent of all women over 65 in the population—were eligible for benefits as retired workers. At the end of June 1962 some 3,211,000 women over 65 years of age—33 per cent of all women over 65 in the population—were eligible for benefits as retired workers. This increase in the proportion of women qualifying on their own work records has focused increasing attention on the question of whether or not a working woman who is potentially eligible for benefits on her husband's earnings and her own earnings gets sufficient recognition of her own contributions to the program. This is a question that will be given a great deal of study in the next few years.

In addition to the basic social security protection that grows out of their work, many people have additional protection under programs for veterans. In 1961 the number of the aged with income from veterans' pension and compensation programs reached 1.9 million, exceeding for the first time the number with income from the special programs for railroad and government employees. This number will rise as more and more people potentially eligible for veterans' payments reach age 65. It should be kept in mind, though, that to get payments under the veterans' program for a nonservice-connected disability, an aged person must meet an income test, and the growing effectiveness of the old-age and survivors insurance program and other forms of retirement protection will tend to limit the number of those potentially eligible who will actually get veterans' payments.

Realistically, of course, the amount of the average old-age and survivors insurance benefit is still not high enough so that by itself it makes a veteran ineligible under the income limitations. Since July 1, 1960, there has been a sliding scale of income and pension payments for people coming on the veterans' pension rolls that replaces the all-or-nothing concept whereby a full pension was paid to veterans whose income was barely within the limitation and no payments at all were made to those whose income exceeded the limitation by even a dollar. Under the new sliding scale a veteran without dependents gets the full pension of $85 a month if his income is $600 or less a year; if his income is between $600 and $1,200 he gets a pension of $70; and if his income is between $1,200 and $1,800 a year, he gets a pension of $40. A veteran could get the $40 pension, even if he had the maximum old-age insurance benefit of $127, if he did not have substantial income from other sources. Many veterans will, of course, have other income.

As might be expected from the increase in the relative number of the aged getting payments related to past work or military service, the proportion of the aged getting payments under the old-age assistance program has been declining. While it is well known that as the old-age, survivors, and disability insurance program has expanded over the years the roles of the insurance and public assistance programs in maintaining income have been reversed, I think this point needs to be emphasized because the role the insurance program is playing cannot be fully appreciated except in contrast to the situation before it took hold. In 1940, only 7 out of every 1,000 people over 65 years of age were getting old-age and survivors insurance benefits and 228 out of every 1,000 were getting old-age assistance payments. At the end of

June 1962, 686 out of every 1,000 people over 65 were getting old-age and survivors insurance benefits, and the number getting old-age assistance payments had dropped to 128 out of every 1,000 people over 65. Despite the great increase in the number of aged people in the nation, the number of the aged on assistance has been slowly declining over the past 12 years, and only about 2.2 million are on the rolls today compared to about 2.8 million in 1950.

The decline in the role of the old-age assistance program as a source of support for the aged is reflected also in the declining proportion of old-age and survivors insurance beneficiaries who get assistance payments—a trend that started in the early 1950's. In 1951, about 12 per cent of the old-age and survivors insurance beneficiaries were getting payments under the assistance program compared to about 6.5 per cent in 1961. Thus, as the old-age and survivors insurance program has grown in effectiveness, fewer and fewer of its beneficiaries have required assistance to help meet their basic needs. This decline in the role of old-age assistance is expected to continue. It should be kept in mind, though, that even with virtually universal coverage under the old-age and survivors insurance program there will always be those who, for one reason or another, will need an assistance program to which they can turn. The extent to which old people will need assistance will depend in considerable part on what action is taken to provide health insurance for the aged under old-age and survivors insurance.

While the growth of old-age, survivors, and disability insurance has resulted in a decline in the role of public assistance, employee pension plans have grown side by side with social insurance. The social security program appears to have stimulated rather than supplanted these other forms of protection. In 1960 some 21.5 million workers were covered by private pension plans and about 1.8 million people were beneficiaries of these plans. Since most of these people are also covered by the old-age and survivors insurance program, private pension plans represent an important supplement to the basic social insurance system. It should be kept in mind, though, that while we can expect even greater coverage under private pension plans in the future, such coverage will never be universal. Private pension plans are not feasible in certain types of work—for example, domestic and farm work, work in the service industries, and work for small firms generally. Also, unless early vesting provisions become really common under private pension plans, much of the coverage that does exist will not be translated into retirement benefits in old age. Unlike the basic protection provided under the social security program, which follows the worker into almost any kind of employment, the protection provided by private pension plans often ends when the worker changes jobs. The lack of vesting tends, of course, to induce employees to stay with the particular employer, and this result is one of the objectives an employer has in mind when he sets up a private plan. In recent years, however, there has been a growing recognition that vesting may have advantages both for the employer and for the economy as a whole.

In addition to these major sources of retirement income, there are, of course, others that are available to some of the aged—for example, annuities purchased individually or elected as settlements under life insurance policies, interest, dividends, and rents. These forms of supplementation, as well as private pensions, are encouraged by the payment of old-age, survivors, and disability insurance benefits without regard to other resources. Over the past 10 years, there has been a small but steady increase in the number of annuities providing current income. In 1952 income was being provided under 645,000 individually purchased annuities and contracts for paying life insurance policy proceeds as lifetime income, while 807,000 such annuities and supplementary contracts were providing income in 1961. To judge from a 1958 survey, perhaps three-quarters of this annuity income is going to people 65 or over.

So far as the over-all proportion of the aged who have a source of retirement income or who will have such a source when they retire is concerned, then, the picture is quite encouraging. Most of those now over 65 get benefits under the old-age and survivors insurance program or the retirement programs for government employees and railroad workers, the vast majority of those turning age 65 are eligible for such benefits, and eventually almost everyone over age 65 will get such benefits. In addition, many people have protection under veterans' programs, private pension or deferred profit-sharing plans, and individual arrangements.

Now, what do we know about the level of retirement income that the aged can expect from these sources? Early in 1963 the Bureau of the Census will conduct for the Social Security Administration a survey of the aged population. We will identify those among the aged who are beneficiaries of old-age and survivors insurance and, from the information obtained in the survey, we will be able to tabulate data showing the retirement income that these people had in 1962. Tabulations of data will be available in the fall of 1963. At present, the national survey of beneficiary income conducted by the Bureau of Old-Age and Survivors Insurance in 1957 is still our best source of data on the retirement income that people get. Although the 1963 survey will undoubtedly show that retirement income is now at a somewhat higher level—particularly in view of the higher level of old-age and survivors insurance benefits today—the data collected by the 1957 survey give some indication of the kind of retirement income the aged receive from the sources available to them.

The data indicate that a large proportion of old-age and survivors insurance beneficiaries have only their benefits as retirement income— that is, as independent income that can reasonably be expected to continue in about the same amount as in the survey year. About 32 per cent of the married couples included in the survey had no source of retirement income except old-age and survivors insurance benefits, and these couples had a median annual retirement income of $990; two-thirds of the couples with old-age and survivors insurance benefits as the only source of retirement income had less than $100 a month and almost none had more than $150 a month in retirement income. A larger proportion of the nonmarried retired workers included in the survey—44 per cent—had no source of retirement income except old-age and survivors insurance benefits. These beneficiaries had a median annual retirement income of $620; almost half had less than $50 a month and close to 90 per cent had less than $75 a month. As for widows, 43 per cent had no source of retirement income except old-age and survivors insurance benefits. These widows had a median annual retirement income of $530; two-thirds had less than $50 a month; all had less than $75 a month in retirement income.

Now, how does this compare with the retirement income of those with more than one source of retirement income? The beneficiaries who had income from privately purchased annuities in addition to their old-age and survivors insurance benefits had the largest retirement income of all those included in the survey. Only 2 per cent, though, had income from this source. Most of this 2 per cent had one or more sources of income—most frequently income from assets—in addition to their old-age and survivors insurance benefits and annuities. The median annual retirement income of these beneficiaries was $2,900 for couples and $2,400 for nonmarried beneficiaries.

The beneficiaries who had income from employer pension plans (either public or private) ranked second in size of retirement income. About 25 per cent of the couples and 15 per cent of the nonmarried retired workers had pensions from former employers. Survivor employer pensions were almost nonexistent, only 2 per cent of the aged widows reporting this income. Many beneficiaries with employer pensions also had another source of retirement income. Again, this additional source was most frequently income from assets. The median annual retirement income for this group of beneficiaries was $2,440 for couples and $1,690 for nonmarried beneficiaries.

Beneficiaries included in the survey who had veterans' payments had less in retirement income than those who had income from annuities or employer pensions, but their income was considerably higher than those who got all of their retirement income from the old-age and survivors insurance program. For half of the beneficiaries who were getting veterans' payments, these payments and old-age and survivors insurance benefits were the only sources of retirement income; most of the others had some interest from savings accounts. The median annual retirement income of the 6 per cent who had veterans' payments in addition to their old-age and survivors insurance benefits was $2,270 for couples and $1,500 for nonmarried beneficiaries.

Income from assets was reported by almost three-fifths of the married couples and almost half of the nonmarried beneficiaries included in the survey. In half of these cases the income from assets was interest earned on savings accounts. For over two-fifths of the nonmarried beneficiaries and over one-third of the married couples with income from assets, this income amounted to less than $75 for the year. The retirement income of beneficiaries reporting income from assets was on the average relatively low. In the majority of these cases old-age and survivors insurance benefits and income from assets were the only sources of retirement income. The median annual retirement income for this group of beneficiaries was $1,890 for couples and $1,010 for nonmarried beneficiaries.

We find, then, that a large proportion of those included in the survey had old-age and survivors insurance benefits as their only source of retirement income and that these people had a relatively low level of retirement income. Only a small proportion of those included in the survey had income from privately purchased annuities or the veterans' programs. A larger proportion had income from employer pension plans or assets, but income from assets often amounted to no more than a little interest on savings accounts.

Those who had earnings, of course, had more in total income than those who relied entirely on their retirement incomes; and those who had more than one-half of their income from earnings had the highest incomes of all. It should be kept in mind, though, that most beneficiaries are unable to work or cannot find jobs and that old-age and survivors insurance benefits are their main reliance. About 63 per cent of those included in the survey had no earnings, and earnings represented more than half of the total income of only 15 per cent. Many of those who did have earnings had already terminated their employment at the end of the survey year. And it is unlikely that many of these people, or many of those who did not work in the survey year, will ever work again. About 7 out of 10 beneficiaries who were not employed at the time of the interview said they were not well enough to work again.

As for total income, old-age and survivors insurance benefits represented half or more of the total income of about 56 per cent of the beneficiaries included in the 1957 survey and the only source of income for about 15 per cent. The median total money income of all beneficiaries included in the survey was $2,250 for married couples, $1,140 for single retired workers and $880 for aged widows.

In considering what we learned about the level of retirement income the aged received from various combinations of sources from the 1957 beneficiary survey, it is important to keep in mind the fact that the information is about 5 years old. The sample used in the 1957 survey was selected from the beneficiaries on the rolls in December 1956. Since that time the level of benefits paid under the program has increased. At the end of 1956, the average old-age and survivors insurance benefit being paid was $60 for a retired worker alone; at the end of June 1962, it was $72. At the end of 1956, the average benefit was $106 for a married couple; at the end of June 1962, it was $127. At the end of 1956, the average benefit was $50 for an aged widow; at the end of June 1962, it was $66. This increase in benefit levels has resulted from changes in the law—such as the general benefit increase enacted in 1958 and the increase in widow's benefits and minimum benefits enacted in 1961—and also from the fact that the benefits awarded under the program have been based on progressively higher levels of covered earnings because both earnings levels and the maximum amount of earnings creditable for use in computing benefits have increased over the years.

It can also be expected that a survey of old-age and survivors insurance beneficiaries taken today would show that more beneficiaries have additional sources of retirement income. The number of people getting payments under private pension plans increased by about 670,000 from 1956 to 1960—an increase of about 60 per cent. Of course, the proportion of old-age and survivors insurance beneficiaries getting such income would not be very much different today from what it was in 1957, since the number of aged old-age and survivors insurance beneficiaries has grown at about the same rate.

Now what can we expect in the future?

As for the old-age, survivors, and disability insurance program—the major source of retirement income for our people—I think that the Congress will continue its past practice of adjusting benefits from time to time to take account of changes in the economy. It should be recognized, though, that past legislative action has been only partly successful in keeping the protection of the program from deteriorating. Benefits have been increased somewhat more than prices; there has been no loss in purchasing power. Nevertheless, the program has not kept up with the increased productivity of the American economy and the consequent rise in the level of living of the American worker. What has happened is that as wages have risen the maximum wage and contribution base has not been increased sufficiently. The maximum base is only $4,800 today as against the original $3,000, while wage levels have considerably more than tripled.

It is generally recognized by students of social security that the maximum amount of earnings that is taxable for social security purposes and that can be used for figuring the average monthly earnings on which benefit amounts are based must be adjusted as wage levels rise. Unless such adjustments are made, more and more people will earn above the maximum and fewer and fewer people will get benefits that are related to their full earnings. In this way, the program becomes progressively less adequate for those earning average wages and above. As improvements in the benefit level are made from time to time, it will be important to consider not only the lower paid worker but also those earning average and above-average wages.

There is a question, too, about how these adjustments to keep the program up-to-date should be made—that is, should we continue to depend on periodic amendments of the law or should we adopt some method for automatically adjusting benefit levels and the ceiling on covered earnings to changes in economic conditions? Some foreign systems have adopted automatic adjustment provisions. The desirability and the feasibility of adopting some more nearly automatic method of adjustment in this country is being studied.

As for supplementary retirement income, the most important source will be private pension plans. The benefits paid under these plans are typically paid as a supplement to the basic old-age and survivors insurance program. While most people are not covered by such plans and we do not know how much of the coverage that exists will translate itself into retirement income, the trends are encouraging. Coverage is growing and there is a trend toward giving an employee a vested right to retain accumulated pension credits even though he may leave his job before normal retirement age. In 1958 about half of the employees covered by pension plans were members of plans that provided for vesting and the number is steadily increasing.

As for benefit amounts, the trend in these private pension plans has been in the direction of liberalizing benefits by substituting "final average pay" formulas for "career average pay" formulas and increasing the flat dollar amount or percentage of compensation credited for each year of service. I hope that these trends will continue.

In summary, so far as the proportion of the aged with some source of retirement income is concerned, the present trend and the outlook for the future are quite good. The challenge that we face is to assure that the amount of retirement income that the aged get from these sources will be adequate.

In delivering the opinion of the Supreme Court of the United States upholding the constitutionality of the Social Security Act back in 1937, Justice Cardozo said, "The hope behind this statute is to save men and women from the rigors of the poor house as well as from the haunting fear that such a lot awaits them when journey's end is near." He went on to say, "The number of persons in the United States 65 years of age or older is increasing proportionately as well as absolutely. What is even more important the number of such persons unable to take care of themselves is growing at a threatening pace." In the twenty-five years that followed, our developing institutions for maintaining the income of the aged have largely eliminated the "haunting fear" that Justice Cardozo spoke of and our confidence in the effectiveness of these institutions as a method of coping with the problem of a growing proportion of dependent aged in the population has made this problem seem much less threatening than it did in 1937. We know that it is within our capabilities to provide adequate retirement income for the aged, and we know that we can find the means of doing so.

IV. The Economic Status of the Aged:
The Older Person as Consumer

CHAPTER 9

OLDER PEOPLE AS CONSUMERS

Jean A. Crockett

Consumption patterns differ among age groups in a number of respects. In this paper we shall be concerned primarily with the percentage of income devoted to consumption and the percentage of total
consumption assigned to certain major categories: food, housing,
clothing, medical care, house furnishings and equipment, and auto purchase. We shall compare the consumption patterns of older with
younger families in these respects and shall also point out consumption
differences among certain subgroups of the older population. While
no direct evidence on the comparative consumption needs of the aged
is presented, it is occasionally possible to make certain inferences as
to these needs from the data on actual consumption patterns.

The 1950 Bureau of Labor Statistics *Survey of Consumer Expenditures* provides the main body of data used,[1] though reference will also
be made to the 1956 survey carried out by *Life* magazine.[2] The BLS
study covers the urban population only and refers to families rather
than individuals, so that age data are consistently available only for
the family head.[3] This means that some older persons, belonging to
families with relatively young heads, will be excluded from the aged
group studied here, while some younger individuals, belonging to families headed by older persons, will be included. This problem is reduced
by restricting family size to 1, 2, or 3 persons in the greater part of
the analysis. Since most 2- and 3-person families contain the wife of
the family head and since the ages of husband and wife are highly
correlated, we may expect that a sizable majority of all individuals in
1- to 3-person families with older heads properly fall in the aged
group. For larger families this presumption is not so clear. The family
size restriction eliminates only a small proportion of families with aged
heads.

It is well known that average consumption expenditures are much lower for older than for younger families. The BLS 1950 study shows consumption falling from $4300 or $4400 for families in the 35–55 age group to $2600 in the age group 65–74 and to $2100 in the age group over 75. Similar results are obtained from other studies. The *Life* 1956 data show consumption falling from around $4800 in the 30–49 age group to $2400 in the group 65 and over.

However, the major part of this very substantial discrepancy is accounted for by the smaller mean income and family size of the aged. The first of these implies fewer resources to use for consumption; the second suggests somewhat smaller consumption needs per family.

In the BLS 1950 sample two-thirds of the 65–74 age group and four-fifths of the 75 and over age group had incomes under $3000 (in 1950 dollars), as compared with only three-eighths of all age groups combined.[4] 80 per cent of the age group 65 and over were 1- or 2-person families, with over 90 per cent in the 1- to 3-person category.

When income and family size are held constant the consumption differences among age groups are much less dramatic. Since our present interest presumably centers on these differences, which may be attributed to age itself, and not those due to the smaller average income and family size of the aged, we have held income and family size relatively constant throughout this paper by making separate comparisons for each of 9 income classes and, as previously indicated, by limiting family size to 1 to 3 persons.

CONSUMPTION AS PROPORTION OF INCOME

Table 1A compares, both for all families and for 1- to 3-person families, the percentage of income consumed in each income class by families with head over 65, families with head under 55 and families with age of head in the range 55–64. The last group in many respects is intermediate between the other two and so has been shown separately. Tables 1B through 1G make similar comparisons for the percentage of total consumption devoted to specific categories. Data are drawn from the 1950 BLS survey and are in 1950 dollars.

From Table 1A we observe that in general the consumption-income ratio greatly exceeds 100 per cent for incomes under $1000, remains somewhat above 100 per cent for incomes under $4000, and falls to less than 70 per cent for incomes over $10,000. For the age group 65 and over the ratio is much lower in the lowest income group than for the age group under 55 and remains moderately lower (5 to 15 percentage points) throughout the income distribution. When we consider only 1- to 3-person families, the differences are somewhat reduced for incomes under $2000 and perhaps increased for incomes over $6000. It should be noted that figures for the aged in income brackets over $4000 or $5000 are based on rather small samples and thus are subject to considerable sampling error. However, they are of great interest if we are concerned with the probable results of a significant increase in the income of the aged.

TABLE 1A

Comparison of Consumption Patterns for Older and Younger Families: Total Consumption Expenditures as Per Cent of After Tax Income

Income class (after tax)	All family sizes, with age of head			1–3 person families, with age of head		
	Under 55	55–64	65 and over	Under 55	55–64	65 and over
Under $1000	286.3	262.0	164.9	249.3	234.7	165.2
$1000–$1999	117.9	115.6	111.0	115.6	116.4	112.2
$2000–$2999	109.2	104.5	101.1	108.1	103.8	100.7
$3000–$3999	103.5	101.1	91.8	102.0	100.2	90.2
$4000–$4999	100.9	95.9	91.9	98.9	93.2	90.6
$5000–$5999	97.4	93.9	*87.8	94.4	91.6	*85.4
$6000–$7499	92.7	88.1	*79.1	90.1	*83.0	*73.9
$7500–$9999	85.1	*84.2	*77.8	80.0	*82.1	*74.1
$10,000 and over	69.1	*66.1	*60.0	*64.0	*62.2	*53.1

SOURCE: Basic data are drawn from the Bureau of Labor Statistics Survey of Consumer Expenditures, 1950.
* Based on less than one hundred families.

The consumption-income ratio for the 55–64 age group is slightly lower than for the group under 55 (usually 2 to 4 percentage points, except in the lowest income group where the discrepancy is larger). This small difference is further reduced when family size is restricted.

The very large discrepancy between the group under 55 and the group 65 and over in the lowest income class probably reflects the fact that the younger families are more likely to consider so low an income as a temporary phenomenon. They are therefore more willing to borrow and to use up past savings for consumption purposes in the expectation of rising income in the near future. This is equivalent to saying that many of the younger families in the lowest bracket are not really so poor as their current income would indicate, since their income is normally higher than it happened to be in the survey year. Among the older families, it is probable that a much smaller proportion of those in the lowest income group can look forward to a substantial improvement in their income position. The great majority must therefore bring their consumption into reasonably close balance with this very low income.

Even though no increase in income is expected, some older families in the lower income brackets may be much wealthier than others, in terms of assets accumulated over their working lives which may now be used to sustain consumption. While no attempt was made in the BLS 1950 study to determine total wealth, two types of asset data were collected: home ownership and holdings of cash and deposits. These asset items are not only important in themselves but are somewhat indicative of total wealth. Turning to Table 3 we observe that aged homeowners spend a substantially higher proportion of their income than renters at incomes under $2000 and a somewhat higher proportion at incomes under $5000. Aged families with high liquid assets spend a far higher per cent of income than low cash families with incomes under $3000 and in fact have consumption expenditures entirely comparable with the age group under 55 in this income range (though lower than the high cash subgroup among the younger families). In other words, where resources other than current income are available, the aged appear to spend about as freely as younger families at low incomes. This suggests that the lower average consumption of the aged in the income range under $3000 results in large part from a more serious inadequacy of resources; and there is no clear inference that consumption needs are lower than for younger families of the same size.

Equally interesting is the fact that at incomes above $3000 even the wealthier groups among the aged—the homeowners and the high cash families—have substantial current savings which far exceed those of younger families with the same income. To the extent that the family head is still employed this may mean that the imminence of retirement provides unusually strong motivation to save, but such motivation cannot be attributed to the group with head not gainfully employed, which saves a little less than the employed group but still clearly more than younger families. While it must always be remembered that the sample is rather small for aged families in the income range above $3000, we may perhaps infer from the relatively high saving in this range that consumption needs are relatively low as compared with younger families.[5] It is also interesting to note that the aged begin to save a substantial proportion of their income when income exceeds $3000 ($4000 for the not gainfully employed), while families under 55 begin to save substantially only with incomes over $6000. Perhaps the first $3000 worth of needs are equally urgent for younger and older families and only above this level do differences appear.

DISTRIBUTION OF CONSUMPTION AMONG MAJOR CATEGORIES FOR OLDER AND YOUNGER FAMILIES

The consumption of the aged is not only less than for younger families of similar income and family size, but is somewhat differently distributed. There are two categories to which families 65 and over clearly devote a smaller proportion of total consumption than do families under 55: clothing and housefurnishings and equipment (see Tables 1B and 1C). Discrepancies are greatest for clothing at low incomes

TABLE 1B

Comparison of Consumption Patterns for Older and Younger Families: Clothing Expenditures as Per Cent of Total Consumption

Income class (after tax)	All family sizes, with age of head			1–3 person families, with age of head		
	Under 55	55–64	65 and over	Under 55	55–64	65 and over
Under $1000	9.1	5.9	4.7	8.2	5.8	4.5
$1000–$1999	11.5	7.8	6.2	11.6	7.3	6.0
$2000–$2999	11.1	9.2	7.6	11.1	9.0	7.3
$3000–$3999	11.0	10.2	9.2	10.7	9.7	8.8
$4000–$4999	11.6	10.9	10.5	11.0	10.1	10.1
$5000–$5999	12.3	12.7	*10.1	11.6	11.3	*9.5
$6000–$7499	12.9	12.5	*12.1	12.1	*11.2	*11.5
$7500–$9999	13.8	*13.3	*11.1	13.8	*11.7	*7.8
$10,000 and over	14.6	*12.7	*12.6	*15.2	*11.7	*10.2

SOURCE: Basic data are drawn from the Bureau of Labor Statistics Survey of Consumer Expenditures, 1950.
* Based on less than one hundred families.

and for housefurnishings and equipment at high incomes. The 55–64 age group is intermediate between the other two but closer to the group 65 and over. It seems reasonable to suppose that these are areas in which consumption needs may be lower for older than for younger families, particularly in the case of housefurnishings and equipment, where the basic stock of these durables has been built up over the years and only occasional replacement is required.

Clothing expenditures as a percentage of consumption tend to rise with income throughout the income distribution, going from 8 or 9 per cent to 14 or 15 per cent for the younger families. For the older groups clothing expenditures start much lower, rise more rapidly until an income level of $4000 or $5000 is reached, and then level off without ever quite catching up with those of the younger group.

TABLE 1C

Comparison of Consumption Patterns for Older and Younger Families: Housefurnishings and Equipment as Per Cent of Total Consumption

Income class (after tax)	All family sizes, with age of head			1–3 person families, with age of head		
	Under 55	55–64	65 and over	Under 55	55–64	65 and over
Under $1000	4.8	3.9	4.1	5.0	4.2	4.4
$1000–$1999	5.3	5.1	4.3	5.3	5.0	4.4
$2000–$2999	6.8	5.6	5.6	7.0	5.9	5.9
$3000–$3999	6.7	6.0	6.5	7.3	6.4	6.6
$4000–$4999	7.7	6.4	5.6	8.2	6.6	5.8
$5000–$5999	7.4	6.9	*5.0	7.8	7.3	*5.5
$6000–$7499	7.7	5.7	*3.7	8.2	*5.9	*3.0
$7500–$9999	7.0	*5.2	*3.5	7.6	*6.2	*3.0
$10,000 and over	9.9	*5.4	*4.5	*9.0	*5.3	*4.5

SOURCE: Basic data are drawn from the Bureau of Labor Statistics Survey of Consumer Expenditures, 1950.
* Based on less than one hundred families.

Expenditures for housefurnishings and equipment by younger families rise from 5 per cent of consumption to about 8 per cent, leveling off for incomes over $4000. For the two older groups these expenditures start a little lower, reach a maximum in the $3000–$6000 income range and decline thereafter. At incomes above $4000 the group 65 and over falls 2 to 5 percentage points below the under 55 group.

Medical care and food expenditures, on the other hand, account for a somewhat higher proportion of consumption for the aged than for younger families (See Tables 1D and 1E). In the case of medical care at least, this clearly reflects greater need for such expenditures on the part of the aged. Medical care, which amounts to 4.5 to 5 per cent of consumption for the group under 55 (except in the lowest income bracket), runs 1 to 3 percentage points higher for families 65 and over. The 55–64 group is only slightly above the younger families in medical expenditures.

TABLE 1D

Comparison of Consumption Patterns for Older and Younger Families: Medical Expenditures as Per Cent of Total Consumption

	All family sizes, with age of head			1–3 person families, with age of head		
Income class (after tax)	Under 55	55–64	65 and over	Under 55	55–64	65 and over
Under $1000	7.0	5.4	8.0	7.5	5.1	8.4
$1000–$1999	4.6	5.6	6.8	4.6	5.4	7.2
$2000–$2999	4.8	6.0	7.4	4.8	6.0	7.8
$3000–$3999	5.1	7.1	6.7	5.1	7.3	6.9
$4000–$4999	4.9	5.7	6.9	4.9	5.9	7.4
$5000–$5999	4.8	4.4	*6.3	4.7	4.7	*6.2
$6000–$7499	4.7	5.9	*5.6	4.5	*5.8	*5.8
$7500–$9999	4.8	*5.9	*8.3	4.7	*4.6	*9.7
$10,000 and over	4.0	*4.0	*5.3	*4.1	*4.2	*3.4

SOURCE: Basic data are drawn from the Bureau of Labor Statistics Survey of Consumer Expenditures, 1950.
* Based on less than one hundred families.

In general, the proportion of total consumption devoted to food falls from about one-third for incomes under $3000 to about one-fourth for incomes over $6000. The two older groups run a little higher than the group under 55 throughout the income distribution (except for the group 65 and over in the two highest income classes where the sample is very small). The discrepancy is about 1 percentage point if all family sizes are considered, but rises, when family size is restricted, to 2 to 4 percentage points for the group 65 and over (again excepting the two highest income classes).

TABLE 1E

Comparison of Consumption Patterns for Older and Younger Families: Food Expenditures as Per Cent of Total Consumption [1]

Income class (after tax)	All family sizes, with age of head			1–3 person families, with age of head		
	Under 55	55–64	65 and over	Under 55	55–64	65 and over
Under $1000	31.7	33.6	35.4	33.0	34.3	37.1
$1000–$1999	34.3	34.4	36.0	34.0	34.8	36.7
$2000–$2999	33.0	33.5	33.3	31.3	32.6	33.6
$3000–$3999	31.0	31.9	31.6	28.7	30.8	31.1
$4000–$4999	29.1	30.1	30.6	26.9	29.0	29.3
$5000–$5999	28.1	29.2	*28.7	25.9	28.4	*26.9
$6000–$7499	26.9	27.9	*29.8	25.0	*27.2	*29.6
$7500–$9999	26.7	*28.2	*24.7	25.0	*25.6	*22.7
$10,000 and over	22.1	*23.6	*21.6	*20.5	*21.8	*17.9

SOURCE: Basic data are drawn from the Bureau of Labor Statistics Survey of Consumer Expenditures, 1950.
* Based on less than one hundred families.
[1] Excludes alcoholic beverages.

There is little systematic difference among the three age groups in the proportion of consumption expenditures assigned to housing (exclusive of fuel, utilities, and household operation), except that at incomes under $1000 and over $5000 the ratio is slightly higher for the group 65 and over than for the group under 55 (See Table 1F). The general pattern for 1- to 3-person families is for housing expenditures to fall as income rises from about one-fifth of total consumption to one-eighth or less, leveling off at incomes over $4000. For the group 65 and over, however, housing expenditures reverse the downward trend and actually increase in relative importance at higher incomes instead of simply leveling off.

Automobile purchase as a per cent of consumption tends to rise sharply with income in the lower brackets and then level off at incomes over $5000 (See Table 1G). At incomes under $5000 the families 65 and over fall below the group under 55, but at incomes above $5000 automobile purchase continues to rise for this oldest group until it

TABLE 1F

Comparison of Consumption Patterns for Older and Younger Families: Housing Expenditures as Per Cent of Total Consumption [1]

Income class (after tax)	All family sizes, with age of head			1–3 person families, with age of head		
	Under 55	55–64	65 and over	Under 55	55–64	65 and over
Under $1000	16.4	17.6	20.7	19.1	19.4	21.2
$1000–$1999	15.1	15.8	16.6	16.5	16.4	16.8
$2000–$2999	12.9	12.9	12.4	14.2	13.7	12.4
$3000–$3999	11.5	11.1	12.7	12.4	11.6	13.4
$4000–$4999	10.9	10.8	10.9	11.9	11.9	11.9
$5000–$5999	10.3	9.8	*11.0	11.4	10.4	*13.2
$6000–$7499	10.4	9.3	*11.6	11.2	*10.5	*12.1
$7500–$9999	10.1	*8.6	*12.6	10.6	*11.3	*15.9
$10,000 and over	10.3	*11.8	*11.8	*11.8	*12.4	*13.6

SOURCE: Basic data are drawn from the Bureau of Labor Statistics Survey of Consumer Expenditures, 1950.
* Based on less than one hundred families.
[1] Excludes fuel, utilities, and household operation.

exceeds that for the group under 55. The 1- to 3-person families over 65 devote 2 per cent of consumption to automobile purchase at incomes under $2000, 5.5 per cent in the range $2000–$5000, about 9 per cent in the range $5000–$7500, and about 12 per cent above $7500 (the last figure being based on a small sample, however).

In summary we may say that the aged at incomes under $3000 devote a much smaller proportion of their consumption to clothing than younger families, a little less to automobile purchase and housefurnishings and equipment, and about the same to housing. However, at incomes over $5000 we find the aged coming fairly close to younger families in clothing expenditures and exceeding them in the relative importance of automobile purchase and housing expenditures, with only housefurnishings and equipment continuing to lag substantially. Food and medical expenditures run consistently higher for the aged throughout the income distribution except at the upper extreme.

The 55–64 age group occupies an intermediate position between the under 55 group and the 65 and over group with respect to per cent of income spent for consumption and the relative importance of expenditures for food, clothing, and housefurnishings and equipment.

TABLE 1G

Comparison of Consumption Patterns for Older and Younger Families: Auto Purchases as Per Cent of Total Consumption

Income class (after tax)	All family sizes, with age of head			1–3 person families, with age of head		
	Under 55	55–64	65 and over	Under 55	55–64	65 and over
Under $1000	3.5	5.1	2.2	2.7	5.7	1.8
$1000–$1999	3.4	3.5	2.1	3.3	3.8	2.2
$2000–$2999	4.6	5.0	5.5	5.0	5.5	5.2
$3000–$3999	6.5	5.4	4.9	7.8	6.2	5.4
$4000–$4999	7.2	6.8	5.7	8.5	7.1	5.8
$5000–$5999	7.9	7.9	*10.7	9.5	8.3	*10.3
$6000–$7499	8.3	8.3	*7.2	9.6	*9.2	*7.6
$7500–$9999	7.7	*9.2	*8.6	8.5	*10.4	*10.7
$10,000 and over	6.5	*6.7	*10.3	*9.0	*7.2	*13.0

SOURCE: Basic data are drawn from the Bureau of Labor Statistics Survey of Consumer Expenditures, 1950.
* Based on less than one hundred families.

AGE EFFECTS AS DERIVED FROM MULTIPLE REGRESSION ANALYSIS

So far our discussion of consumption patterns has been in terms of the per cent of total consumption represented by particular categories. It is also of some interest to compare the dollar value of expenditures in these categories for older and younger families. For example, food represents a higher proportion of total consumption for the aged but consumption itself is a smaller proportion of income, so that the dollar value of food expenditures for given income and family size is not much different for the aged than for younger families.

Multiple regressions are available, based on both the BLS 1950 and the *Life* 1956 data, which give some indication of age effects in dollar terms when a large number of family characteristics, in addition to income and family size (e.g., liquid assets, tenure of dwelling unit, value of home, race, education, and others), are held constant. Unfortunately, these studies include only the employed portion of the aged population and only the income range $1000–$10,000.

Table 2, which is based on the 1950 BLS data, shows the average amount by which various consumption expenditures of the age group 65 and over fall short of (—) or exceed (+) those of specified younger age groups with the same income and other family charac-

TABLE 2

Differences in Consumption Expenditures between Families with Head over 65 and Younger Families, 1950 [1]

Item	Difference in dollars between the Age Group 65 and over and	
	Age 35–49	Age under 35
Total consumption	$— 402	$— 340
Food [2]	— 57	+ 30
Housing [3]	— 27	— 12
Clothing	— 89	— 54
Medical expense	+ 27	+ 48
Housefurnishings and equipment	— 118	— 175
Automobile expense [4]	— 97	— 210
Personal care	— 16	— 9
Reading, recreation and education	— 61	— 59

SOURCE: Bureau of Labor Statistics Survey of Consumer Expenditures, 1950.
[1] Based on multiple regressions for white employee families in the after-tax income range $1,000–$10,000, with income, family size, liquid assets, tenure of dwelling unit, value of home, city class, and other variables effectively held constant.
[2] Excluding alcoholic beverages.
[3] Excluding fuel, utilities, and household operation.
[4] Includes gas, oil, and repairs as well as automobile purchases.

teristics. We observe that in total consumption the aged fall $300 to $400 below the younger groups. In food expenditures they fall below one younger group but above the other, while clothing expenditures run $50 to $100 lower. The largest discrepancies, $100 to $200, are for housefurnishings and equipment and automobile expense (a broader category than automobile purchase). Medical expenditures are $25 to $50 higher, and reading, recreation, and education about $60 lower.

The *Life* 1956 data are conceptually different from the BLS data in several respects and the multivariate analysis was slightly different. Again, the not gainfully employed and the families with incomes under $1000 or over $10,000 (in this case, before taxes) are not covered. Comparisons are available only between the age group over 50 and younger groups.

Total consumption runs more than $400 lower for the group over 50 than for the 35–49 age group, but the former group is only slightly below the group under 35. Food expenditures for the families over 50 are a little below those for the 35–49 group but substantially (over $100) above the under 35 group. Housefurnishings and equipment for the oldest group fall below those for the two younger groups, but the discrepancies are less than half as large as in the corresponding 1950 comparison. Automobile expense for the oldest group falls below that for the two younger groups by about $100. Medical and personal care, which are grouped together, are about $20 higher for the group over 50 than for the group under 35. Since the older families tend to spend more on medical care but less on personal care, two offsetting effects are combined in this comparison. The 35–50 group are similar to the oldest group with respect to the combined category of medical and personal care. The above results all check reasonably well with the 1950 BLS figures, when we allow for the fact that the oldest group includes the 50–64 age range as well as the 65 and over group in the 1956 analysis.

With respect to housing and household operation, the oldest group falls below the 35–49 age group, and particularly the under 35 group, by a much wider margin than in the 1950 BLS comparison. This probably reflects the broader definition of housing expenditures, which in the 1956 study includes household operation and, more important, mortgage repayment.

Clothing expenditures show quite different age effects in the 1956 *Life* study than in the 1950 BLS study, with the oldest group falling very little below the 35–49 age group and substantially exceeding the under 35 group. In this case the inconsistency of the results cannot be attributed to differences of coverage, but implies either large sampling error or a shift in consumption patterns as between the two periods.

CONSUMPTION PATTERNS FOR SUBGROUPS OF THE AGED POPULATION

It has been indicated already that considerable variation in consumption behavior occurs within the age group 65 and over, even for given income and family size. Accumulated assets, particularly those in liquid form, provide an alternative source of funds for consumption and are probably spent relatively freely by older families, since in many cases they were acquired for the specific purpose of providing for the needs of life after retirement. It seems reasonable to suppose that current income plays a somewhat smaller role and accumulated assets a somewhat larger role in financing consumption for the aged than for younger families. Thus, among the aged in particular, we may expect homeowners and holders of sizeable liquid assets to spend a higher proportion of income than other families; and this pattern is clearly demonstrated in the first part of Table 3, particularly for incomes under $5000. We may also expect differences in the distribution of consumption among major categories, and these are shown in the second part of Table 3 and in Tables 4 and 5.

Another consideration which may affect consumption is the employment status of the family head, and perhaps also his occupation, if employed. Patterns for various occupational groups are also shown in Tables 3, 4, and 5.

In comparing homeowners with renters, we find that the former spend a higher percentage of income on consumption at income levels under $5000 and a much higher percentage for income under $2000. A considerably higher proportion of homeowners' consumption is accounted for by expenditures on durables—both housefurnishings and equipment and automobile purchase—in the $1000 to $4000 income range. Aged homeowners in this range do not devote any smaller proportion of consumption to either category of durables than do families in the age group under 55 (though they spend somewhat less than younger homeowners). Aged renters devote a much smaller proportion of expenditures than do younger renters to each durables category in the lower income ranges and to housefurnishings and equipment throughout the income distribution.

Food expenditures run a little higher for aged renters than for aged homeowners at incomes under $5000, while housing expenditures run

TABLE 3

Consumption Patterns for Subgroups of Older Families: Total Consumption and Durables Expenditures
(1–3-person families with age of head 65 and over)

Income class (after tax)	All families	Home-owners	Renters	Self-Employed	Professional or clerical	Manual workers	Not gainfully employed	Cash and deposits Less than $500	$500 and over
Total consumption expenditures as per cent of after tax income									
Under $1000	165.2	186.1	147.3	258.5	197.6	152.6	160.5	138.6	259.6
$1000–$1999	112.2	117.7	105.5	122.7	105.2	103.6	114.5	103.5	134.3
$2000–$2999	100.7	102.1	97.9	106.5	95.8	98.2	103.1	96.6	107.2
$3000–$3999	90.2	91.2	88.5	83.8	87.3	85.0	100.0	88.3	92.8
$4000–$4999	90.6	92.0	*88.0	100.6	87.3	92.2	88.2	88.6	*91.7
$5000–$5999	*85.4	*84.0	*88.7	74.5	85.3	72.4	95.6	*92.8	*78.0
$6000–$7499	*73.9	*71.3	*81.2	67.9	73.9	85.0	73.5	*71.5	*75.8
$7500–$9999	*74.1	*79.9	*59.0	56.7	78.0	79.0	88.5	*56.5	*79.3
$10,000 and over	*53.1	*54.2	*41.0	51.6	46.6	75.8	57.3	*45.9	*61.9
Durables expenditures as per cent of total consumption									
Under $1000	6.0	5.8	6.2	13.8	2.4	4.3	5.6	4.9	8.1
$1000–$1999	6.7	9.4	3.0	5.2	3.8	5.6	7.3	4.9	10.1
$2000–$2999	12.1	15.1	5.7	15.8	10.2	11.6	12.2	11.8	12.6
$3000–$3999	12.9	15.5	8.5	8.7	13.5	13.3	13.7	10.8	15.6
$4000–$4999	13.5	14.3	*12.0	20.5	13.9	12.5	12.0	12.6	*14.9
$5000–$5999	*16.7	*17.9	*14.1	17.9	19.8	10.4	15.2	*18.3	*14.9
$6000–$7499	*12.3	*10.8	*15.7	9.1	12.5	19.9	8.5	*8.4	*15.0
$7500–$9999	*14.1	*13.0	*17.9	15.7	9.7	34.4	13.3	*11.7	*16.7
$10,000 and over	*18.2	*18.6	*13.0	31.5	22.4	2.1	5.6	*13.6	*22.5

SOURCE: Bureau of Labor Statistics Survey of Consumer Expenditures, 1950

140

(1–3-person families with age of head 65 and over)

Income class (after tax)	All families	Home-owners	Renters	Self-Employed	Professional or clerical	Manual workers	Not gainfully employed	Cash and deposits Less than $500	$500 and over
Food expenditures [1]									
Under 1000	37.1	35.4	39.0	33.6	40.1	38.1	37.3	40.9	30.0
$1000–$1999	36.7	35.0	39.0	37.3	40.2	39.4	35.6	38.9	32.4
$2000–$2999	33.6	33.2	34.3	30.3	34.3	34.7	33.3	35.2	31.2
$3000–$3999	31.1	30.3	32.3	29.7	28.1	34.7	29.4	32.3	29.5
$4000–$4999	29.3	28.7	*30.6	26.1	27.3	32.1	28.9	29.9	*28.9
$5000–$5999	*26.9	*26.8	*27.1	33.2	28.2	32.7	21.4	*26.1	*27.7
$6000–$7499	*29.6	*30.8	*26.8	33.6	26.5	24.8	35.1	*30.2	*29.2
$7500–$9999	*22.7	*23.0	*21.4	23.8	30.0	9.4	18.8	*26.6	*18.2
$10,000 and over	*17.9	*17.5	*24.3	19.5	17.4	19.7	16.6	*17.6	*18.2
Housing expenditures [2]									
Under $1000	21.2	15.9	26.9	15.9	25.1	19.6	21.8	21.7	20.1
$1000–$1999	16.8	12.6	22.4	13.4	19.3	16.5	17.2	17.3	15.8
$2000–$2999	12.4	10.0	17.7	12.3	14.1	11.3	12.8	11.9	13.2
$3000–$3999	13.4	10.7	18.2	12.9	17.3	11.2	14.0	13.1	13.9
$4000–$4999	11.9	9.6	*16.7	11.9	12.5	10.6	12.8	11.5	*12.5
$5000–$5999	*13.2	*12.1	*15.8	3.1	11.6	8.9	20.7	*11.9	*14.7
$6000–$7499	*12.1	*11.7	*13.0	12.3	14.5	9.6	9.3	*13.6	*11.0
$7500–$9999	*15.9	*14.9	*19.6	8.1	14.5	8.9	23.1	*11.5	*20.9
$10,000 and over	*13.8	*13.0	*22.7	7.6	11.6	14.7	20.3	*16.5	*11.1

141

SOURCE: Bureau of Labor Statistics Survey of Consumer Expenditures, 1950.

* Based on less than fifty families.

[1] Excludes alcoholic beverages.

[2] Excludes fuel, utilities, and household operation.

higher by 5 to 10 percentage points (Table 4). Clothing and medical expenditures are fairly similar (Table 5).

Turning now to the effect of liquid asset holdings, we find the group with more than $500 in cash and deposits spending much more than the low cash group at incomes under $3000 and generally somewhat more throughout the income distribution. This group tends to devote a considerably higher percentage of its relatively high expenditure to durables. While this may reflect the fact that the families with large assets are better able to afford durables, the direction of causation is not entirely clear, since liquid assets may have been accumulated— either by saving or by conversion from less liquid form—in anticipation of the durables purchase. Food expenditures account for quite a low proportion of consumption for the high cash group at income levels under $3000, while medical expenditures are a little high in this range. Clothing expenditures run somewhat low above the $3000 level.

The not gainfully employed spend a slightly higher proportion of income on consumption than aged families as a whole except in the lowest income group. This becomes clear if we combine adjacent income classes above $3000. On this basis the not gainfully employed ordinarily exceed each of the other occupational groups at incomes over $3000. This undoubtedly reflects the fact that those families which are still earning anticipate an imminent decline in income upon retirement. At incomes under $3000 the retired fall short of the self-employed, and under $1000, of the clerical and professional, as well.

With respect to the distribution of consumption expenditures, the not gainfully employed are about the same as all families combined, except that food expenditures tend to run somewhat lower and housing expenditures somewhat higher.

The manual workers spend a considerably smaller proportion of income on consumption than aged families as a whole at incomes under $6000. (They are numerically insignificant above this level.) A relatively small percentage of consumption goes into durables and a relatively large percentage into food in the $1000–$5000 range and into housing throughout the income distribution.

In summary we may say that homeowners and families with high liquid assets have much higher consumption-income ratios than renters and low cash families at income levels below $2000 or $3000, and moderately higher ratios in the $3000–$5000 range. Both groups devote a relatively high proportion of these relatively high expenditures

Consumption
(1–3-person families with age of head 65 and over)

Income class (after tax)	All families	Home-owners	Renters	Self-Employed	Professional or clerical	Manual workers	Not gainfully employed	Cash and deposits	
								Less than $500	$500 and over
Clothing expenditures									
Under $1000	4.5	4.3	4.6	5.9	4.5	4.9	4.3	4.2	5.0
$1000–$1999	6.0	5.8	6.3	7.7	7.1	6.3	5.6	5.9	6.2
$2000–$2999	7.3	7.2	7.6	8.4	7.6	7.0	7.2	7.4	7.1
$3000–$3999	8.8	8.6	9.0	9.9	7.1	7.9	9.9	9.4	7.9
$4000–$4999	10.1	10.3	*9.5	7.3	11.0	10.0	10.5	10.9	*8.9
$5000–$5999	*9.5	*10.0	*8.4	7.0	8.9	11.2	10.0	*8.5	*10.8
$6000–$7499	*11.5	*10.0	*15.0	10.6	12.2	12.4	10.4	*12.7	*10.6
$7500–$9999	*7.8	*7.5	*8.8	4.7	12.0	12.2	6.6	*9.9	*5.5
$10,000 and over	*10.2	*10.2	*10.2	10.0	10.2	16.1	9.5	*12.3	*8.2
Medical expenditures									
Under $1000	8.4	10.4	6.3	7.6	3.4	7.3	8.8	6.4	12.3
$1000–$1999	7.2	7.6	6.5	7.2	3.9	6.4	7.6	6.8	7.9
$2000–$2999	7.8	6.9	9.6	6.1	8.3	9.1	7.1	7.0	9.0
$3000–$3999	6.9	6.5	7.5	8.0	7.5	6.8	6.3	7.6	5.9
$4000–$4999	7.4	7.4	*7.3	8.6	8.1	6.5	7.4	7.2	*7.2
$5000–$5999	*6.2	*6.2	*6.1	4.9	7.3	6.1	5.0	*8.0	*4.0
$6000–$7499	*5.8	*5.9	*5.6	7.1	5.6	3.0	7.2	*4.6	*6.7
$7500–$9999	*9.7	*11.2	*4.7	13.8	1.8	4.5	12.8	*8.3	*11.1
$10,000 and over	*3.4	*3.5	*3.2	3.2	3.0	2.7	4.0	*4.4	*2.6

143

SOURCE: Bureau of Labor Statistics Survey of Consumer Expenditures, 1950.
* Based on less than fifty families.

to durables at incomes below $5000 (and for high cash families, throughout the income range). Food expenditures run a little low for both groups at low incomes and housing runs substantially lower for homeowners than for renters throughout the income distribution.

The not gainfully employed among the aged have relatively high consumption-income ratios except in the lowest income class, while manual workers have low ratios, particularly at incomes under $2000. Both groups devote a relatively high proportion of expenditures to housing, while food expenditures are low for the not gainfully employed and high for the manual workers. The latter run a little low on durables.

SUMMARY

The great difference in average consumption expenditures between aged and younger families results primarily from the lower mean income and smaller family size of the aged. However, even when income and family size are held roughly constant we find the age group 65 and over spending a somewhat smaller percentage of their income for consumption than the group under 55, with the 55–64 age group intermediate. The discrepancy, as computed from the 1950 BLS consumer expenditure data, runs from 5 to 15 percentage points for most income classes, but is much larger than this for incomes under $1000. In the low brackets all age groups spend more than their income but the aged exceed income by a smaller percentage than younger families.

The greater willingness of younger families to dissave at low incomes may reflect the fact that a large proportion of them can look forward to an increase in income in the near future, while this is less likely to be true for the aged. In this connection it is interesting to note that where aged families with low income have other resources in the form of assets—particularly liquid assets—accumulated in the past, their consumption behavior closely resembles that of younger families. However, at incomes above $3000 even the high asset holders among the aged save substantially more than younger families. This creates some presumption that the urgency of consumption needs, beyond some basic minimum, is less for the aged than for younger families.

In addition to being relatively low, consumption expenditures of the aged are somewhat differently distributed among major categories than those of younger families, particularly at low incomes. At incomes under $3000 the aged devote a much smaller proportion of their consumption to clothing than younger families, a little less to automobile purchase and housefurnishings and equipment, and about the same to housing. However, at incomes over $5000 we find the aged coming fairly close to younger families in clothing expenditures and exceeding them in the relative importance of automobile purchase and housing expenditures, with only housefurnishings and equipment continuing to lag substantially. Food and medical expenditures run consistently higher for the aged throughout the income distribution, except at the upper extreme.

Homeowners, holders of substantial liquid assets, and the not gainfully employed all consume a higher proportion of income than aged families as a whole, in most income classes. The first two subgroups devote a relatively high proportion of consumption to durables expenditures; and all three spend a relatively low proportion on food at incomes under $5000.

NOTES

[1] A much more detailed study of these data for older families has been made by Sidney Goldstein, *Consumption Patterns of the Aged* (Philadelphia: University of Pennsylvania Press, 1960). Some of the results shown in this paper are necessarily somewhat repetitious of material presented there.

[2] The analysis of the data from this survey has not been published.

[3] Some information on the age distribution of children is also available.

[4] In Chapter 5 by Charles Lininger, two-thirds of the age group over 65 were found, on the basis of 1961 Survey of Consumer Finances data, to have incomes below $3000 (in 1961 dollars), while 84 per cent fell below $5000.

[5] The consumption-income ratio tells nothing, of course, about the absolute strength of consumption needs, but only about the relative urgency of consumption and saving motivations. However, it is not obvious why the aged who have already retired should have stronger motives for saving than younger families who must still provide for the rearing of the children and the retirement of the parents.

CHAPTER 10

BUDGETING FOR OLDER PEOPLE

Helen H. Lamale

The topic, budgeting for older people, is somewhat ambiguous even in a conference dealing with aging and the economy. To some, it implies a discussion of how older people, on the average, spend their incomes and how their spending pattern and manner of living differ from those of younger persons. To others, a discussion of budgets should provide recommended spending plans for individual families—guides for preparing individual retirement budgets. Both of these aspects of the subject are important, but I shall limit this discussion to what are commonly called "standard" or "normative" budgets. Such budgets define the goods and services required to provide a *specified standard of living* for a *specified type of family.* Estimates of the cost of such budgets are an essential part of the measurement of the income needs of older persons and the adequacy of resources to meet them.

In recent years, the tabulation and analysis of information for older persons and families obtained in surveys of income, expenditures, and savings have greatly increased our knowledge of how older persons live, what income and resources are available to them, and how their expenditures vary in different circumstances.[1] Similarly, excellent materials and programs for planning individual retirement budgets have been developed by labor and business organizations and by educational and social agencies. There has been considerably less progress in evaluating budgetary requirements for an adequate standard of living for older persons in different circumstances, or in properly relating such estimates as we have to understanding and solving problems of the aging.

"The BLS Interim Budget for a Retired Couple," [2] published by the Bureau of Labor Statistics and priced in 20 large cities in the autumn of 1959, is the most recent budget of this type. Although it is limited in scope, when used with other budgets and with income and expenditure data, it provides some answers to questions being considered at this morning's discussional. It has already been referred to in several of the papers of the Conference. The concept of this budget and the assumptions and methods used in developing the list of goods and services included in it are discussed in detail in the published report and in other papers.[3] I will outline them only briefly here, as necessary for understanding the cost estimates.

Living costs depend on many different circumstances, and standard budget estimates reflect the assumptions made with respect to each of them. The following are the most important factors and the budget assumptions related to them:

Living costs depend on:	The budget assumes:
1. The standard of living maintained.	"Modest but adequate," meeting psychological and social as well as physical needs.
2. Family size and status.	Self-supporting husband and wife, aged 65 or over, and not employed.
3. Where they live.	In a 2- or 3-room rental dwelling in a *large* city or its suburbs. Cost estimates are available for only 20 cities, including 12 with populations of more than one and a quarter million, and 8 with population from one-quarter to one and a quarter million.
4. The size and condition of their inventory of household goods.	The home is assumed to be equipped with housefurnishings and mechanical equipment usually considered to be household necessities, such as a gas or electric cook stove, mechanical refrigerator, and small electrical appliances. The quantities of these items, as well as clothing items, specified for the budget are primarily replacement rates, since it is assumed that the family has an average inventory. 22 per cent of the families were assumed to own automobiles, except

Living costs depend on:	The budget assumes:
	in three cities (New York, Boston, and Philadelphia), where ownership was 14 per cent.
5. The state of their health.	In reasonably good health, able to take care of themselves, and to manage the home. The wife does all of the cooking and most of the cleaning and laundry—some laundry is sent out and there is occasional paid help.
6. Life insurance and income taxes.	No provision for life insurance or income taxes. This assumes that payments on life insurance policies have been completed before retirement, and that most of the income of retired couples at this level is tax-exempt because of source and the remainder insufficient to require payment of taxes.

Having thus indicated the essential features of the budget, let us look at the autumn 1959 cost estimates for 20 large cities. Total budget costs ranged from $2,641 in Houston to $3,366 in Chicago. Costs in 8 of these 20 cities, ranged between $3,025 and $3,125, were under $3,025 in 6 cities, and over $3,125 in 6 cities. Estimates were modified by including a lower-cost food budget and eliminating provision for automobile ownership. The costs of the reduced standard ranged from $2,390 in Houston to $3,112 in Chicago, about a $250 difference from the higher standard. There was a difference of $277 in the cost of the two levels in Washington, D.C., the median-cost city.

Other modifications in the standard and manner of living might be made which would also affect the level of the budget costs. For example, limited research into the relative cost of owned and rental housing of retired couples, indicated that the budget housing costs might be reduced by one-fourth to one-third for couples who owned mortgage-free homes. At the median budget level, this would amount to a reduction of about $230 to $300. Considering the magnitude of these differences, it is reasonable to conclude that average costs of an adequate standard of living for a retired couple in these large cities are not likely to be below $2500. It is considerably more hazardous to extend this generalization to small cities. Such generalization is entirely unwarranted with respect to villages and rural areas where the manner and standard of living of the young employed families, as well as the retired, are sufficiently different to make the budget goods and services an inappropriate measure of adequacy for most purposes. This is not to imply that the cost of the list of goods and services specified in the budget for retired couples residing in large cities would be substantially lower if priced in small towns and rural areas (the importance of intercity differences in price levels is frequently exaggerated), but rather to point out the danger of adopting for small town and rural families the budget standards developed for large-city families without evaluating them and their appropriateness for the specific use.

We have found that most people believe that there are greater differences in living costs among cities than our budget studies indicate. They also seem to think that high-cost cities are high for all categories of goods and services and low-cost cities are low-cost in all respects. The cost of the total budget increased by about one-fourth from the lowest- to the highest-cost city, but there were many variations in the relative cost positions of the cities with respect to the different types of goods and services. For example, the total budget cost in all four of the West coast cities was above the average, but the cost of rent, heat, and utilities was at or below the average. Philadelphia, which was relatively low-cost with respect to the total budget, rent, and goods and services other than food, was relatively high-cost for the food budget. If estimates were available for more and different types of cities, greater differences in living costs might be found. However, in this day of mobility, rapid communication and transportation, and national markets, it is rather unreasonable to expect to find the same manner and standard of living costing substantially less in one place than another. Greatly reducing one's living costs without changing one's manner and standard of living appears very improbable.

If this is the situation with respect to changing one's place of residence, it is probably more likely regarding budget requirements before and after retirement. One's living costs are not suddenly and greatly reduced when one reaches 65 and decides to retire, unless one

TABLE 1

Annual Costs of the Retired Couple's Budget, by Major Components, 20 Large Cities and Suburbs, Autumn 1959

Item	Atlanta	Baltimore	Boston	Chicago	Cincinnati	Cleveland	Detroit	Houston	Kansas City	Los Angeles
Food and beverages[1]	$768	$781	$953	$889	$879	$860	$899	$758	$841	$894
Food at home[2]	714	734	900	838	824	806	847	711	797	840
Low-cost plan	600	610	779	743	728	715	750	595	706	731
Moderate-cost plan	827	857	1,021	933	921	897	944	827	889	949
Food away from home	29	28	32	33	36	34	32	28	27	32
Housing	1,010	1,067	1,298	1,331	1,062	1,265	1,122	928	1,183	1,105
Rent, heat, utilities[3]	778	802	1,029	1,067	821	1,015	858	694	942	862
Housefurnishings	98	103	97	100	98	99	106	99	101	106
Household operation and communications	134	162	172	164	143	151	158	135	140	137
Clothing	208	216	213	232	215	233	226	197	221	213
Husband	80	79	83	84	82	87	84	76	82	79
Wife	103	109	100	114	102	113	108	92	106	101
Clothing materials and services	25	28	30	34	31	33	34	29	33	33
Medical care	241	247	316	317	240	327	298	260	250	366
Transportation[4]	153	180	144	195	168	170	170	161	175	166
Automobile owners	516	584	656	653	523	566	536	530	576	579
Nonowners of automobiles	51	66	61	66	67	59	66	57	62	50
Other goods and services	340	349	380	402	361	389	381	337	364	367
Reading and recreation	101	102	111	124	112	122	119	95	105	105
Personal care	75	75	73	83	75	78	79	75	81	81
Tobacco	35	37	38	35	35	35	36	41	34	33
Gifts, contributions, etc.	129	135	158	160	139	154	147	126	144	148
Total cost of goods and services	2,720	2,840	3,304	3,366	2,925	3,244	3,096	2,641	3,034	3,111
Estimated annual cost comparable in content with original budget[5]	2,467	2,571	3,067	3,112	2,698	3,011	2,865	2,390	2,802	2,851

150

151

Food and beverages[1]	$846	$945	$939	$956	$887	$870	$920	$900	$938	$864
Food at home[2]	795	892	889	899	830	824	866	848	875	816
Low-cost plan	*701*	*776*	*769*	*780*	*724*	*729*	*755*	*735*	*763*	*685*
Moderate-cost plan	*889*	*1,009*	*1,008*	*1,018*	*936*	*920*	*976*	*961*	*988*	*948*
Food away from home	31	32	30	39	36	28	32	33	40	29
Housing	1,216	1,124	1,003	1,116	1,078	1,210	1,172	838	1,196	1,163
Rent, heat, utilities[3]	962	849	754	863	817	970	919	595	921	921
Housefurnishings	97	99	98	104	102	96	107	105	109	95
Household operation and communications	157	176	151	149	159	144	146	138	166	147
Clothing	231	215	213	221	222	213	224	211	222	216
Husband	85	83	79	81	82	77	82	85	85	80
Wife	111	101	100	107	105	102	106	100	103	106
Clothing materials and services	35	31	34	33	35	34	36	26	34	30
Medical care	319	262	260	264	326	273	346	222	336	271
Transportation[4]	162	134	133	180	181	183	174	162	169	176
Automobile owners	534	652	589	571	597	595	627	543	574	583
Nonowners of automobiles	57	50	58	69	63	66	46	55	55	61
Other goods and services	361	364	361	365	355	350	387	348	391	357
Reading and recreation	100	111	107	105	103	93	114	115	107	102
Personal care	75	69	79	78	78	76	86	70	91	78
Tobacco	37	39	37	34	29	34	34	35	38	32
Gifts, contributions, etc.	149	145	138	148	145	147	153	128	155	145
Total cost of goods and services	3,135	3,044	2,909	3,102	3,049	3,099	3,223	2,681	3,252	3,047
Estimated annual cost comparable in content with original budget[5]	2,906	2,812	2,684	2,842	2,792	2,858	2,949	2,429	2,990	2,770

SOURCE: Margaret S. Stotz, "The BLS Interim Budget for a Retired Couple," *Monthly Labor Review*, 83 (November, 1960), 1144.

[1] Includes small allowances for guest meals and for alcoholic beverages.

[2] The cost of food at home used in the calculation of the total cost of the budget is an average of the low- and moderate-cost food plans shown in italics, including the suggested additional allowance of 10 per cent for small families.

[3] Average contract rent for tenant-occupied dwellings that conform to the housing standards specified for the budget plus the cost of required amounts of heating fuel, gas, electricity, water, and specified equipment.

[4] Weighted average cost of automobile owners and nonowners.

[5] Costs based on the low-cost food plan, and excluding allowances for automobile ownership and alcoholic beverages.

is willing and able to make some reductions and changes in his manner and standard of living. We do not have comparable budget estimates for couples before and after retirement, but the "Scale of Equivalent Income for City Families of Different Size, Age, and Composition," [4] published by the Bureau of Labor Statistics, indicates that couples with husband aged 65 or older need 94 per cent as much as couples with head aged 55 to 65 to maintain an equivalent level of living, i.e., net income available for consumption goods and services. This same scale both disproves the old adage, "two can live as cheaply as one," and establishes that neither can one live at half the cost of two. It indicates that a single person, aged 65 or older, would require about 60 per cent of the cost of the budget for a retired couple. The costs of the "Retired Couple's Budget" ranged from 56 to 62 per cent of the cost of the 4-person "City Worker's Family Budget" in these cities in 1959, reflecting the differential needs and consumption pattern and different size of the younger family.

It is important to recognize that the budgetary requirements of retired persons as a group are constantly changing—not because the prices of goods and services are changing appreciably, but because the composition of the group itself is changing, and the social and economics factors affecting the group are highly dynamic. The retired population of the mid-60's will be very different from that of the mid-50's, in terms of its pre-retirement social and economic status and its standard and manner of living. They will have had a higher real income, higher level of education, a larger and different inventory of household goods, and perhaps what is most important, different attitudes. Their retirement resources and the capacity of the economy to meet their budget needs will also be very different. The Technical Advisory Committee stated this very succinctly when evaluating the standard budgets of the late 1940's:

"Such a budget is not an absolute and unchanging thing. The prevailing judgment of the necessary will vary with the changing values of the community, with the advance of scientific knowledge of human needs, with the productive power of the community and therefore with what people commonly enjoy and see others enjoy." [5]

Much more research in estimating budgetary requirements is needed to provide estimates appropriate for the many different purposes they serve. This is particularly true since such estimates are being used with national income estimates in macro-economic research and in developing national policies.

Greater care should be taken when applying standard budget cost estimates to the income distribution for all persons over 65 years of age to obtain estimates of aggregate need. There should also be more discretion in how the results are labeled. "Poverty," "need," "deprivation," and even "substandard" are relative terms, but, more importantly, they are emotionally charged terms and highly controversial.

Estimating the budgetary requirements of older persons is a very complex problem, and rarely, if ever, do complex problems have simple answers. Estimates of the cost of standard budgets, such as the BLS "Retired Couple's Budget," are research tools and should not be used indiscriminately to arrive at general conclusions. Properly used, they shed considerable light on the problem of measuring the adequacy of incomes of retired persons and the capacity of the economy to support older persons in retirement.

NOTES

[1] See, for example, Sidney Goldstein, *Consumption Patterns of the Aged* (Philadelphia: University of Pennsylvania Press, 1960).

[2] Margaret S. Stotz, "The BLS Interim Budget for a Retired Couple," *Monthly Labor Review*, 83 (November, 1960), 1141–57.

[3] See, *Retirement Income of the Aging*, Hearings before the Sub-committee on Retirement Income of the Special Committee on Aging, U.S. Senate, 87th Congress, July 12–13, 1961 (Washington, D.C.: U.S. Government Printing Office, 1961). See also Helen H. Lamale and Ewan Clague, "Standard Budgets for Elderly Persons: Problems of Concept, Methods and Interpretation" (Washington, D.C.: Bureau of Labor Statistics, 1960) (mimeographed).

[4] See Marsha Froeder, "Estimating Equivalent Incomes or Budget Costs by Family Type," *Monthly Labor Review*, 83 (November, 1960), 1197–1200.

[5] U.S. Bureau of Labor Statistics, *Workers' Budgets in the United States: City Families and Single Persons, 1946 and 1947*, BLS Bulletin 927 (Washington, D.C.: U.S. Government Printing Office, 1948), p. 7.

V. The Economics of Aging: Implications of Pension Funds

CHAPTER 11

PENSION FUNDS AND ECONOMIC POWER

Paul P. Harbrecht, S.J.

My purpose in dealing with the problem of pension funds and economic power is to show how, in attempting to deal with the problem of economic security in our society, we are evolving a system that will change the nature of our society itself.

Our subject is pension funds, of course, and I will not maintain that they alone will work the radical social changes of which I speak. The pension funds, however, are a dramatic example of the evolutionary process now going forward. My thesis is briefly stated: *the drive of our modern society is for economic security; the unintended result of this drive is a change in the structure of society itself.* The private pension funds will serve as a model to demonstrate this thesis.[1]

What is the basis of the economic power of the pension funds? How big are they? The assets of all pension and retirement funds in the United States amounted to $114 Billion at the end of 1961. This total was made up of government funds amounting to $59 billion and private funds totaling $55 billion. The government block breaks down this way: state and local funds amounted to $21.7 billion; the Old-Age and Survivors Insurance Fund amounted to $19.7 billion with the rest of the funds accounted for by various other federal types of old age insurance programs, railroad retirement, civil service, and federal disability insurance. Our concern here will be exclusively with the private funds.

In the private sector, the $55.3 billion is divided in this way: 59 per cent are in the form of noninsured pension funds and 37 per cent are of the insured type. 4 per cent more are made up of noninsured funds managed by multi-employer groups, nonprofit organizations and unions.

If we relate the pension funds to some of the other benchmarks on our economic landscape we get a better idea of the relative importance of pension funds than these numbers can give us. The private funds have $55.3 billion in assets, the national debt is pushing upward toward $300 billion, the defense budget is $48 billion, total reserves of all life insurance companies have reached $128 billion.

But these comparisons of scale are not nearly as telling as an analysis of the impact of the pension funds upon the lives of those who depend on them and the impact they have upon the capital markets of the United States.

PENSION FUNDS AND PENSIONERS

Let us consider first their impact upon the individual. There can be no question that the pension movement is a great benefit to the nearly 23 million people who are covered by private pension plans. They are undoubtedly looking forward to a degree of security that the workingman in society has never before anticipated. Private pensions have come as a much needed supplement to the more modest amounts that will be supplied to older people by social security benefits. Indeed, as with social security, we may well wonder what we ever did without them.

It is hard to overestimate the gains that flow from the financial independence that a person over 65 will enjoy as a result of his monthly pension checks. The older person will no longer be dependent upon the generosity of relatives or charitable institutions who care for him if he is destitute. He can now live with dignity, if not in affluence, drawing upon a source of income that he has earned himself in his active lifetime.

At the present we can only begin to estimate some of the economic consequences of the pension movement. The Institute of Industrial Relations at the University of California in Berkeley has undertaken a series of studies analyzing the impact of social security upon the lives and spending habits of persons of retirement age. The National Bureau of Economic Research is doing similar work with regard to the pension funds. As these studies are not yet completed, we will have to wait for results. One measurable impact that social security seems to have had is the creation of communities of older people in Florida and elsewhere.

As time goes on, however, and a greater proportion of the population begins to enjoy the fruits of pension plans, the economic impact of retirement incomes will be much more profound and more easily measured. The Life Insurance Institute estimates that under the pension plans already placed with life insurance companies, older people will receive an annual income at retirement of more than $3 billion. We have no similar figure for the noninsured plans, but taking the same percentage of their total assets we arrive at an estimate of $4.5 billion. This, of course, is only an extrapolation from the insurance company figures, but it does give us some idea of the impact pension incomes will have upon the economy. Thus, we can guess that approximately $7.5 billion will be spent by people over 65 when the pension plans now in force begin to dispense their benefits to employees now at work.

At the present time the noninsured pension plans are paying about $1.1 billion per year to retirees. The insured plans, though an accurate figure is not available, are undoubtedly paying less than this. It would be conservative to estimate that when most of the pension plans now in force mature, older people will have more than four times the income now available to them from private pensions. Their additional income will undoubtedly be even greater than this as many will accrue additional benefits by continuing to work after retirement age. Furthermore, as time goes on, pension benefits will undoubtedly be increased. The Department of Labor estimates that pension and welfare benefits are renegotiated at least every three years and recent experience has shown that pension benefits tend to be increased upward constantly. How much of these increases will go to offset inflation, I leave to the economists.

This is a bright picture, but the pension movement has not yet brought us to the millennium. The benefits provided by these plans, with the exception of those designed for executives, are modest, even including social security benefits. The pensions and social security will have to be supplemented by some other source of income in order to reach a standard of living that we have come to regard in America as acceptable. The pension movement, however, is making progress toward liberalization of eligibility requirements, scale of benefits, additional benefits, vesting, etc. We may confidently expect that as time goes on pensions will more and more enable retired persons to live in a manner to which they have become accustomed.

We can conclude, therefore, that the economic position of older people will be greatly improved by the pension system, at least with regard to that third of the work force now covered by pension plans. But there are features in the pension system that militate against the security of pension expectations.

THE RESERVE CLAUSES

In nearly every pension plan there are provisions stating that the employer may terminate or amend the plan at will. These clauses are necessary because, if a company falls upon hard times, an employer could be bankrupted by pension commitments.

If management should decide to avail itself of these escape clauses, except in the case of the strictly insured type of plan, the only recourse employees have is an appeal to their union contract. If there is such a contract, the corporate management need only wait until the contract runs out and refuse to renew it. Certainly, there are situations in which a corporation operating from a large base could afford to wait out the resulting strike. It has happened before. In the absence of a union, management's task would be easier. In the light of such a possibility, how safe, how secure are the pension expectations of the employees of the smaller corporations in our economy?

The situation described above is possible, though hopefully unlikely. But there are other conditions under which it might be necessary to terminate a pension plan. According to Internal Revenue reports, there have been relatively few terminations thus far in the history of the pension movement. During the fiscal years 1956–59 about 1,400 plans were discontinued. The best available data on causes for pension termination covers only three months in 1957. Of 51 plans discontinued during that time, the most frequent causes of termination were mergers (14), sale of the company (8), financial difficulties (13), and dissolution of the corporation (5).

Such data as we have from other sources suggest that, in some cases at least, employees covered by private pension plans are deprived of their accrued pension rights when plans are terminated. Before sounding an alarm we need more information, but it should be remembered that during the short time the pension fund system has been in force, economic conditions have been relatively good; moreover, heavy demands upon the pension funds have not yet begun.

We might sum up the situation by saying that except for those employees who have actually retired—and in some cases they must be included too—the guarantee that a promised pension will actually be paid or paid in full is only as good as the solvency of the corporation and the continued willingness of the employer to carry out his promises.

LEGAL PROTECTION

What protection is available to the employee whose pension plan is jeopardized by the action of his employer? First of all he can appeal to the courts. If he can convince a court that the funds invested in a pension plan are in fact a true trust, he might successfully argue that funds already committed to payment of his pension are being misused. But his remedy is of doubtful value. Very few decisions in this matter have recognized a right that accrues to the pensioner because he is the beneficiary of a trust.

Even if the pensioner does surmount the hurdle of getting a court to agree that his pension plan is indeed a trust, there is no way in which he could compel the employer to continue contributing money to the trust. This would probably be true of any trust, but it certainly obtains in the case where the employer expressly reserves the right to discontinue the pension plan at any time.

Another source of protection for the assets of a pension plan is the law on the taxation of pension trusts. Since a pension plan can receive great tax advantages if set up to comply with certain conditions, nearly all plans of any size are set up in conformity with the requirements for tax exemption. One of these requirements is that the employer must segregate, irrevocably, any funds that are to be part of a tax-free plan. The employer who would like to recover funds set aside for pensioners faces tax disadvantages great enough to discourage him in most cases.

But this does not guarantee that an employer will continue to pay into the pension trust at the same rate at which he began. Furthermore, the employer who can show valid reasons for his action will be allowed to terminate a plan without being taxed for previous contributions. He cannot, of course, recover these contributions.

The power of his union is perhaps the strongest weapon the employee has in seeking to protect his pension plan. But union contracts are subject to renegotiation and a union might be forced to agree to smaller pensions.

The federal and state legislation thus far enacted in the pension field is aimed only at the prevention of fraud or the looting of trust fund assets. As yet, few legislatures have attempted to force employers to fund pension plans (that is, to lay aside in advance sufficient assets to pay pensions out of the interest they earn) or otherwise guarantee the promises they make. Such legislation would be rather drastic at this time, but compulsory funding is likely to be considered seriously in the future. We have, after all, the precedent of compulsory workmen's compensation insurance.

VESTING

Many of these problems could be solved, of course, by the introduction of vesting into existing pension plans. Vesting refers to an employee's right, on leaving employment before retirement, to receive all or part of the benefits purchased in his behalf by the employer's contributions. It is usual to have some requirements of age, service, or membership in the plan as a requisite for vesting of contributions made for the employee. The purpose of these requirements is to exclude casual or transient employees and to keep the cost of financing the program from becoming unduly high. Vesting would enhance the employee's chances of urging his legal right to protect his pension from the hazards of mismanagement or theft. A recent study by the Bureau of Old-Age and Survivors Insurance surveying all the data available on the prevalence of vesting among pension plans reveals that vesting has been on the increase ever since 1950.[2] These studies show what great variety there is in the vesting arrangements in different pension plans. For example, a plan may not begin to vest until age 60 with 20 years of service, or it may vest immediately.

In order to be really effective against the problems we have been discussing, a vesting provision ought to take effect no later than age 40 and 10 years of service, but the BOASI study concludes that probably no more than one-fourth of all employees with pension coverage in the late 1950's could obtain vested rights within 10 years of service and no age requirement or an age requirement no more than 40. The study estimated that no more than half the plans in force had vesting provisions. There is much progress to be made here.

One other factor which gives rise to uncertainty about pension benefits ought to be mentioned. Where a pension plan fails to provide for vesting, an employee who leaves his employment loses all his pension credits. Thus, he becomes, as he grows older, more closely tied to the job he has. Unfortunately, statistics with regard to labor turn-over are relatively meager, but those we do have indicate that job stability is not very high. While we may think rather highly of an employee's right to change his job, yet the fact that a valuable employee may be bound to his job by the prospect of a pension is undoubtedly one of the major advantages an employer derives from instituting a pension plan. To require a high degree of vesting in all pension plans might well discourage many an employer from introducing a plan into his business.

A QUESTION OF EQUITY

Here a neat question of economic equity presents itself. What is the nature of an employee's right to receive a pension? Can the employee's right to a pension be regarded as a true property right in fact, or is it really only a claim upon his employer which may be realized on the fulfillment of certain conditions? In order to understand the question better, let us examine the typical pension fund situation.

In a pension plan wherein an employer agrees to provide a certain level of benefits at retirement age and where there is no vesting, the cost of the plan to the employer is in part determined by the fact that a certain number of his employees will not remain with him long enough to reach retirement age and claim pension benefits. It is part of the employer's agreement, then, that he will provide sufficient funds only for those employees who remain with him until they reach retirement age. Looked at this way, it is not possible for any one employee to say that any given portion of the pension fund is earmarked for him. It is for this reason in part that the courts have been extremely slow to admit that an employee has the kind of interest in a pension fund that would enable him to sue his employer or a trustee for mismanagement of the pension plan.

This is a legal issue and a social one, too, which has not yet been resolved, though there is a tendency to regard these funds as a deferred wage. This is probably the best of the competing theories with regard to employee rights in pension plans, but it obviously does not solve the problem of whether or not an employee has a genuine property interest in a pension fund. Employee rights in pension funds, prior to retirement, are still the subject of debate.

The solution to the problem of protecting employee rights in pension funds that is slowly emerging in the legislation of a handful of states and the federal government is to assign to public authority the protection of individual rights in pension funds. The theory seems to be that the attorney general of the United States or of a state is the only person with sufficient standing in the law to call the employer or the union to task for misuse of employee welfare or benefit funds.

But the theme of my discourse is pension funds and economic power. And this is a good point to return to it. We can see from the analysis, as far as we have gone, that while the employees who are covered by pension funds achieve a degree of security thereby, they certainly have no economic power. Whether the average citizen has less economic power than he did before the rise of the pension system may be hard to determine. But we know, at least, that there is a new alignment of powers controlling him and that certain decisions he once could make are now no longer his. In most cases, the most evident decision-making power he has lost is whether or not he will save. With this have gone the consequent decisions as to his rate of savings, the form his savings will take, and the amount he will save. Certainly, it is true that the worker has lost the power of decision he would have gained if his salary increases had appeared in his pay envelope rather than on the credit rosters of some pension fund. If the effect of the pension funds is to make the employee a capitalist as many have said, he has only one of the prerogatives that make it desirable to be a capitalist—security. He gains little in the way of economic power or the freedom that economic power carries with it. Capitalist he may be, but certainly not in the sense that Marx and Adam Smith used the term.

PENSION POWER

Though the beneficiaries may not have access to it, the pension funds do represent a force of considerable economic power. Let us turn our attention now to the *noninsured* corporate pension funds, which amounted to a total of $32.4 billion at the end of 1961. Approximately 85 per cent of all this money at book value was invested in corporate securities. The most significant portion of their portfolio composition for our purposes has to do with their purchases of common and preferred stock.

It is reliably estimated that all financial institutions hold about a third of all shares listed on national stock exchanges. The Securities and Exchange Commission reports that the market value of the stock holdings of the pension funds was more than 30 per cent of the total held by all financial institutions, or, about $20 billion worth of stock, of which $19.5 billion are common shares. If these figures are correct, the pension funds own approximately a tenth of all the shares outstanding.

When we consider the rate at which the pension funds are buying shares of stock, it will come as no surprise that they own so much. Corporate pension funds have since 1959 purchased more shares of common stock than any other class of investor. In 1961 they made net purchases worth $2 billion, while their nearest competitor, the investment companies, purchased $1.2 billion worth of corporate equities. Furthermore, pension funds are accelerating their rate of stock purchases each year. They have larger amounts of new capital to place each year, and they spend a larger percentage of that amount on shares of stock. In 1961, 55 per cent of pension fund receipts was used to purchase common stock, as against 50 per cent the year before; net acquisitions of common and preferred stock by pension funds were equal to almost 40 per cent of net equity issues. In the three years from 1959 through 1961 pension funds have accounted for almost one-half of all institutional net purchases of common stock.

The quantity of pension fund holdings becomes truly impressive when we consider that the pension funds have been buying significant quantities of stock for only about 10 years. Dollars will continue to flow into these trusts in increasing amounts for approximately 10 years more and if the present trend continues, it is quite possible that the pension funds will own a good deal more than 10 per cent of all corporate shares outstanding. The likelihood has been denied, but I would maintain that it is quite possible the pension fund trustees may eventually be in a position to exercise great influence, if not control, in a significant number of American corporations. This is especially true when we realize that the fund trustees now concentrate their purchases in a rather narrow range of securities. Obviously, they are not investing in all of the stocks in the United States, or even in the majority of those listed on the New York Stock Exchange. They, more than other purchasers, are interested in blue chip securities.

Even now it is a fact that these institutional investors are watched very closely by the managers of top corporations. If a large financial institution, representing several pension funds, began to sell off its holdings in a certain issue, the effect upon the market value of the shares of that corporation could be catastrophic. Something like this did happen when the pension funds liquidated their holdings of tobacco stock at the time of the first cancer scare.

CAPITAL MARKETS

The possibility of major influence upon the financial markets of the United States becomes more real when we consider the degree of concentration that exists in the field of private pensions. The Securities and Exchange Commission reported in 1958 that 14 per cent of all corporate, noninsured pension funds held about 84 per cent of all assets and that funds of $100 million and over (1.5 per cent of all funds) held 55 per cent of all assets.[3] But the story is not complete until we consider that many individual pension funds go to the same bank for servicing their plans and grant to the bank trustee a great amount of independent judgment as to how assets should be invested.

The New York State Banking Department reported that in 1953 the 13 largest banks in the state handling pension fund assets held more than 98 per cent of all such funds and administered over 60 per cent of all the noninsured pension funds in the United States.[4] A careful scrutiny of the New York figures leads to the suspicion that the pattern of pension fund concentration in New York banks is such that about 95 per cent of New York assets are concentrated in 6 or 7 banks. Indeed, one bank with the Bell Telephone Company pension trust in hand, amounting to more than $3 billion, and 2 automobile funds may well have more than all the rest of the New York banks put together.

At this point it is important to observe that there is no evidence whatsoever that either the pension funds themselves or the bank trustees are seeking control of American industrial corporations by means of pension funds. The employer corporations seek the services of extremely well-qualified experts in the investment field to handle their funds. The bankers, in turn, seek to invest the money entrusted to them in the most profitable way. The result is the economic power structure we have been observing.

Though this is not their primary intent, the fact is that the pension funds, along with other large financial institutions like the mutual funds, the life insurance companies, and the personal trusts are rapidly buying control of the industrial corporations of the United States.

The economic movement so dramatically displayed by the pension funds is only one aspect of the drive toward collective security that capitalism has fostered in America. In my opinion the private pension reserves amounting to $55 billion, the life insurance reserves amounting to $128 billion, the personal trust funds in the hands of our banks amounting to $60 billion and mutual fund assets, consisting primarily of shares of stock amounting to $23 billion, are massive evidence that the American property system and with it American society are in a state of rapid evolution, taking us constantly farther away from the traditional patterns of private property and individual ownership toward a kind of collectivized economic system in the control of a class of professional managers.

Though in America today more people own their own homes than ever before, and we have a higher standard of living than the world has ever known elsewhere, we are basically a society that is integrated around the productive economic process. As a result it is the form of ownership and control of productive property that gives our society its economic structure.

About 75 per cent of our productive property is owned by large corporations. These corporations are in turn coming to be owned by financial institutions like the pension funds. In the large corporation the individual stockholder now has little or no voice and in most of the new or newly significant financial institutions the individual contributor has not even the paper title to a say in management that the common stockholder has.

But on the other hand, the fruits of capitalism, that is returns on capital investment, are being shared by upward of 100 million persons, whereas corporate stockholders number at most 15 million. Thus are we socializing our wealth.

At the same time it is a mere mockery to call these people capitalists for they have in reality only one prerogative that attaches to ownership, namely a claim upon income. The truth is there are few capitalists left. The role of the capitalist is carried on by a group of corporate managers who are responsible to a large public which makes itself felt either by a kind of economic vote in the market place or through its agent, government.

This system is neither socialist nor capitalist, in the classical sense at least. It is a kind of public but nonstatist system of economic organization. I have called it the paraproprietal society, the society beyond property.

As a third new form of socio-economic organization, such a society presents an interesting contrast to our European neighbors, who are also in a state of evolution from their capitalist origins. For the most part their economies are marked by a much higher degree of government intervention. The private pension funds are much more highly regulated in Europe than they are in the United States, and the official who is charged with their supervision usually has more far-reaching powers to make substantive as well as procedural rules. But in Europe the tendency to enlarge the benefits and contributions under social security laws seems to be driving out private pension plans for wage earners.

The Europeans with their predominantly governmental pension funds reap certain advantages. Their systems permit more flexible control of these funds by the public managers of the credit system.

They can preserve their capital markets from the distortions to which we are subject by the influential presence of the pension funds in the capital markets.

There is greater mobility for the workers whose pensions do not depend on staying with one employer.

ADVANTAGES TO THE U.S. SYSTEM

However, the American system is not without unique opportunities of its own that have not yet been fully realized. Neither the trustees who administer these funds nor the unions and employee groups who are the beneficiaries have exercised much more than technical control of these vast aggregations of capital. The trustees apparently administer these funds in general solely to secure a reasonable rate of return, with adequate security. The unions thus far have not been eager to exercise financial control, though some of them have made suggestions regarding the investment of employer-managed funds.

What I have in mind is that our pension guardians could exercise a good deal more imagination in the investment of the funds entrusted to them. It does not seem unreasonable to ask that a modest proportion of these funds be invested in projects that would be of social use to workers both before and after retirement.

It is not necessarily inconsistent with the financial soundness required by these funds that they be invested in housing projects, recreation centers, or nursing homes and community housing for retired persons. If we are to have such institutions they will have to be financed in some way, and there is no good reason why pension funds which are always seeking new avenues of investment cannot be tapped for a purpose consistent with the basic interests of the people for whom they are invested.

The freedom of these funds to follow new and creative paths of their own choosing suggests that we are only at the beginning of this revolutionary process whereby our society will find new and better ways to free the individual person to develop his own potentialities from the beginning to the end of his life.

NOTES

¹ For a further exposition of the author's thesis, see Paul P. Harbrecht, S.J., *Pension Funds and Economic Power* (New York: The Twentieth Century Fund, 1959), and also Robert Tilove, *Pension Funds and Economic Freedom* (New York: The Fund for the Republic, Inc., 1959).

² U.S. Bureau of Old-Age and Survivors Insurance, Division of Program Analysis, Analytical Note No. 120 (Baltimore: The Bureau, 1960) (mimeographed).

³ Based on statistics developed by the SEC to update its *Survey of Corporate Pension Funds, 1949–1954,* October, 1958.

⁴ George A. Mooney, *Pension and Other Welfare Plans* (Albany: N.Y. State Banking Department, 1955), p. 31.

PRIVATE PENSION PLANS AND ECONOMIC POWER

William Haber

Father Harbrecht's excellent paper is concerned largely, in fact almost entirely, with private pension plans in American industry. The development, as his figures indicated, has been phenomenal. While some plans are quite old, the major expansion came during World War II and especially after 1950. And in that development collective bargaining has had an unusually important place. In fact, it is clear to me that without the push given to company financed pension plans by unions, this development would not have reached its present magnitude providing, as Father Harbrecht indicated, certain benefit rights to over 23 million wage and salary earners and accumulated reserves exceeding $55 billion. He is particularly concerned in his discussion with about 60 per cent of these reserves—about $32 billion in noninsured pension funds.

This clearly fabulous growth as he and others have emphasized is bound to continue. It has been estimated that nearly $4 billion is being added to these reserves annually and that by 1965 private pension funds may have financial reserves of quite fantastic amounts and may, after that time, grow at the rate of $4 to $6 billion per year, reaching a total of $77 billion by 1968.

It should be borne in mind, however, that the reason why these private plans developed, to a very large extent, is directly related to the limitations of the public social security system which we adopted in 1935. It is essential to recognize this point in any discussion. The public scheme is, after all, the real bulwark for old-age security, particularly for American wage earners. While its reserves are much smaller than those of the private plans, being somewhat less than $20 billion, social security covers at least twice as many persons. Altogether, over 90 per cent of wage and salary earners in the United States are entitled to retirement benefits under social security plans.

This program, now over 25 years old, provides the basic underpinning for retirement income for the bulk of our wage earners. It is a social insurance system. Participation is (with few exceptions) compulsory. Its early weaknesses, particularly its inadequate coverage and its strikingly low monthly benefit payments are largely responsible for collective demands for private employer financed supplementary retirement pension plans. Thus, this program, which advanced rapidly during World War II and mushroomed after 1950, is still growing and will, no doubt, eventually cover many more than the 23 million persons now entitled to some private pension benefits. It is important to bear in mind that any basic weakness in the public scheme which provides for nearly universal coverage is bound to increase pressure for expansion of the private plans and their benefit rates. It is, therefore, of utmost importance that the public system of old-age, survivors, and disability programs be subjected to continuous examination with regard to the adequacy of its benefit structure in relation to general living standards and particularly to the purchasing power of the pension dollar.

It is important to emphasize, however, that under the best of circumstances, the social security plan can never be adequate for everybody. It is, after all, a "floor of protection." It cannot hope to meet the larger needs of the more favorably situated wage earners, the skilled workers, technicians, those in the higher wage brackets. Consequently, the private plan serves an important social and economic function as a supplementary system to provide a sort of second story over the floor of basic protection contemplated by the social security system.

While the private plans in American business and industry today have made an immense contribution to increasing the economic security of retired people, the problem of old-age security is by no means "solved." The major weakness of these private plans, in my judgment, is the absence of vesting. In view of this, there is no assurance that a person who has worked for an employer under a retirement pension scheme will in fact be eligible to receive a benefit at a particular age. It is almost universally required that he remain with the same employer. Vesting provisions are slowly being introduced, and the most forward movement in increasing the economic importance of these plans would be a rapid expansion in vested pensions at age 40 after 10 years' employment. Such a development would go a long way toward reducing the danger of pension plans inhibiting occupational and geographic mobility of wage earners. It would also increase pension benefits, since a retired person would be eligible to receive a benefit from more than one fund. On the other hand we cannot be blind to the fact that pensions are the costliest item in the "fringe package"; they are a part of production costs; they are not free. If such costs are to be met without price increases, productivity must also increase.

In my judgment the danger to mobility said to be inherent in private pension plans is greatly exaggerated. It is common to refer to these plans as introducing a modern form of feudalism—a system which ties a worker to his employer and keeps him there, since he would lose his benefits if he left. Mobility is important to our economy. It helps to allocate labor where it is most productive. It should be encouraged and vesting of private plans at a relatively early year would do so. Nevertheless, other factors are more responsible for such immobility which may exist than pension plans. The *age* of the worker is probably much more important; *older workers* do not take the risks of seeking newer jobs. Union seniority is, in my judgment, a greater "impediment" than pension plans. A wage earner with 15 or 20 years seniority has a valuable economic asset he is strongly disinclined to gamble away by moving to a new occupation or to another city. These and similar personal and social factors are probably much more important in discouraging mobility than pension plans, with or without vesting.

Fear has often been expressed that pension plans, public and private, interfere with or discourage individual thrift. Father Harbrecht suggests that the insured person (whether covered by social or private insurance) has certainly lost any influence over the *rate* and *form* of his savings. This may be true. It cannot be said, however, that the amount of thrift has been adversely affected. To begin with the compulsory tax deduction for social security is, in itself, a setting aside of present earning for future use. This is also true of employer payments into a pension fund. The question often is between so many cents for an increase in the basic wage rate or an increase in the employer's contribution to the pension fund. When the latter step is taken, current earnings or potential earnings are set aside for future use. Perhaps even more important is the fact that the very existence of public and private pension plans providing a minimum retirement income has actually led to an increase in private saving to supplement that income. Home ownership of old people is far higher today than it ever was. And more people own private insurance annuity policies than ever before. Old-age security is expensive, too expensive for the ordinary wage earner. The "lift" given by the public and private schemes makes it possible for the individual to supplement the monthly amount with private saving whether in the form of home ownership or annuities.

The major focus of Father Harbrecht's paper is upon the theme that one of the unintended results of private pension funds is likely to be a dramatic change in the nature of our society. The thesis is that these funds really do not belong to anyone. There is some truth in that—in a very technical sense. They cannot be claimed by the union which may have negotiated the plan and whose representatives sit as trustees. They cannot be claimed or controlled by the company which may have made the payments and which is also represented on the board of trustees. They certainly cannot be claimed by the individual pensioner. He has no title until he retires or quits (assuming there is vesting), and even that title is often of questionable legality. Consequently, it is said that some $30 billion increasing after 1965 at the rate of over $4 billion a year is available for investment by trustees or bankers representing them in securities, and these possibly lead to the control of significant corporations.

That there is such a danger is quite clear. Note has been taken of this by committees of the Congress and by the chairman of the Federal Reserve Board. Father Harbrecht has made a real contribution in highlighting the danger in his book on the subject. It seems to me, however, that the threat that pension fund trustees may so manage their investments as to gain control of important corporations is exaggerated. The potential is there and may sometimes erupt. But it can be said with Professor Harbrecht that "no evidence whatsoever" can be found that either bank trustees or pension funds are seeking control of important corporations by means of fund assets. This observation is attested by others. Bankers and trustees seek to invest reserve in industry where the best returns can be had and if they appear to concentrate on 200 or so common stocks it is because these stocks appear (or should one say until recently appeared) to have a good profit potential.

What disturbs Professor Harbrecht more, however, it seems to me, is a philosophical idea that we are tending to modify our social system from one of private capitalism to one of collective security. The evidence he suggests is massive; that we are slowly shifting from private property and ownership toward a collectivized economic system in control of professional managers. One should point out, however, that this has been taking place without pension funds and their alleged economic power. This is a development which has been operating in our society for half a century and is probably being accentuated by the role of the large corporation and investment funds in control of insurance companies, mutual funds, trust company assets, as well as private pension funds. I am not too disturbed about this development. Our society is not static and our institutions are being changed by time and circumstances. So long as these institutions can continue to provide a maximum degree of economic freedom, so long as they can continue to protect the dignity of the individual human being, so long as our institutions can make it possible for our society to improve standards of living, education, economic security, and maintain free government, we need not fear the fact that our institutions are changing. That fact is too clear to be challenged.

INTERNATIONAL PERSPECTIVES WITH RESPECT TO PENSION FUNDS AND ECONOMIC POWER

Robert J. Myers

In the United States, the investment of the assets of the various social insurance systems, which total some $30 billion, do not have any *direct* economic power in the sense that they effect private industrial growth and development through direct investment. The reason for this is simply that, by law, all such investments must be in government obligations. Indirectly, however, there may be a very considerable effect, because if these government bonds were not held by the several trust funds, they would be held by private investors, who would then have less monies available for private investment. It is hardly worthwhile to try to trace through these intricate economic effects. Instead of considering further the situation in the United States, I should like to describe how the investments of foreign social insurance systems result in their having a significant amount of economic power.

I believe that it can be said that in all economically well-developed countries, the same practice is followed in connection with the investment of social security funds as is done in the United States— namely, any investments that are made are in government securities. In the developing countries, however, there is a considerably different situation. A substantial proportion of the assets of their social security systems—particularly those dealing with pension benefits—is invested in a wide variety of areas besides government bonds. The reasons underlying such a procedure are not always clearly thought out, but rather are often the result of circumstances.[1]

In many instances, the social security institutions are semiautonomous organizations and have great freedom in investment procedures. Frequently, as a practical matter, investment in government securities is not financially advisable because of the relatively weak fiscal situation of the government. Then, too, investment in private securities carries with it the advantages not only that relatively higher interest rates and/or greater security of principal are available, but also this procedure may be very desirable for the social and economic growth of the country.

In many instances, the legislative policy is clearly directed toward the social security institution having this goal. In other instances, however, this is merely a haphazard and fortuitous result; the system may be established with relatively high contribution rates and with relatively low benefit outgo in the initial years of operation (due to long qualifying periods and to benefit formulas that relate the amounts to the length of coverage under the program).

Investments in other than governmental obligations by foreign social insurance systems occur in many different ways. In some instances, such investments are in bonds of private corporations, and even at times in common and preferred stocks. Such investments are also frequently in mortgages—both commercial and industrial, and also residential. Frequently, persons covered by the system have a priority to obtain home mortgages from its funds—and, even at times, personal loans for other purposes. Going further into the field of private enterprise, the assets of some social security institutions are invested in commercial real estate enterprises, such as hotels and office buildings, which are frequently leased to private operating companies, but with a share in the profits going to the social security institution and with the ultimate ownership remaining in its hands.

Frequently, social security institutions utilize their accumulating funds to build medical facilities and hospitals for use in connection with health-benefit provisions. Under such circumstances, there should be proper accounting procedures to charge the costs of these facilities against the health-benefits provisions and, thus, to safeguard properly the investment and financial status of the remainder of the system. Such a procedure will, of course, present some difficult and complex accounting problems, but it can be performed.

At times, the general government compels the social security institution to make investments of certain types. For example, institutions sometimes must make substantial investments in low-cost housing projects. Although such programs may be highly beneficial to the nation they may prove very poor investments to the social security institution—both because of unduly low interest rates being charged and because rents are not established at economic, self-liquidating levels—and even then there may be great delinquency in payment of rent. In fact, the tenants might feel no necessity for paying the rents falling due, if they make the fallacious argument that "after all, the apartments are built from our own money, so why should we be concerned about paying ourselves?" In actual fact, what this means is that some of the covered workers are being subsidized by the entire group of covered workers.

There are valid arguments both in favor of and against the investment of social security funds in other than governmental obligations, especially in economically developing countries. On the "pro" side, there is the major point that economically developing countries generally have a great shortage of capital available for economic growth. Intelligent, planned use of social security funds available for investment can significantly help the economic development of the country. In addition, if such investments in private economic development are wisely made, there will be a good investment return with ample security (and even perhaps more than if the money were invested in government obligations).

On the "con" side, the investments made in private economic enterprise by an autonomous or semiautonomous social security institution may not aid economic development sufficiently. Investments may be made in such areas as luxury apartments, expensive office buildings (including one for the social security system), and sports facilities—rather than in productive economic enterprise. Moreover, the responsibility for investing such large funds is placed in the hands of a relatively small number of individuals, who may, accordingly, possess great economic power—and, in fact, possibly more power than the top government officials who are concerned with fiscal and economic planning matters. This procedure can be not only bad in theory, but also in practice there may arise great financial temptations to the persons who have the responsibility for virtually uncontrolled investment of the social security funds.

In summary, the social security systems in many of the developing countries throughout the world are building up relatively large funds that are available for direct investment in private industries or in enterprises that compete with or take the place of private industries. There are both great advantages and possibilities of economic development if this process is carried out—and also possibly great disadvantages and dangers. From the social welfare viewpoint, much of the potential gain resulting from the development of the economy as a whole—or, conversely, much of the danger of economic wastage, if this should eventuate—would be foregone if the benefit structure were established so that more benefits would be paid out in the early years than is frequently the case. It might perhaps be best if this more immediate payment of benefits were made, and if the necessary monies needed for economic development came directly and clearly from other sources established for this specific purpose and goal.

NOTES

[1] It should be pointed out that in many cases the decisions as to types of investments have depended mostly on expediency. Considerations of the long-range effects of various investment procedures has perhaps been underemphasized.

PENSION FUNDS AND ECONOMIC POWER: USES OF FUNDS IN OTHER NATIONS

David S. Blanchard

The question of aging in relation to employment and other related problems was of particular interest to the International Labor Organization in 1962 as it constituted the main subject for discussion at our annual conference held in Geneva, Switzerland, in June. This Conference is the supreme body of the ILO in which the representatives of 102 governments come together to discuss related problems and attempt to find solutions to them. But the ILO is unique among intergovernmental organizations, and among its sister organizations in the family of the United Nations, by virtue of its structure, for we have not only direct representation by governments but by management and labor organizations from the member countries as well.

So that while the ILO is particularly preoccupied with questions affecting older workers at present, this is not a new subject for us. In fact, the constitution of the ILO which was adopted in 1919 numbers "provision for old age" as one of the elements of the improvement of social conditions entering into the ILO's field of competence. Now, while we usually think of technical assistance as being aid given by developed to underdeveloped countries, you will no doubt be interested to know that shortly after the United States joined the ILO in 1934 (which was, incidentally, the first organization of this kind in the work of which the United States decided to participate) it called upon the Organization to send to this country social security experts from its staff in Geneva to assist in drafting the Social Security Act in 1935.

This then is the first difference I note between practice here and in some other countries, namely that social security plans, particularly as regards pensions, have been in existence a good deal longer than they have here. Second, in many countries, particularly in Europe and Latin America, social security measures often cover a much wider field of risks than purely pensions. In many cases these would also include coverage for family allowances, accident and unemployment insurance, and medical care. This means that for these risks, short-term accumulation of funds is more usual than long-term, as in the case of most pension funds, and therefore the economic impact is different. Also, in most of the cases that I shall be referring to, social security plans are operated and controlled by public or semipublic institutions and their capital reserves are controlled or regulated by the government. This does not mean that private pension plans are not important in many other countries, because they are, particularly in Europe. But their importance and influence is probably not as great as in this country, and the information available relates to public or semipublic plans.

It seems to me that one can consider the question of pension funds and economic power from three points of view: (1) of the individual considered mainly as the recipient of social benefits; (2) of the employer, where much of the income of social security plans are collected, and (3) of the community as a whole. As far as the individual is concerned, the main effect is that he is compelled to save, or, as Father Harbrecht points out, the choice of whether to save or not is removed from him. Whether such saving would have been carried out in any case is difficult to prove.

In many countries, the contributions paid by lower income groups of insured persons are usually at the expense of immediate consumption. However, benefits they receive in terms of short-term insurance, unemployment insurance, family allowances, etc., usually more than make up this loss. The contributions of middle income groups to social security are probably at the immediate expense of both voluntary saving and consumption. In most European countries and in some countries in Latin America, including Argentina, Chile, and Uruguay, pension plans have already matured to such an extent that the middle class as a whole benefits greatly. In some other countries, where this stage has not been reached, the reduction in voluntary savings by the middle class is probably more than offset by compulsory savings for later entitlement to old-age and survivors pensions.

While the burden of contributions of employers to social security varies from country to country and depends upon the number of risks covered, it is usually large enough to represent an appreciable amount. However, it is generally agreed that these costs on industry are often passed on, either wholly or partly, to the consumers by raising prices or to the workers by withholding or reducing the increases in wages they would otherwise have been granted.

From the national standpoint, the relative burden of the social security system on the economy as a whole can be gauged from the level of receipts and expenditure. Figures on this subject are not often collated and itemized in official publications, but we do know that expenditure for social matters varies greatly from one country to another. In gross terms it is said to account for 10 per cent of the British national income and over 17 per cent of the French national income.

Thus, by reason of the contributions it levies, the benefits its distributes, and the number of individuals it directly affects, a social security system is bound to influence the operation of the economic mechanism and to sway the behavior of its members. How then are the funds accumulated in various countries invested or otherwise safeguarded until they are ready to be paid out as pensions?

In general, the nature and function of any accumulated assets of a social security system are for two major purposes—to provide a contingency fund to meet any adverse fluctuation in the balance of income and outgo, and to provide investment income to help finance the program. Indirectly, it might be said that under systems following the capitalization principle—particularly when it is on the individual basis —the accumulated assets are intended to be available to guarantee payment of benefits. In the long run, however, it can be assumed that social insurance systems will be perpetual in nature, and so, if adequately financed on a long-range basis, they are not required to liquidate these responsibilities at any one time.

In considering the invested assets of the old-age pension plans in most countries we should certainly bear in mind that the funds involved are pooled and cover various risks—always one or more long-range risks in addition to old-age pensions and, quite frequently, short-range risks such as sickness benefits as well. In other words, in statistics published by these countries, there are no particular assets assigned to the old-age pension risk as such.

The assets of the systems of many Central and South American countries are in a wide variety of investments. Thus, in almost all these systems, there are investments in government bonds, stocks and bonds of private companies, housing loans, both to government agencies and to private corporations and individuals, real estate loans for construction of hospital and other medical facilities in connection with sickness benefits payable under the general social security system, and even, in some cases, loans to persons covered under the system (not only for housing, but also for other purposes).

In the Japanese system, all the funds of the scheme that are available for investment are turned over to the Ministry of Finance, which pays an interest rate of 6.5 per cent and which lends out part of these funds to local public housing authorities for building hospitals, recreation centers, and houses.

In a number of the other Latin American countries, government bonds constitute about 40 per cent of total investments; at the other extreme, as in the case of the Brazilian system for commercial workers and in the Mexican system, the corresponding figure is only about 5 per cent. In only one instance—the Dominican Republic plan—is there a significant investment in bonds of private business organizations. Likewise, in only two instances—the systems of Chile and the Dominican Republic—are there significant investments in shares of private business organizations.

A number of the programs have sizeable investments in mortgages; in the Brazilian system for commercial workers and in the programs of Costa Rica and Panama, the proportion is one-third or more. Further, in regard to mortgages where subdivided data were available, there appears to be virtually no investment in farm mortgages and relatively little investment in business mortgages; in other words, the bulk of the activity is in home mortgages (including those in respect to the residences of insured persons). In the Panamanian system, which has the highest percentage of investments in mortgages, about one-fourth of the mortgages are on business properties, and the remaining are on homes. Relatively few plans have any investments in the form of loans to insured persons (other than home mortgages). Real estate constitutes a very significant proportion of total investments in certain systems—about 30 per cent in the Brazilian system for transport workers and in the Dominican Republic system, and as much as 44 per cent in the Brazilian scheme for commercial workers (it will be noted that the latter has over 75 per cent of its investments in either mortgages or real estate) and 63 per cent in the Mexican system (about a quarter of this is in so-called "workers' colonies"). Most of the systems have from 5 to 10 per cent of their investments as cash balances.

From what I have said, it seems clear that many countries, particularly in the less-developed parts of the world, are anxious to safeguard the purchasing power of pension funds. This accounts for the increasing number of investments in real estate and real property. One thing should be emphasized: In many of the underdeveloped parts of the world where patterns of saving and accumulation of funds differ from those followed in other regions, the introduction of old-age pension plans has had a very beneficial effect on the accumulation of capital for investment. It is, of course, imperative that measures be adopted, where this has not already been done, to insure that these funds, including their value, are safeguarded for the benefit of future pensions, but also that in the interim they are used as wisely as possible for the sound economic development of those countries, which, of course, is another way of insuring the soundness of the pension funds themselves and of the social security system as a whole.

VI. The Economics of Aging: Social Policy and Social Values

CHAPTER 12

AGING AND NATIONAL POLICY

Charles R. Sligh, Jr.

I have been asked to make some predictions here, and the first one I would like to make is that our national problems, including the problems of the aging in our population, never will be solved.

I hope it will always be this way, because in a dynamic society such as ours we can never be satisfied with things as they are. As we cross one hill, there is always another to be climbed, and if we ever reach the point where we have no more problems, we will lapse into complacency and stagnation.

But in developing solutions as we go along, we must be careful not to beget problems greater than the ones we are trying to solve. All of our solutions in the end—and this applies to present problems as well as those which will develop in the future—depend on the productive capacity of our society. It will only defeat our purpose if, in trying to solve a problem of today, we create additional problems which detract from our ability to cope with the challenges of tomorrow.

In this connection, I think we must avoid solutions which call for more than the problem really needs—which, to borrow a term from the military, "overkill" it. And this applies particularly to the problems of the aged.

Competent research, which I will cite later, indicates that the financial difficulties of the aged as a group are not nearly as great as is claimed by those who advocate drastic solutions to their problems.

In approaching my own assignment here, "Aging and National Policy," it may perhaps be best if I break the subject down into these three aspects.

First, what national policies will help the aged and the aging lead useful and productive lives?

Second, what is the best way to meet the needs of those who can no longer be productive?

And *third,* how can these needs be met with the least burden on the productive potential of the population as a whole?

This conference, composed of persons who seriously study all the many aspects of the problems of the aging, well realizes that no simple act of Congress, once and for all, will dispose of the difficulties of each of our older people. We realize that there are many older people who have no difficulties at all, and some whose problems are so many and varied that no piece of legislation could envision them.

We also know that never before has any society's aged members been so well off, on the average, as ours are today. This is, of course, a direct result of the wealth our society has created—and which most of these older persons have helped to create. And we know that there are many sources of assistance to the aged now—family, private, and institutional, as well as local, state, and federal governmental sources.

GUIDELINES FOR NATIONAL POLICY

A national policy for the aged, then, may not be formulated in a vacuum, but should be for the purpose of improving the present condition of the aged. Bearing this in mind, I would suggest that any such national policy should include consideration of these points:

1. Present nonfederal sources of help and comfort for the aged—sources which are still increasing in numbers and in effective service—must not be discouraged or forced from the field. They should be encouraged to take a larger part.

2. As federal resources are not unlimited and are already severely strained, and as the majority of older people are not without resources of their own, or are eligible for assistance from nonfederal sources, our policy should avoid making all of our aged citizens wards of the government—like the unhappy Indians who have had so much experience with this status.

3. And, as more of our citizens are living longer because their health is becoming better year by year, national policy should encourage older people to be as self-reliant as possible. This is as important to them as it is to the nation.

4. Finally, our national policy should preclude the imposition of programs for the supposed benefit of the aged that have such burdensome costs that they prevent our citizens from providing for their own old age, and at the same time slow or halt the remarkable advances in providing for old age that have been taking place in the private economy.

ACCOMPLISHMENTS OF INDUSTRY

As a spokesman for industry, I naturally take pride in the accomplishments of industry in matters pertaining to the aging, the aged, and the retired. I would like to cite these as an example of concern outside government.

For some years, the National Association of Manufacturers has been conducting a program of educating employers to the possibility and the desirability of lifting age barriers to employment, and we have met with considerable success.

Today, the employer-operated retirement systems in America, exclusive of plans conducted through insurance companies and plans administered by unions and supported by employers, have accumulated about $40 billion in reserves. At present, because many of these plans are fairly new, annual income of these pension funds is about four times the annual payments out of the funds.

In addition, many companies have set up medical insurance programs so that retired employees receive paid-up medical care policies on retirement, or are able to continue such insurance at very moderate cost.

There are signs, too, that many companies are taking a hard look at compulsory retirement ages. The astonishing progress made in medicine has made the retirement of many 65-year-olds seem as ridiculous as retirement of 45-year-olds. And the introduction of technological improvement in materials handling, automation, and such developments have both reduced the drudgery that ages men and women and changed the nature of available jobs, so that youthful strength is no longer required in many which once required it.

Meanwhile, safety and health programs in industry have reduced accidents and illness—contributing to the unimpaired vigor of many older workers—and actually helped to prolong life. Many of the older people with whose problems we are concerned in this meeting simply wouldn't be here except for the improvement in industrial health and safety practices.

ROLE OF THE FEDERAL GOVERNMENT

I am sure that we are aware that so far as the general public is concerned today, most of the argument assumes that if the problems of the elderly are to be met, the federal government is the agency to meet them and this means new federal commitments. This approach contains real dangers for our older people. I'd like to take a brief look at where we stand today with the programs already in being.

The Social Security system is calculated to be obligated to the extent of $350 billion to present participants in the program. The Social Security fund is less than $20 billion, and it is not growing. By contrast, the pension funds of private companies, as I have noted, contain twice this amount of reserves against much smaller obligations.

The federal employees' retirement system has an unfunded accrued liability of $32.5 billion. The Railroad Retirement unfunded liability is more than $5 billion.

What is quickly apparent is that in our eagerness to provide for elderly persons, we have obligated ourselves to collect in taxes during the lifetimes of present participants in these programs some $367 billion—a figure far larger than the national debt that everyone worries so much about these days.

Unlike the national debt, this obligation must be paid out of current earnings of the economy. The only alternative is to add it to the national debt as it comes due. Furthermore, as Senator Harry F. Byrd recently reported, the total calculable obligations of the federal government now amount to one trillion, 242 billion dollars.

Now I can't imagine a figure like that, and I don't suppose you can. What does it mean? Well, according to the National Bureau of Economic Research, in 1958 (the last year available) all the nongovernmental assets in the United States had a value of one trillion, 340 billion dollars. So, you see this figure means that the federal government has pledged to pay almost everything that all of us own. Homes, cars, farms, factories, stores—everything in America. These tremendous obligations have a direct bearing upon the economy's ability to support its older citizens. This is so, because the obligations must either result in increased taxes or in increased federal debt.

Problem of Excessive Tax Burden   The present administration has come to the conclusion that the present tax burden already is too great and that it actually is slowing down economic growth and preventing the creation of employment opportunities. It is a conclusion the NAM arrived at quite some time ago. Increasing tax rates obviously will slow still more the growth of the economy and impair the economy's ability to support its aged.

If the obligations are met by increasing federal borrowing (which on such a scale could only be done by the creation of bank credit) we will have accelerated inflation. This means that the obligations to our aged citizens will be paid off in cheap dollars of lower buying power. As one of the concerns of this conference is how to meet the problems of aged persons on fixed pensions and incomes which have been eroded by the relatively mild inflation we already have had, I do not need to labor the point that such a solution would create incalculable damage to our elderly population.

There is a third possible solution to the problem that these enormous obligations pose, and that is to reduce them. Social Security benefits, despite the general impression, are not paid out of funds contributed by those who draw them. They are paid out of taxes collected from men and women who currently are earning, and from their employers. Nor is there any legal guarantee that benefits will be continued at any particular level or, indeed, that they will be continued at all. There is the political possibility that at some future time the current working population will become so incensed at the magnitude of the tax burden on them for the benefit of their elders that they will demand congressional reduction of the benefits to lighten the load.

I believe that anyone who has real concern for the welfare of the elderly must bear in mind the possible consequences of higher taxes or inflation when considering federal programs ostensibly of benefit to the aged. I would hope that more attention will be paid to the possibilities of private solutions to such problems. By contrast with the federal solutions which involve assuming that future voters will be willing to carry the load we assign them, all private plans are based on present investment whose earnings in future years will meet the obligations of those years. The private plans represent actual accumulated resources to which the retired persons will have vested property rights rather than assumed political rights.

We must also bear in mind that a rising cost of public programs for the care of the aged will inevitably reduce the capabilities of our working people to provide for their own retirements, and therefore assure still greater cost of public programs indefinitely into the future.

Confine Benefits to the Needy   One way to hold down the cost of such programs is to confine benefits to those who need them. I know that there is much emotional opposition to any so-called "means test." Much of this opposition comes from persons who approve of "means tests" in other fields. For example, one and the same man may oppose any proof of need as a condition to federal payments of medical expenses, while holding that means tests are needed in public housing so as to reserve the available accommodations for persons who cannot afford to pay full rent.

Such a position is based on the fallacy that while public housing accommodations are quite evidently limited, federal money is not. A moment's thought certainly should produce recognition that federal money can only represent a portion of the national income. And when the federal share is increased, as it has been increasing in recent years, a point of diminishing returns is reached. An economy which is shorn of too much of its income becomes first static, then declining, as income is consumed rather than invested for future consumption.

The virtue of private systems is that they are based upon investment for future consumption, and thus are self-supporting and self-perpetuating. The danger of the federal approach is that it merely redistributes the income of current earners to nonearners, and this can continue only so long as the earners allow it. They will not allow it so long if they become aware that their earnings are being redistributed to persons who may be better off than themselves.

It seems to me, then, that the present situation dictates that the way to meet the needs of those who can no longer be productive is to take full account of the individual status of such people, and of the private and local provisions that are made for them.

ECONOMIC CONDITION OF THE AGED

In the present debate over one phase of the problem, medical care, the aged are pictured by some spokesmen as almost universally indigent. Perhaps you are familiar with the study made by James W. Wiggins and Helmut Schoeck of Emory University.[1]

The Emory professors, after a cross-section study of considerable size and statistical validity in 78 communities, found these facts about those over 65:

Less than one in 10 reported they had any uncared-for medical needs. Less than one in 20 owed a medical bill. Two-thirds described their health as good, and only one in 10 said his health was poor. Far more than half had some form of health insurance.

I was particularly interested in Charles Lininger's paper, which showed among other things that slightly more than half of all spending units where the head is aged 65 or over are living in their own homes free of mortgages, while only about one-fourth are living in rented quarters. And that while 84 per cent of those studied had no installment debt, only 21 per cent had little or no assets, and 65 per cent had assets from "moderate" to "very substantial," which means upward of $5,000 in all these cases.

If we treat everyone over 65 as a hardship case, regardless of such findings, we will place an intolerable burden upon our working population, and we may very well give help to persons who need no assistance—and at the expense of those who need help desperately. And so the picture that emerges is that while the condition of our older citizens is not all we might wish it to be, it is not generally desperate, and it is improving.

ACHIEVING ECONOMIC SECURITY

For the future the greatest security for the elderly will be achieved by setting aside investment from current income which will care for tomorrow's older citizens. This, obviously, cannot be accomplished within the federal government, where the approach is frankly that today's worker is taxed to help today's elderly, and little or nothing is set aside for the future under any of the several federal plans.

If the political dangers are avoided, I believe that America will be able to support its aged citizens in increasingly greater comfort and security. As we all know, there are more aged citizens today than ever before, and this proportion will for some time continue to grow. At the same time, we are keeping children in school and out of the work force longer. These factors are offset, however, by the fact that more women are employed—and in recent years the active work force has grown at a faster rate than the population as a whole.

This means that there will be a broader base of support available for retired persons in our economy. The economy also has the opportunity to grow, provided sufficient investment is made in technological improvement. When productivity is increased by new methods, again the base of support for retired citizens is improved.

In short, America's retired persons will share the future of the economy as a whole. If it is a growing economy, it can support its elderly in better style. If it does not grow, the prospects of the aged in our country are dubious. Therefore, all who are genuinely concerned with the problems of the aged must consider the effect of their proposals upon the whole economy as well as the immediate benefits to be gained for present beneficiaries. The incomes of all of us can come only from current production of goods and services.

There is increasing evidence of greater awareness of the needs of a growing economy. I will not go into these details here. I will merely say that the economy is an engine, which stalls when too great a tax load is placed upon it. But as it gains speed, it gains power and can carry heavier loads. We must be careful not to be tempted to start in high gear; but to start in low, start with modest loads, and add to the loads in such ways and such quantities that we won't stall out.

NOTES

[1] James W. Wiggins and Helmut Schoeck, "A Profile of the Aging; U.S.A.," *Geriatrics*, 16 (July, 1961), 336–42. [Ed. note: As with other research reported in this volume, the nature of the sample should be noted. Since the purpose of this survey was to study the nondependent or "normal" aged, a quota sample was employed in place of the standard area-probability type and all nonwhites and persons receiving Old-Age Assistance or living in public housing were omitted. This permitted the elimination of over 20 per cent of the aged population, representing the lowest economic segment.]

CHAPTER 13

AGING AND GOVERNMENT POLICY: OUTLOOK FOR PROGRESS IN THE 1960's

Donald P. Kent

To a sociologist turned federal administrator, the topic you have given me is especially challenging. For it is the goal of the Kennedy administration to promote progress in dealing with problems of aging by every means within its power. And the demands of this task, which have taken me to virtually every part of the nation in the past few months, have left little time for introspection or analysis.

Yet it is the function of the sociologist to be objective, to be critical, to take nothing for granted. It is his role, for example, to ask searching and sometimes embarrassing questions like these: "What *is* progress?" "How do you measure it?" "Are we really moving *ahead?*" We are moving, there seems little doubt of that. But we should be careful not to fall into the age-old trap of assuming that motion and progress are necessarily one and the same.

Both as a sociologist by training and a federal official by present occupation, I am concerned that we not confuse more activity with advancement to the disadvantage of our ultimate objective. So I am glad that you have forced me to spend some time in taking stock.

I am even more glad to be able to say to you, after this process of assessment, that I think we *have* made demonstrable progress during the first months of the 60's, and that we will make even more during the years immediately ahead. But I have been sobered also by the realization that there is so much to do if we are not to fall behind, let alone to make headway in a situation where the needs are growing with almost incredible rapidity.

One of the responsibilities which the Office of Aging has undertaken is an effort to assess the probable changes of the next decade, both within the older population and in the world of which it is a part, and to develop programs to cope realistically with these changes. I would like to give you a preliminary view of the direction of our thinking as we proceed with this effort.

In the first place, the sheer numbers of older people are increasing at a rate which is really quite difficult for us to comprehend. You have heard and read the raw statistics many times, but numbers alone have a disturbing way of turning human beings into statistical abstractions. We have been trying to understand what they mean in terms of human needs.

Perhaps it may help us all to assess the magnitude of these needs if we recognize that the number of people in this nation who have passed their sixty-fifth birthday now exceeds the total number of all ages still living on farms. It may impress us, too, to realize that our elderly citizens now increase each year by an amount which slightly exceeds the entire population of the state of Vermont.

Think for a moment of the problems we would face if we were actually to add to United States territory a state of this size every year —complete with people, but in a relatively undeveloped condition, and sorely lacking facilities and services to meet the needs of its citizens. Imagine further that all the citizens of this new state were 65 or over, with special needs which accompany advancing age but with the declining strength and relatively modest financial resources also characteristic of most people in this stage of life.

This is a fairly good way of indicating the magnitude of the task which confronts us. But it is a very bad way to express the *nature* of that task, because, of course, older people are not a separate group in our society. Fortunately for them and for all of us, they are thoroughly intermingled with the rest of the nation's citizens. Fortunately, too, they continue to think, act, and vote as free and independent individuals, just as they did when they were younger. In fact, recent research evidence appears to indicate that in some respects at least, advancing age *increases* individuality. It makes inherent personality characteristics stand out more clearly; it causes the individual to be less responsive to the external pressures of society and more attentive to demands originating within himself.

In every measure we take for the benefit of our older citizens, we must be careful to respect this essential individuality. By the same token, we in the administration are convinced that continued vigorous effort by the nation to improve the lot of its older people is one of the best possible ways to insure that they will always continue to behave as independent citizens and will not be forced in self-defense into the position of a self-seeking pressure group.

Our programs in aging must take account, too, of another basic fact: that just as American society is changing with unprecedented rapidity, its older people are changing too. There is virtually a complete turnover of our elderly population every 20 years; and just as the present "generation" of elderly is quite different from the last, the next probably will differ even more. As we plan programs which are meant to be applicable not merely to the needs of the present but for a substantial period in the future—say, until the mid-1970's at least—we must try to think in terms of these future changes.

What will some of them be? Prediction is always quite risky, but of one thing we are reasonably certain. Virtually every need, characteristic, and individual difference now associated with aging will grow in its importance to the society and will demand more attention from the society as represented by government. The increasing numbers virtually guarantee this.

There will be many more older people who are well, but there will also be many more who are sick. They will need increasing amounts of services ranging from doctor visits, through brief hospital stays, to complete long-term care. There will be more older people who are able to get along on their own resources through savings and private pensions, but an even greater absolute number who will be dependent on financial support through government channels. More and more, this support will be furnished through old-age and survivors insurance, rather than through the less satisfactory method of old-age assistance.

By the mid-1970's there will be more older people who are married and continuing to pursue a "normal" family life. But there will be an even greater increase among those who will be bereft of spouse and essentially alone in the world. As you know, while medical advances have increased the life expectancy of all persons reaching age 65, they have extended the life span of women far more than that of men. This tendency is likely to continue at least in the immediate future. Thus, while women outnumber men in our older population today, their margin will increase even further in the decade to come. And the number of older women without husbands will increase at an even more rapid rate. By 1975 we can anticipate an increase of about 30 per cent in the number of older men who are married and living with their wives, but of well over 50 per cent in the number of older women without a husband present. At that not-too-distant date, there will be almost 8.5 million women 65 and over not living with husbands. That's almost the size of the entire elderly population at the beginning of World War II. And of these millions the great majority will be widows, for whom single status requires a drastic readjustment in living patterns at a time of life when changes come hard.

Quite obviously, our programs of the future most focus increasingly on the needs of lonely people—and especially of lonely women. They are the ones who most need help from the larger society at present; and they will need it even more in the years to come.

On the other hand, continuing improvements in and utilization of our techniques for providing economic support to older people will almost certainly bring an increase in the number of couples and single persons who are relatively independent and relatively free from the anxiety and demeaning restrictions imposed by inadequate incomes. If we can only find some way to implement a broad-scale program of providing insurance for medical expenses, we will have removed the last remaining hurdle to achieving economic security for the great majority of the elderly.

Continuing health improvements will also mean that more persons retain their vigor for longer periods. And older people will become steadily better educated. These facts mean that older people will represent a steadily increasing pool of usable talent; and this talent will, I predict, increasingly desire and even demand opportunities to express itself in socially useful ways. If we can but find the key, the growing talents of the elderly may form one of our most valuable resources for meeting the increasing needs of the elderly.

The older people of the future will also be more accustomed to leisure and better able to handle the free time placed before them by retirement. Our fathers, for the most part, did not spend most of their working lives in the happy circumstances of the 5-day, 35- to 40-hour week. Retirement will not be as severe a wrench for the older person of the future; and if we can develop adequate counseling services and other techniques to bridge the transition, we may yet be able to make retired status the grand opportunity for self-fulfillment which it is supposed to be and which studies show it increasingly to be.

Yet if we are to use the full potential of America's older people and simultaneously to provide them with experiences which fittingly reward their long contribution to their descendants and to the entire society, we must somehow come to terms with the problem of assigning them positive roles in this same society. We have extended the lifespan and made it possible for the great majority of elder people to be retired. But the only expectation we have yet developed for them in their retirement is that they will not compete with those whom they raised to adulthood, and who consequently are younger and still part of what we rather thoughtlessly call the "productive" segment of the population.

Assigning positive roles does not necessarily mean the same roles as those of the middle years. The aged may wish to disengage, though there is a real question whether this wish stems from an internal desire or from external circumstances that force disengagement. Be that as it may, the fact remains that roles for older people are the least clearly defined within our society.

At the same time, I think it is becoming increasingly clear that the complex problem of the relationships between old and young will not be solved via the simple route of admonishing the young to respect and care for their elders. A lot has been spoken and written about the growing gap between generations; but most of it has been based more upon "armchair" philosophizing than upon sound fact.

Where facts have been gathered scientifically, they have provided a much more encouraging picture of the changing relationships. It is a picture which emphasizes not an enforced dependency of one generation upon the other, but a healthy independence in which there remain close family ties based upon affection, reciprocal contribution, and mutual respect.

Our modern society is, of course, a tremendously mobile one, and work opportunities often take children many hundreds or even thousands of miles from the place of their upbringing. It is also an increasingly urban society, and our urban structure does not lend itself as well to the sharing of dwelling space by different generations as did the family farms of yesteryear. Census data suggest that as economic advances and a growing supply of housing have increasingly enabled the generations to live in separate homes, they have increasingly taken advantage of this opportunity. We can only conclude from the existing evidence that this is usually the preferred relationship for all concerned, except where economic or health needs dictate otherwise.

During the decade of the 1950's there was an increase of over 12 million units in the nation's housing stock, while the total number of families increased by only about half that amount. Together with a general rise in real incomes, this enabled many American families who had previously been forced to live "doubled up" with others to acquire separate quarters.

The change was reflected dramatically in the housing situation of older persons. In 1950, about 31 per cent of people 65 and over did not live in their own households but in households headed by others. By 1959 this proportion had declined to less than 23 per cent. And the end of the decline was not yet in sight, because between 1959 and 1961 the proportion decreased over one percentage point more.

A substantial part of the drop was accounted for by a decline in the per cent of older people living in the households of relatives. But there was an even more dramatic decrease among elderly lodgers in the homes of nonrelatives. Today, the percentage of older people living as lodgers is only about one-third that of 1950. There has also been a decline in the per cent of older people living in institutions, which may provide some statistical backing for the frequent contention that institutionalization is sometimes a last resort when more suitable accommodations are unobtainable.

Many people have jumped from facts such as these to the conclusion that the old family relationships are breaking up. But recent research suggests a quite different situation. Shanas, for example, reported from her nationwide surveys that only one older person in seven lives more than a short ride away from his or her nearest child, and a majority live within walking distance.[1] They may not live together as much any more, but they still live close enough to visit frequently.

Furthermore, the popular notion that children are abandoning their parents to the mercy of the state has taken a sharp rebuff from the findings of surveys that children quite consistently show a greater feeling of responsibility for their parents' welfare than the parents themselves appear to desire.[2] The parents are more inclined to want independence of their children, especially in a financial sense. And they are generally disposed to feel that financial support, if needed to supplement their own resources, should be provided through governmental channels.

Factual knowledge discloses still another fallacy in popular thinking about the responsibility of children for parents' welfare. As medical science increases the life-expectancy, we develop a situation for which there is no precedent in human experience: substantial numbers of elderly parents whose children, themselves, are past retirement age. In this instance there is really no meaning to the admonition that the "young" should support the "old," for in fact both generations are past the age where they support themselves by their own labors.

In Shanas' surveys, one older person out of 9, when asked to name the person other than husband or wife to whom he would turn for aid in a health crisis, named someone 65 years of age or more. An additional 13 per cent named someone aged 55 through 64.[3] Couple this with the fact that about one older person out of every 5 has no living children, and one can see clearly the basic flaws in the still disturbingly current notion that the needs of older people in such areas as housing, health, and even income could be met without governmental intervention if only children would recognize their responsibility to their parents.

I think that many of the things I have mentioned point clearly to the responsibility of the entire society, through its governmental bodies at the federal, state, and local levels, for the welfare of aging persons. We intend to do our best to advance the fulfillment of governmental responsibility, to the end that older people will be not *more* dependent but less dependent, and that they will be able to achieve their utmost potential in terms of their own happiness and in terms of constructive contributions to their families, their communities, and the nation as a whole. We also want to do everything possible to stimulate and aid efforts in the private sphere, for the relative flexibility and freedom to experiment of private action provide prime dynamic forces in American society.

These, then, are some of the things about which we in the Office of Aging are thinking as we try to develop program objectives which will serve the needs of older people well into the foreseeable future. What progress has been made in meeting the needs, and what important gaps exist? Progress, to a sociologist, has two main attributes: The first is change and the second is direction. The direction of the change must be one which is desirable in terms of the ultimate welfare of the whole society. Can we indeed see change in a desirable direction? I think that a balanced view should not lead us to be complacent or smug about our achievements to date; but neither should it cause us to despair.

In assessing progress in aging, I think there are four critical components that should be kept in mind. The first is our store of knowledge; we cannot expect to get very far in solving any problem if we lack basic factual knowledge. The second is the personnel needed to deliver this knowledge in the form of sound action. The third is the organizational structure necessary to enable skilled personnel to work effectively. And the fourth is the finances required to support a level of effort adequate to the problem. I think we can see changes in all of these areas; not as many as we would like, perhaps, but for the most part in desirable directions. We can also see gaps which should be filled. I would like to talk about both.

First, about our basic knowledge. Here, we can see a dramatic and vast extension. We can appraise the increase in knowledge in terms of both quantity and quality.

All of us are aware of the vast increase in research in gerontology. One measure of this is the number of items appearing in bibliographies compared to those of a decade ago.

Take, for example, those items appearing in the *Journal of Gerontology* for the two-year period of January 1950, through December 1951, and compare it with the two-year period of January 1960, through December 1961. The journal lists 4,726 items in the first period and 7,321 items in the first two years of the present decade.

However, if it were possible only to indicate a gross increase of activity without a concurrent increase in level of sophistication, I would have qualms about claiming progress. But I think one can make a case for improved research design, increased comprehension of the interrelatedness of factors, growth of longitudinal studies, use of more adequate statistical tools, and most important, a growing conceptualization. Studies are moving beyond the state of mere description and becoming increasing analytical with at least some theoretical components being present in many of our present studies.

Of vast significance in our quest for knowledge is the bill introduced into Congress to develop an Institute for Child Health and Human Development.[4] Tentatively, the plans for this institute call for a major institute devoted to the study of human development with a special section on gerontology. It has two attributes of critical importance. In the first place, the emphasis of the proposed institute is not upon disease but upon the promotion of health, not upon pathology but upon sound development. In the second place, the institute would be an interdisciplinary center in which no one approach is paramount but all scientific disciplines are called upon to contribute their best in team research.

Two other hopeful legislative developments are the Fogarty-McNamara Bill and the new Senior Citizens Act of 1962 introduced by Congressman Bailey. Both would make available grants for research and demonstration projects through which our knowledge of aging and constructive approaches to the needs of older people may be advanced. Although the point is not spelled out specifically in either bill, each would permit the development of positively oriented, nonpathology-centered research programs, which would allow for interdisciplinary projects. In the event either bill or a similar one is passed,[5] I hope that many such projects will be developed and submitted, and I think that many of the people present here should be in a position to see that they are.

At present, there are many gaps in our knowledge which still demand the contributions of research. One critical gap I have already mentioned: how to develop positive roles for older people in American society. Another large area of ignorance lies in the effect of the aging process upon the older person's feelings about himself and the world around him. Those of us who are not old may only dimly grasp how it feels to be old. And older people have difficulty in telling us; most of them are not very articulate about it, and those who can express their feelings in ways we can understand may not be representative of the rest. Until we know, however, we may have great difficulty in developing approaches which do not conflict with older people's basic psychological needs; we may too often inflict upon them not needed aid but needless annoyance.

Another area of neglect is the problem of the slightly confused: those no longer quite able to make all the right decisions for themselves, but still not so completely disoriented that they require constant surveillance. How can they be helped without impressing upon them the dire and ego-shattering fact of their declining mental competence?

I think the very nature of these gaps in our knowledge indicates how far we have come in our search for knowledge. We have gathered many of the simpler but basic facts; we now enter the shadier and more complex areas which we must comprehend if we are to make the best use of the knowledge we possess already. And this task will not be easy; it will tax our research techniques to their utmost limits, and in many instances call for research that has the sophistication and conceptual component alluded to before.

In regard to the second critical area, personnel, I regret to say that the shortage of adequately trained people is still critical. We may well be falling behind in comparison to the rapidly increasing demands. Nor are we making the rapid strides I would like to see in developing training programs to fill the needs in future.

Information compiled by Harold L. Orbach for the Inter-University Council in Social Gerontology in the fall of 1961 indicates that there are now 10 active institutes or divisions of gerontology in U.S. colleges and universities, or about one for every 200 institutions of higher education in the country.[6] This, of course, does not correctly indicate the full extent of academic resources being applied to the problem, since there are also a small number of university research centers and inter-departmental co-ordinating committees on aging, and there are many institutions offering limited course work under the general aegis of other programs. Nonetheless, when only a fraction of 1 per cent of our institutions for higher learning have given major status to programs for comprehensive training in meeting the problems of almost 10 per cent of our population, I feel that we have a long way still to go.

Nonetheless, there are encouraging developments to report. In Oregon, Mount Angel College is launching the first undergraduate curriculum in social gerontology under the direction of Dr. Carrol H. Mickey. It is sure to be the forerunner of other programs in many parts of the nation. The American Public Welfare Association, whose pioneering work in planning of services for the aging under the leadership of Mr. Jay Roney is well known, has just received an additional grant of $800,000 from the Ford Foundation to be used primarily for developing training programs for public welfare personnel.

The National Council on the Aging, in addition to its series of conferences on planning for the aged, is sponsoring an Institute on Housing which will have important implications for training of personnel.

We ourselves, at the Office of Aging, are engaged at present in formulating a curriculum for graduate training in the management of housing for older persons. This, we believe, is one of the areas of most serious personnel deficit at present, especially in light of the rapid development of special housing projects for the aging. Purdue University expects to put this curriculum into operation during its next academic year, and we have had expressions of interest from other institutions as well.

The Office of Aging and its regional staff have been working with educators in North Dakota in developing a program within the secondary schools which will have important long-range consequences for the field.

Again, let me refer back to my earlier remarks about the definition of progress. It seems to me that we can feel some satisfaction at the systematic way in which we in the aging field are going about applying our knowledge to pioneering entirely new curricula and endeavoring to make these curricula the most advanced possible in light of the needs. We are, I believe, building a solid framework for the training programs of the future. We are not making the all-too-frequent mistake of beginning a new activity without first inquiring what purpose it should serve and how it might best serve that purpose.

The number of specialists in aging we turn out next year will be very slight in relation to the demand, but we have some assurance that their training will be of use to them and to the problem. This, to me, means more than simply being able to say that we have started x number of training programs with x thousand students, although I would hope that within a very few years we will be able to cite such statistics as well.

With regard to the third area, organizational structure, let me say that my travels around the country have left me both impressed and depressed about the present status of services for the aging. I have been greatly impressed by the tremendous growth of services. In many areas interesting programs exist which have come into being only in the past couple of years. While it is too early in many cases to evaluate these programs, many of them obviously possess the vital asset of imagination. They represent bold experiments in meeting newly recognized needs, and they augur well for our ability to meet the challenges of a rapidly increasing elderly population.

Yet I have been somewhat depressed to note the spotty coverage of these programs. Each is local and meets only a tiny percentage of the national need which might conceivably be served by programs of its type. Furthermore, each community has tended to devote most of its resources to developing one or two particular type programs, which meet only a fraction of the total spectrum of needs in that community itself.

One community will have a foster name placement service, another meals-on-wheels, home care in yet another, some will have activity centers, a few referral centers, and here and there a nursing home placement service. Too often these and the dozens of additional services we can name are operating as demonstration projects reaching only a small fraction of the community's older citizens.

Yet more crucial, I do not know of any community which has developed a co-ordinated full-range approach. This is essential in the long run, and until at least one exists as a model we still will have a long way to go in the development of services. I am glad to note, however, that community after community is setting up the rudiments of an organizational structure by which a comprehensive pattern of services may ultimately be provided. The Community Councils are an encouraging development; they are at least a large first step toward the goal.

A large part of the reason why we have not made more progress in organization unquestionably lies in the problem of finances. As yet, we as a nation have not developed the willingness to pay for the level and extent of services we must provide to our aging population. Published recently is a report on "How the Government Works for Older People." [7] It was prepared by the Federal Council on Aging, which has been replaced by the new President's Council on Aging, established under an executive order which clearly defines responsibilities and which enables it to have a staff commensurate with its responsibilities. I am sure you will be interested in the wide scope of services provided by the federal government to older persons. This scope is neatly illustrated by a brief list of examples on the very first page of the text:

"How the Federal Government worked for the Nation's older people in 1961 can be measured in many ways.

" · By the $15 billion it spent, or administered, for the economic welfare of persons 65 and over. [8]

" · By the pleasure a 57-year old widow in Cleveland gets from her new apartment, built in 1961 partly with Federal funds under the new 'Housing for the Elderly' program

" · By the scientific research sponsored or conducted by the Public Health Service to wipe out cancer, heart disease, and diabetes.

" · By the special job-finding help of the Federal-State Employment Security System that returned many older people to employment.

" · By the hospital care the Veterans' Administration gave to many thousands of World War I veterans who couldn't afford it elsewhere.

" · By the new interest in the plight of older people created by the White House Conference on Aging.

" · By the many who received assistance in setting up small business to help supplement their retirement income.

"But, no matter how you measure the Government's help—with cold statistics, in warm, human terms, or as a new dimension of dignity—the end result is an amazing phenomenon of recent years."

But one of the items in this report which interested me most is found near the end, in the discussion preceding the tables on how much the government spends. There it is indicated that programs for income maintenance account for $19 out of every $20 spent by the federal government to aid people 65 and over. The remaining dollar is spread over all the other types of services which the government provides, the description of which takes up the bulk of the booklet.

Now, I certainly would be among the last to argue that we should redistribute the existing funds a different way. Every cent that is spent today on income maintenance is needed by those who receive it. In fact, there is an urgent need to revise upward virtually all of our programs relating to income maintenance. Yet I would like to see that one remaining dollar increased at least threefold within the next few years so that we could begin to provide the amount and variety of services older people need.

I would also like to see increased contributions from state and local governments as well as from private sources. The magnitude and complexity of the problem as well as its essentially community-centered nature argue against programs totally controlled and financed from Washington. We at the Office of Aging have been attempting to stimulate the formation of state and local organizations which can take a guiding hand in programs suited to particular local needs. While these organizations will almost unquestionably receive aid from the Federal Treasury, I think there will always remain a need, as there is at present, for contributions from the localities themselves. And this need for funds will grow with the older population to be served.

I am quite sure that the ultimate solution to the financing problem will come about through some rational combination of federal, state, municipal, and private funds, perhaps allocated according to a flexible formula which permits variations to meet local situations. The proper approach, however, cannot be determined wholly from Washington, but must draw on the wisdom of people representing all regions of the nation, large cities and small towns, and both private organizations and governmental bodies at all levels.

At present, however, the financing situation is a vast jumble, with large and irrational variations from one place to another and, most important, with huge gaps where nobody is paying the bill and consequently the needs are not being met. Drawing order out of this chaos will be one of the most important tasks of the years immediately ahead.

In trying to deal with the topic of the outlook for progress in the 1960's, I have found myself devoting a good portion of my time to predicting the needs of the 1970's, and a considerable part to discussing not what has been accomplished but what remains to be done. But I do not think the emphasis has been misplaced, for we cannot think about progress without considering goals, nor can the goals of the present be separated from those of the future in this rapidly changing world. And we cannot very well assess how far we have progressed toward a goal without attempting to measure the distance which remains.

We have, I believe, a long way yet to go. But what we have done is, by and large, good. The tasks of the years ahead will be to fill in the gaps, to delve deeper into the causes and complexities of the problem, to develop co-ordinated approaches to replace the fragmentary efforts which exist at present, and perhaps most important, to continue our efforts to develop the widespread public awareness and sympathy which is essential to continued progress. These tasks will not be easy. But with the best efforts of all of us, I am sure they can be accomplished.

NOTES

[1] Ethel Shanas, *Family Relationships of Older People,* Research Series 20 (New York: Health Information Foundation, 1961), p. 14. [Ed. note: Shanas' studies are based on a nationwide area-probability sample of the entire non-institutional older population.]

[2] See for example, *ibid.,* pp. 30–31.

[3] *Ibid.,* p. 9.

[4] This measure was enacted and signed into law by the President on October 17, 1962. (P.L. 87–838.)

[5] No congressional action was taken on either bill in the 87th Congress.

[6] Harold L. Orbach, "Training and Research in Social Gerontology in American Universities and Colleges," Report Presented to the 14th Annual Meeting of the Gerontological Society, Pittsburgh, November 10, 1961 (Ann Arbor: Inter-University Training Institute in Social Gerontology, 1961). (Mimeographed.)

[7] U.S. Federal Council on Aging, *How the Government Works for Older People* (Washington, D.C.: U.S. Government Printing Office, 1962).

[8] Another $6.6 billion represents the total of income maintenance programs for persons 45 to 64, health and older worker programs for persons 45 and over, housing programs for persons 62 and over, and special tax provisions for persons 65 and over.

CHAPTER 14

Panel on
SOCIAL ATTITUDES TOWARD RETIREMENT
AND SUPPORT OF OLDER PEOPLE

TIBBITTS: The outstanding achievement of our generation, I think, is the increase in the expectation of life at all ages up through 65. Parallel with this, not entirely a function of it, is the appearance of retirement. *The Handbook of Social Gerontology* contains a chapter entitled "Retirement: the Emerging Social Pattern." This chapter was written by the two organizers of this conference—Wilma Donahue and Harold L. Orbach—with some help from Otto Pollock of the University of Pennsylvania. In very scholarly fashion these authors have shown that retirement has become a common expectation of all American workers and, moreover, that it has become a right to which all people are entitled. These, along with other changes in our culture and in our economy, raise many questions of the kind explored over the years in Michigan conferences. In this conference our thinking has been directed to such questions as: *When should retirement take place? How much income should people have in retirement? How much does it take to live in the later years? Where should the income come from? How much responsibility should be borne by the individual, by the family? How much intervention by government is justified?*

Last night another question was raised: *What is the effect of collective or social action on individual initiative?* I'm glad the word "collective" was cleaned up last night so that we now may use it.

How these questions are eventually resolved will depend partly on the kind of knowledge that was presented during the last two days, but mainly on the attitudes of people who in the end make the decisions in our society. Attitudes, in turn, are a function of the background that people have, the experience they accumulate, and of values acquired over the years.

The topic for our discussion this morning is "Social Attitudes Toward Retirement and Support of Older People." To discuss a number of questions we have four people of different backgrounds and widely different experiences and, presumably, people who grew up in different but, to some extent, common value systems. John Convery is consultant to the National Association of Manufacturers. Mr. Convery participated in one of the first University of Michigan conferences. He was interested in aging at that time and has continued to be. He is concerned also with the employment of the physically handicapped and works with the National Safety Council. He is a staff member of the Committee on Employment of Mature Workers of the National Association of Manufacturers, and he has worked with the Department of Labor's Wage and Hour Advisory Committee for Sheltered Workshops.

David Livingston is president of District 65 of the Retail, Wholesale, and Department Store Union in the New York area. This is an extremely vigorous union of 30,000 members. Mr. Livingston is a trustee and officer of the 65 Security Plan, which is one of the most far-reaching and liberal plans in the country. Mr. Livingston has been a pioneer in trial retirement, in retirement preparation, and in the development of programs by the union for retirees as well as in the whole area of pension benefits.

Ormond Loomis is now well established in his third career. He started out as a publisher in Boston and as a real estate trustee, gaining a good deal of financial experience. At the beginning of the New Deal he went to Washington in the Home Owners Loan Corporation and remained with that organization until it had completed its task. When Mr. Loomis retired he went to Clearwater, Florida. He dislikes the word "retire," and he has done so only in the sense of changing to new forms of activity. When he went to Florida he founded a business. Shortly, however, he decided that he was more interested in other things. He found that Clearwater was not undertaking to create what he considered to be a proper climate for attracting the retiree coming to that community. Mr. Loomis founded and is president of the Senior Citizens Services of Clearwater, which is a voluntary, self-initiated planning group for the community and which is having success in interesting the community in providing services that will make Clearwater a much more attractive place to retire.

Dr. Ethel Shanas is research associate with the rank of associate professor with the Committee on Human Development and the Department of Sociology at the University of Chicago. I'm sure all of you know her for her studies, published by the Health Information Foundation, on income, family relationships, and responsibilities. She is now the first individual in the social sciences to be participating as the over-all director of a cross-national survey of "Income, Family and Status, and Other Aspects of Aging"—a study which involves the United Kingdom, Denmark, and the United States.

The people on the panel are the product of many different educational backgrounds. John Convery is a graduate of the University of Pennsylvania, David Livingston of Columbia, Ormond Loomis of Harvard, and Ethel Shanas of Chicago.

Two totally different opinions have been expressed at this conference regarding retirement. In one of the two opening papers, Professor Jaffe of Columbia said categorically that we do not need all of the workers who are available to the work force or to the economy at the present time and that we have a right to a period of retirement and freedom to do things that we want to do. Last night Professor Haber of the University of Michigan said that work is the most ennobling activity in which people can engage and that older people should be enabled to work as long as they live. Question: *Should we encourage and facilitate retirement or not?*

CONVERY: Well, it is, I'm afraid, a highly individual problem. Fortunately, for us in our contemplation, people are different and should be allowed to make up their own minds. The question is loaded when it's directed at me because I happen to be in that past-65 group, and I have to work in a set-up where we have fixed retirement. It would be very embarrassing if you were to ask me the question "Why do I continue to work?" because I would feel that I was being put in a corner and would come up with a rationalization that would be pretty good, don't you worry about that. But I wouldn't dare to tell you that maybe the reason I continue to work is the result of habit that somehow or other has been developed over a period of years. You wake up at a certain time and you follow through on that basis. I think we ought to look at the question from two points of view. We should look at it from the workers' viewpoint and his desire. And we ought to look at it from the point of view of the employer and the openings that he happens to have. I certainly agree with those who say everybody has a right to available jobs providing, of course, they are qualified to fill the jobs and provided they're needed. Now when we survey the national scene, we find that practices vary a good deal. Some of the finest companies I know of, with personnel practices that are beyond reproach, have a fixed retirement policy, and there are certain reasons why they have it. Probably in those places it's best that they do have it. There are others where exceptions are made. I don't hesitate to say that any survey of companies with fixed retirements which we tend to equate with compulsory retirement may lead us to an erroneous conclusion. We usually find that companies with fixed retirement policies do retain some workers who are past 65.

LIVINGSTON: Dr. Tibbitts, I would first like to correct your introduction of me, if I may. I am a product of Columbia but I didn't get a degree. I'm much more a product of the depression. Among the distinguished company at this conference, this may make me an expert on something, at least, and in a different way.

I didn't find myself too much in disagreement with Mr. Convery of the National Association of Manufacturers—I don't know whether this is bad or good. I'm sure it's contrary to expectation. I believe, and I think the general position of the labor movement is, that every worker should have the right to retire and the right not to retire. We live in a society in which we are both work- and money-oriented. There is a substantial belief that the ability to "make a living" is a tremendous factor in the peace of mind and in the sense of accomplishment of our senior citizens and that there should be no arrangement which would deny a person the right to work at any given age. I think our society is committed by legislation to the concept of full employment. American society has said that our government should organize our economy to provide a job for our total work force. It didn't say our work force up to this age or to that age or the next. Everybody who wants to work, who is physically capable of working, should be permitted to work. The question is a little bit loaded, in one respect, because the real issue is *not* should we encourage people to retire who are set to retire, but should we encourage all older workers to retire?

I do not believe we should encourage people to retire. It sounds very nice for society to say that the senior citizen should devote his remaining years to something other than work. But what society really means is: isn't it time for you seniors to get out of the labor force and let the young ones in? That's really what is meant! My own belief is that we should not go along with the view that because of automation and a lot of other things, it's time to get the old-timers out of the way and let the young ones in. We have a country where we should provide a job opportunity for everybody, whether he's 68 or whether he's 18.

TIBBITTS: You raised this issue exactly the way I was going to raise a question that's related to it. At the present time, the highest rate of unemployment is among those who are entering the work force, those between ages 18 and 24. *When there is a choice should employers favor those who are entering the work force or those who are in the later years and eligible for retirement?* I know Mr. Loomis has some definite ideas on this matter of retirement and whether or not it's ennobling.

LOOMIS: Generally, I'm in favor of open opportunities for all, and I think we ought to recognize that those coming into a labor force or desiring to come in ought to have opportunities commensurate with their talents and willingness to work.

I think it's unfortunate that we think of work as sort of a lock-step performance. We get into the spirit of enterprise and carry on as workers because others do. Work, to me, is more than just a performance of certain duties and activities for financial compensation. There are opportunities for work that exist outside the labor force while we are workers in the labor force, and I think most people ought to contribute in their activities as workers to the welfare of the community in which they live and by that process develop ability to serve the community other than for compensation. I object to the belief that we are a work- and money-oriented people, that our concepts of a full life are pretty much confined to gainful employment and financial income. It's most unfortunate. To answer your question specifically as to whether preference should be given to those coming into the labor market as against those who have been in it and have had their opportunity for several years, I think you should favor the younger people. However, I think the opportunities are large enough for a great majority of our elderly people to continue to participate. They ought to have that opportunity without arbitrary restrictions and limitations.

SHANAS: You know when I hear this, I'm beginning to feel that those among us who might want to sit down at age 70 are going to feel awfully guilty if we don't keep working. I'm getting the impression— which I don't think is really the one the members of the panel want to give—that somehow we are trying to make people feel that they have to keep working forever. I am more inclined to agree with Dr. Jaffe when he asks: "Shouldn't a man have a right to quit sometime, if he wants to?" What we have to avoid here is building up the kind of social climate where a man, or a woman for that matter, feels guilty if he or she wants to sit down at 65 or even 60. I think what we should stress, but not overstress, is that work may be a good idea for some people. What we have to stress is flexibility. We have to provide for older people what they themselves want, and there are a great many older people who seek to retire from the work force and would welcome an opportunity for this other kind of life or other things if they had enough money to live on. I don't think that it's necessary that everybody should feel that he or she has to keep working forever in order to be a worthwhile person. I think what we have to stress is flexibility and choice and that every American should have the right to quit on a decent income, if he or she wants it. Or have an opportunity, if he has skills that are necessary or needed or wanted, to keep working if he so desires.

LIVINGSTON: Dr. Shanas, don't you agree that the real pressure on the senior citizen, quite contrary to what you said, is to stop working? Isn't the commonly accepted social doctrine now that the desirable thing is to get the senior citizen out of the labor market? You sound as if the real pressure on the senior citizen is to continue working and the poor fellow who quits at the age of 72 is somehow feeling guilty. But is that the fact? Is that the way society is running now?

SHANAS: Well, let's say the real pressure, in terms of social policy, is to quit working, but I'm getting the feeling from this panel that somehow we are projecting the idea that there's something wrong with that. What's wrong with quitting working if you have an adequate income?

CONVERY: Dr. Shanas, I am inclined toward your point of view, though I respect very much Mr. Livingston's statement. We were talking at breakfast about our parents, and the members of the panel all bragged with one single exception that their fathers had continued working until in one case, age 83, he had fallen over, and in another until he died. I kept quiet, and the reason I kept quiet wasn't that my father wasn't just as fine as the others. He was a wonderful gentleman, but he quit working before he arrived at the age that I happen to be at the present time. And I think he exercised that choice very wisely, and I think that he satisfied himself in the process.

As for the social pressure of working, you know that when you meet somebody you haven't seen for a long time the first question is: "What are you doing?" I often wondered how you answered that question if you were retired. I was talking to a conference member yesterday who said he likes to go to Central America whenever he can. He said the study of the ancient ruins is terrific—it really represents a fine frontier. He happens to be the personnel manager of the Burroughs Company in Detroit. He said, however, that if one of those Indians were to ask him what he does for a living, he would have an awfully tough time explaining to him just exactly what his job was.

TIBBITTS: You can see from this discussion that here is one of the major elements in our value system which is in transition. Dr. Shanas led into the next area we wanted to explore a little bit, namely, *Levels of Living*. At the present time I think it's correct to say that retirement income levels are largely what legislators and the public are willing to make them or they are the amounts that are negotiated over the bargaining table. I would like to ask the panel a question. *Are these methods adequate or are there more logical methods that might be used in determining what is appropriate income for the retirement years?*

LIVINGSTON: I keep finding myself saying: That's the wrong question. Maybe that has to do with what's the difference between a specialist and an expert. I'm trying to get the question on which I, at least, have an opinion. I think that it's wrong for us as specialists or experts to attempt to answer the question: "Where should we get our money?" or "What is the proper level of living?" I think the answer to that has to be obtained from the senior citizens themselves. It is our experience in our union that our senior citizens can get anything they choose to organize for and fight for. I'm not speaking of fighting as a power-prop, but I'm speaking of the concept that our senior citizens can, in a society like ours, attain agreement on what should be done and therefore the money to provide for it.

I don't want to sound like a Pollyanna, but I believe that it's a little bit wrong to talk about the problems of aging. Personally, I believe our senior citizens are an asset—they are in our union. The finest members of our organization are our retired members, in every respect. They do better on the picket lines than the youngsters. They do better in every campaign than the youngsters. Their attendance at meetings is, well, I wouldn't say 100 per cent—but it is certainly the highest in our organization. They're terrific. We don't consider that we have a problem with them. We think they have some problems, and they are organizing themselves and directing their efforts to finding solutions to their problems.

Now, what's an adequate level of living? In an affluent society like ours you write your own ticket. How do you get it? How do you pay for it? Well, you organize yourself properly, you express yourself in a democratic fashion, and you attain a concensus among varying groups who will go along with you in saying that life in our senior years should be livable. I don't know whether it sounds like a dream, but I believe that it can be done.

SHANAS: I agree with Mr. Livingston. I think that in a society such as ours no American, regardless of age, ought to be living on a subsistence level. Certainly, older people, like other people, ought to have enough to live on. My researches show that if they can't finance an adequate level of living out of their own resources, older people believe that somehow we—all of us as fellow Americans—should be able to finance this through the resources of our country. Everyone has a right to be able to have enough to eat and a roof over his head and maybe even a little extra and, in this country, we should certainly be able to provide it for everyone.

TIBBITTS: There were a number of very good papers presented which had to do with income, with income requirements, and with the present income situations of older people. Dr. Striner started us off Monday morning with a bold suggestion that incomes could be increased quite markedly and perhaps quite rapidly. *Do you think that some of the knowledge we are accumulating regarding needs of older people should be used as a basis for raising income?*

LOOMIS: With the changes in our income levels, the question becomes a different one depending on the time you retire. Having retired three times I can understand that there are differences! In my first retirement the level of income which was set and necessary was adequate for that period. Within five years it changed substantially, and it's continuing to change. A person who retired, say five years ago, with what he supposed was an adequate income finds that it is quite inadequate at present and is increasingly inadequate. He lives on a fixed income, but the cost of living continues to go up and the value of the dollar continues to go down. The problem with many retired persons is how to adjust themselves to these enforced changes in their own resources and the value of those resources in their own community.

There is also the problem of individual differences. What one person or family can live on differs very materially from what another family even in the same community would require. And those differences are partly in frugality and partly in habits such as in standards of living with respect to clothing and food and travel. You can't arbitrarily fix that level for any family because of these wide differences. My own belief is that the community should help in some way to divide these resources. For example, in the field of health there are many who are comfortably off with a moderate income and with moderate savings and resources, but when ill health develops those resources can vanish almost overnight. These people become medically indigent when they were not indigent before, and they are thereafter indigent because they have absorbed their savings. Now, the level of income for a person who is ill and handicapped must be higher than the level for those who are in good health.

The surprise to me is that the proportion in good health is as large as it is. In our community a recent survey revealed that more than 80 per cent indicated they were in good health and needed no help. Those who were indigent were less than 3 per cent. Now, that group needs outside help and resources that will keep them in good health by reason of adequate food and some recreational enjoyment. What those resources are is difficult to determine, but it ought to be examined by the community and by the state and the national government so that it never falls to a point that makes them destitute while they are still alive.

TIBBITTS: We weren't going to get into the question of health insurance on the panel this morning, but I see that Mr. Loomis, from his close connection with retired people, can't stay away from it.

CONVERY: I think the question involves not only older people but, it seems to me, people of all ages. My recollection is of the problem that I had, as a young married man, of making my wife realize that we couldn't buy whatever we felt we needed. We had to limit our purchases to what we could afford. I think that's something that we have to keep in mind when we're working on this problem.

When we were discussing the economic question earlier at this conference I had the feeling that somehow or other it was assumed that progress is automatic and that somehow or other prosperity is inevitable. I just can't go for that. I have lived long enough to have seen times when we didn't make the progress that we should have made if progress were automatic and prosperity inevitable. Prosperity comes about as a result of things we do and plan. We just can't take this pie for granted and divide it up on the basis of the way we might feel it ought to be divided.

I attended the White House Conference on Aging last year and I noticed that the question of inflation is the one that worries people that are retiring as much as any question that I know of. Inflation is not inevitable either. We should not discuss it only in terms of: "Well, we're going to have it anyway so we might as well arrange so that income will increase with inflation." I'm not sure that that's the way it ought to be done.

Now, the question of someone that's in ill health. If, for instance, we have an older woman who needs medical care. It makes no difference whether she's married or not; it makes no difference whether her son is on the lam or whether he is lying in Flanders Field; *we*—and I mean John Convery—is the individual who ought to do something about the situation if it involves him and his family and his community. It should not be done by government on the basis of a social security number. I resent the idea very much of being listed not as an individual but simply as a number. And I don't believe we should proceed on the assumption that somehow or other this help will come about automatically.

LIVINGSTON: Can I say a word about this? John, I'm sure that you and I were invited here with the specific thought that we'd come to blows—verbal blows, at least. Management and labor were never supposed to agree. I'm sorry I keep violating the expectation, but about one-fourth of the way, labor goes along with you. We don't like to be numbers either.

I think, however, there is an area between the individual and the government that you don't mention, and this is where, I believe, there can be some answers to the question. This is the area of organized individuals. I think we agreed the term "the collective" is legitimate here—the collective, the mass of the people in organized groups. Now, members of our union, in addition to social security, get $5 a month in retirement benefits for each year of service. Let's take a 65-year-old person with 25 years of membership. In our union he will get $125 a month over and above his social security. In addition to that he gets all his medical expenses completely covered for himself and his family—a state of affluence which is not equaled by a great proportion of the American population. Yet, we are very poor workers. The average wage in our industry is well below that which prevails in automobile or steel or other places. We have thousands of members to whom the achievement of $1.50 an hour, which we recently accomplished in New York, was a great step forward. Yet, poor as we are, we have a retirement program that many richer unions would be happy to have.

We attained this program in two ways. First, we organized ourselves and we agreed to engage in co-operative activities, not through the government, not as individuals, but as a group. Then we said we'll set aside a certain portion of our income each week to attain certain objectives collectively. Now, we could say that the employers pay this bill. The amount of the weekly payment is achieved in collective bargaining and it's paid by the employer directly to a fund. However, when we get a certain amount for pension purposes, for example, we take the view that it is really a wage increase we didn't get put on our pay checks. We could have bargained for a direct wage increase instead. So we really are paying for the additional benefits ourselves in a collective fashion.

As a consequence, by organizing ourselves, by being frugal and farsighted and looking to the future, we say to our wives: "Well, we got an increase but you can't spend it because we don't have it available now. Instead, we have arranged that it be put aside for the future because that's what we should do with it in any case and, this way, it's providing us with more security." The result is that we now have a reasonably successful and suitable retirement program. Now, I would hope that the NAM would encourage the development of organizations of senior citizens—organizations of all citizens—who would start dealing with these issues in this fashion.

Actually, we deal with the problem of senior citizens a little better if we divide it in two. One is what do we do about the persons who have already reached the age of 65 or better. The other question is what do we do about ourselves. I'm 47, and before I know it I will be at retirement age. What am I doing about the future problem of retirement? On this, I think—between the government and my own personal savings and the retirement programs of the union and the similar retirement programs developed through other unions and other organizations—we could in 20 years have quite a different picture. But, what do we do about those already retired?

I think we can start with the concept that a retired person should be able to live as well as I would expect to live when I'm 65. Maybe I'll work, maybe I won't. But if I don't work, I'm not going to have to look for some petty little thing to do. I'll be financially well provided for through my union, and I will be intellectually and emotionally stimulated in a variety of ways through many opportunities. Since this is what I want for myself 20 years from now, I should be willing to want the same thing for a man who is already 65, whether he is my father or my uncle or my union brother. And I should be willing to contribute something out of my present income, because of what he has contributed to my union and to my society, to bring him at least to the point where he is almost equal to what I would like to have when I am a senior citizen. I don't know whether or not the NAM agrees with that.

CONVERY: I don't think there's a great deal of disagreement with that, Mr. Livingston. After all, we wouldn't be true to our membership, which manufactures probably 75 per cent of the manufactured goods in this country, if we didn't recognize the principle of saving for the future. There's no question about the attitude of industry, no matter what you hear to the contrary. I would say that long before social security or even long before your union, individual employers promoted pensions themselves. They provided for their people as has been indicated already here.

Now, may I add that, as far as I'm concerned individually, this social security is certainly the best bargain I ever got because, after all, I have contributed less than $1,300. If you match that with what my employer paid on the matching basis, which is part of the employment cost, why, my wife and I would have gotten that back already. We would have gotten it back in less than two years. Now, I'm acquainted enough with figures to know that somebody's got to pay that in the future. There's no question about that. I think when people like ourselves, past 65, are told we're paying our way, that we are being grossly misled. We are not paying for ourselves. We're free riders.

So far as the economy is concerned, I often wonder if some of the younger people will continue to be willing to support those already retired. After all, they have problems, too. This idea that problems are confined to people over 65 I don't think is true. Problems are universal. The problem of aging is almost like the problem of living. I already find people complaining about what they call "take-home pay"; they think too much is being withheld before they get it. It seems to me that recently I read in the paper where the communications workers at their annual meeting in Milwaukee decided that it was about time they stopped paying this contribution to social security—that this payment of theirs should be made by someone else. I just mention that to you, not by way of complaint. Certainly, a fellow who is getting a free ride has no right to complain. However, I can see someone in the future saying: "Well, now, . . . ?"

Let me not take any more time. I could very nicely review what happened after World War I and what happened in the early 1930's, but now we've changed a lot of our ideas. For instance, I notice that social security pensions have a means test tied to them now, the "retirement test" which places limitations on covered earnings up to age 72 in order to draw full benefits. This is unfortunate, but they do have it just the same, and I'm thinking we may get more of it.

SHANAS: I'd like to comment on this. I think my role here is to provide a kind of balance. Researchers, you know, are supposed to be impartial. I think, again, Mr. Livingston, I'd like to restate something you said. I think that we are now in a period of transition. Today's middle-aged people who are going to reach retirement age— whatever it is in the future—are probably going to come into the period of retirement better prepared in every way than those persons who are 65 and over or 62 and over now. There isn't any doubt about it. We've had a revolution in our thinking, and people are more conscious of retirement. You know Americans aren't really squanderers. Even the statisticians who spoke earlier at the conference pointed out that we're really very conscious of saving for the future. Quite a bit of our money goes into savings, into insurance schemes, and so on. Those of us who are middle-aged now are going to become 65 and over, and we're going to have more income, we're going to have more opportunities, and so on.

This, however, doesn't solve the needs of those who are 65 and over now. It's not their fault that they are not drawing social security at the maximum limit. It's not their fault that a lot of them had savings wiped out in the 1930's. It's not their fault that somehow they just weren't able to provide for themselves for every contingency that they face. And I think in a society and a country such as ours—you can't say that we are an inhuman society—I think we face a real need here, and we've got to meet it. We may grumble about deductions from take-home pay, but I think we're willing to make them. We're not that inhuman.

TIBBITTS: There are many other questions related to this subject, but I would like to move on into another area. One of the questions in which there is a great deal of interest and uncertainty at the present time is the extent to which retired people will take part in activities. There is a theory of "disengagement" which has been advanced recently. In essence, as I understand it, this theory holds that older people tend to withdraw from activity and responsibility, and that this withdrawal tendency persists even when the community provides opportunities for and encourages activity. *Do we agree or disagree with this theory of disengagement?* Mr. Loomis, you're having some experience trying to interest retired persons in taking community responsibility. What do you find?

LOOMIS: There are many people who like to retire completely. They stop working, set themselves aside from life, get on the sidelines. In some cases it's a matter of health, in some cases it's a matter of physical laziness, in some cases it's a failure to adjust themselves to the life in the community. Yet, I am convinced that the retired person is happiest when he is doing something. No one can remain in a vacuum; in this world of change he has to change with the changing environment. Everyone, I think, desires a certain freedom of action. Yet, I think the individual ought to feel a pressure to contribute to society as long as he's alive. He not only benefits himself, he benefits the community.

I believe firmly that communities should provide the facilities and the encouragement to participate in community activities. One reason why I'm so against confining the attitude of ourselves and our public to the paid employment field is that there are so many fine contributions that can be made outside of that limited category. We must grow as we live, and as long as we live we must adjust ourselves to changing community needs. I think the real problem is whether there's a concept or desire to continue to grow. If you do not continue to grow, you go the other way. Thus, the real problem is to stimulate growth and interest that will keep us mentally alive and mentally and physically participating in the life of the community.

TIBBITTS: At most of the retirement ceremonies I have observed, people are congratulated on the contribution that they have made and are encouraged to withdraw and enjoy themselves. Now, here's a retired man talking like President Kennedy. You recall that when the President was concluding his inaugural address he said we have a responsibility to find out how we can serve our country and to serve it. *What, specifically, are some of the ways in which we can serve these communities or the country or our organizations?*

LIVINGSTON: I've been trying to think about what the people that are here could do when they return home to translate what we have learned at this conference into some action. I don't have the answer to that, but I do believe that we should be advocates of a certain attitude wherever we are. And that is to develop an attitude of respect for senior citizens.

Now, when you talk about "What will the retired worker do or what will the senior citizen do?" it all depends on your attitude. If you approach him and say: "Poor old John, you're 68 now and you're living on your dole, which you didn't earn, as a free rider. Now, why don't you make yourself useful by some little activity?" He's going to say: "Now, look, please; you're putting me aside on the shelf until I pass on. Don't bother me with this." But if you go to the man and you say: "John, you've lived 68 years and you've made some fine and important contributions in the past. By getting to be 68 you picked up some knowledge and some wisdom. Give us your best advice. Give us your best guidance." Well, I believe then, and only then, will it be possible to encourage the senior citizen to do what he wants to do. In our organization we don't *have* activities for the retired people. The retired people *engage* in activities. You may say it's a quibble, but I don't think it is.

We have a leadership of the retired people. I wish you could have heard Walter Newburgher who is chairman of our group. He must be 70. He spoke at a meeting the other day where we gave awards to Walter Reuther and a few other people for their contributions to senior citizens. He spoke beautifully, and he advanced what he called a creed for senior citizens—what they believe in, what their notion of their contribution to society is. Well, if you were a sentimentalist, you'd be inclined to cry over it. Now, we didn't figure out a program for Walter Newburgher. This is a human being of great quality and capacity, and his years have made him better than he was. We look to him and we ask him: "What do you think?" and he gives answers. He engages in activity useful to society because he knows that he is a useful and respected human being. And I think that until society says that our senior citizens are one of the most precious possessions we have, they won't engage in activities that are useful. On the other hand, if you really respect them, they'll do a million things. You won't have to worry about what to do with their time.

CONVERY: Could I comment on that for just a minute? I certainly couldn't disagree with you on that. There's no question about it because it's a compliment to the older people. And I think one of the fine things about attending these Michigan conferences is the fact that you get the feeling of your own responsibility, and I would like to speak for just a moment on the responsibility of the older person. Retired people can't afford and they can't expect to stand on the sidelines and not be interested in what's going on in the world. They can't expect their children to pay them the right type of attention if they, in turn, don't do their part. I think it's very important that older people become a little more conscious of this fact. You know we have begun, unfortunately, to feel that people owe us respect, and I don't think that's a particularly good thing. Now, I'm talking from the point of view of an individual. I think, probably, that's one of my weaknesses, that I've expected too much of children. Perhaps it's a good thing to come to these conferences and come to a realization that the older person has responsibilities, too.

TIBBITTS: One point of view is that the older person should be free to do what he wants to do. Mr. Convery and Mr. Loomis have said that society should set up expectations for older people. No one prior to retirement is free to choose entirely what he wants to do. Perhaps retirement should not be a period of total freedom either. *Dr. Shanas, from the point of view of a social psychologist, how do you think older people would react if society said: "You are not through with your responsibilities, but you have these and these and these things which you owe to society?"*

SHANAS: Let me say that I think you have asked the question not quite as I would ask it. Really, nobody in life is ever free to do exactly what he wants to do. We're not anarchists, we're living inside of a society with a lot of other people. Really, what we are saying— what we ought to believe—is that we, all of us, have responsibilities for living and we have them all our lives. We expect children to develop and grow up—ideally, to be mature and responsible adults—and we have responsibilities to be mature and responsible adults as long as we live. Now, sometimes, you know, we are not able to do more than just keep house and sit quietly and watch life go by from our window. That's all we're able to do and all that we want to do. If this is all we can do, it's enough.

What we mean, really, is that people should have an opportunity to live knowing that their basic needs are being met and to develop according to their capacity. And I think we would be closing our eyes if we didn't realize some capacities do shrink as we age. Somebody asked me the other day how my tennis was. I said, "I don't play tennis any more." Well, I have freedom of choice. We do have; our capacities do decline and there is some freedom of choice. I think what we really are getting at is that it's our responsibility to function to the best of our ability as long as we can, and for those of us who need help in functioning—as I do with my tennis playing—well, then, it's the responsibility of society to make this help possible.

TIBBITTS: Thank you. Last year the subject of the Michigan Conference was POLITICS OF AGE. We learned during that conference—we actually observed—the process of older people, working through organizations of their own, aimed at improving the level of their income, at obtaining help and medical care, at improving their position in society. The next question is: *Is it helpful for older people to join organizations aimed at improving their circumstances? Is it good for society?*

I'm going to frustrate the panel by not letting them answer these questions. These are important matters that we can all think about as we leave the conference today. We live in a dynamic, constantly changing society. The panel has given a fine illustration of how attitudes vary among people of different backgrounds and of the way in which attitudes are modified in the crucible of discussion.

CHAPTER 15

IMPLICATIONS FOR THE SOCIAL HEALTH OF THE NATION

Jack Weinberg, M.D.

Despairing of his inability to solve his problems, man attempts to separate himself from his human condition, the major source of his suffering, and to tend to his biological needs. He will preoccupy himself with his physical needs in an escape from his lack of a philosophy of life, its meaning and purpose. He complains of his glands when he is really sick at heart. He frets at his financial insolvency when his real troubles lie in a bankruptcy of the spirit and soul. As in an essay on Kafka, Ionesco, a contemporary playwright and a giant in the theater of the absurd, stated, "Cut off from his religious, metaphysical, and transcendental roots, man is lost; all his actions become senseless, absurd, useless." [1]

If the above sounds moralistic and philosophical coming as it does from the mouth and pen of a psychiatrist, may I point out that it is psychologically valid, for those who have to deal with the emotionally tired and ill must deal not only with biological man but also with the human being. As a biological entity man is definable, and the fulfillment of his biological needs are definable, concrete, and definite. However, those characteristics which make him human, his common sympathies, passions, feelings, and failures, are much more abstract, more varied, less concrete, and more difficult of definition. Because of the inability to articulate the ambiguous man takes refuge in the obvious and avoids the latent.

It is, of course, the function of the social scientist as well as the psychiatrist to penetrate the manifest and to bring the latent material to light. However, even as scientists we are often beguiled by the comfortable manifest. As an example, may I quote from Shanas' report on *Family Relationships of Older People*. Shanas states: "Contrary to popular belief, however, most older people are not physically isolated from their children. Findings from this survey by the National Opinion Research Center of The University of Chicago show that most elderly live close to and often see at least one son or daughter. There has been much conjecture about the closeness of family ties of older people, particularly as these affect health and financial circumstance. This partial report . . . explores the subject and shows that there is a mutual feeling of responsibility between older people and their grown children." [2]

Heartening and encouraging. However, mutual responsibility and geographical closeness are a far cry from close affectional ties of a positive nature. The reverse may be more than true. With psychiatric perversity, yet from bitter experience may I offer the following formula: Love, warmth, and affectional regard between grown children and their aging parents frequently increase in inverse ratio to their spatial proximity.

All of us in the behavioral sciences, you and I, are painfully aware of the above. We are acutely aware that of the entire animal kingdom man and man alone is particularly unique in that the imaginative capacities of his human state allow him to alter his environment, influence his evolution, determine and actuate his fate. Human evolution is more often a result of cultural development and not of an organic change. It is therefore one of the reasons that this conference on Aging and the Economy and how they affect one another was convened. It is meant to find ways to free man from his economic insecurity to fulfill his biological needs, so that he can realize more fully his human strivings. Inasmuch as man is human, the satisfaction of his instinctual, biological, animistic needs is not sufficient to make him happy; they are not even sufficient to make him sane.

Man's solution of his physiological needs is, psychologically speaking, rather simple. Reality as a source of suffering can be modified, for here the difficulty primarily is a sociological and economic one. Man's solution to his human needs, however, is quite complex. It depends on a multiplicity of factors—on the way his society is organized and how this organization determines the human relation within it.

From time immemorial as man surveyed the world he has lived in but had not created, he has been consumed by a number of burning motivating forces; first, to master himself and that about him; second, by his productivity to contribute to or alter and modify his environment; and third, to belong to and be accepted by his own species. To the realization of these ambitious dreams man of every generation has spent most of his adult years. He has created a world of man-made things as they never existed before. He has constructed a complicated social machine to administer the technical machine he built.

Yet this entire creation of his stands over and above him. He does not feel himself as a creator, but rather as the servant of a monster which his hands have wrought. The more powerful the forces which he unleashes, the more powerless he feels himself as a human being. He confronts himself with his own forces embodied in the things he has made, apart and alienated from himself. He is owned by his own things and has lost ownership of himself. He has built a golden calf all over again. However, above all he yearns to fulfill the prophecy of Hosea (14:3): "Neither will we say any more to the work of our hands, you are our gods."

To maintain his safety and security he has created governmental machinery, entrusted it with the preservation of his welfare, and then reacted to it as being alien to himself and his needs. He looks with hostility toward its attempts to do just that which he has asked of it. He feels no kinship with it and does not consider himself a partner in its institutions. For he prizes his individuality, the individuality of being human, while his physical self must merge with the herd and submit to its laws if he is to survive.

Furthermore, he is engaged in a titanic struggle with time, another one of his inventions. The measurement of time is the creation of man for his orderliness and convenience. Then he looks upon it with typical human ambivalence. It is a great friend and healer for "time heals all wounds." On the other hand its ticking minutes are a tragic accompaniment to his life pulse. It is a constant reminder of periodicity and all things temporal. It is forever running out on him; he begins to look upon it with hostility, suspicion, and anger. He must kill time, for otherwise it is certain to kill him.

The older person particularly experiences time in a unique fashion. To him it is a static situation during which nothing happens, nobody comes and nobody goes. If one is active one tends to forget the passage of time, one passes the time, but if one is passively waiting, as so often happens to the aged, one is confronted with the action of time itself. In an analytical essay on Proust, Samuel Beckett, another contemporary novelist and playwright, points out man's dilemma in relationship to time: "There is no escape from the hours and the days. Neither from tomorrow nor from yesterday because yesterday has deformed us, or been deformed by us. Yesterday is not a milestone that has been passed, but a daystone on the beaten track of the years and irremediably part of us, within us, heavy and dangerous. We are not merely more weary because of yesterday, we are other, no longer what we were before the calamity of yesterday." [3]

It is only through identification with, and adherence to, values that are timeless that one can experience positive influences on the aging process. The commitment of the self to ideals and values that transcend the time dimension while at the same time participating in the passing fashion without slavish dedication to it, tends to keep the individual in the stream of life, a member of an ongoing society and not really passé. Certainly, clinically the sick aged show a disregard for time which to me seems to be an attempt to do away with that dimension which is most injurious to the façade, the physical self, the body and its transitory aspect.

In a society which is future oriented, it is the aged who can most afford to live in the present. Yet, most of them find it difficult to do so, not only because of the paucity of the present but also because they cannot help themselves. One of society's functions is to transmit to its individual members its cultural value orientations. Cultural patterns play a large part in determining variables in human behavior. These include not only moral standards and mores but also more subtle patterns of motivation and interpersonal relationships. Variations in judgments and systems of belief, such as religions and philosophies, have been integrated with other cultural patterns such as child-rearing practices by cultural anthropologists. As a result of this synthesis, there is now a clearer understanding of the effects of the one or the other on the individual and the cultural pattern he has developed. The values which the child accepts and incorporates into himself have much to do with defining his attitudes toward aging people and later toward himself as an aging person.

We can readily see, therefore, that in our society, which is future oriented, we incorporate this value and apply it to ourselves in later life. Since the older person has the least future chronologically speaking, he is the least desired member of our group. The older person looks upon himself with disfavor. Much as he would like to live in the present, he is unable because of this incorporated time value. As a matter of fact our society is so child centered and oriented that we tend to treat all adults, and particularly the aged, as children!

The type of individual that our culture values is also germane to our discussion. There are three choices—the individual who is concerned mainly with the feelings, impulses, and desires of the moment, called the "being" type; the one who is principally concerned with action, achievement, and getting things done, called the "doing" type; and the individual referred to as the "being" and "becoming" type who is most interested in inner development and the fullest realization of aspects of personality. Americans are noted for their emphasis on doing. While the Mexican mother, who can be classified as a "being" individual, may happily enjoy her child from day to day, the American mother is too often concerned with his progress. She compares him to other children, and in this way measures her own success as an efficient manager or as a force in the community. What the individual does and what he can or will accomplish are primary questions in our appraisals of people. Getting things done and looking for ways to do something about everything are stock American characteristics despite our cultural Pluralism. Our "doing" orientation leads to our comparing and competing to an extreme and intense degree. Here, again, we can readily recognize the impact of such an orientation on the aging organism. Unable to compete with younger groups at his old rate and speed, he is obviously at a disadvantage. He may have stopped "doing" and so, again, he is beyond our pale.

I am acutely aware that I have said: "He may have stopped 'doing,' " and I must hastily add "doing" in our cultural sense. Being pragmatists, our deeds, actions, and accomplishments must be visible to the naked eye of others, if not to the naked eye, then at least to any of the other physical senses. Should we be reading and asked what we are about or doing, we are much too prone to reply: "Nothing. Just reading." As if thinking, evaluating, or reading is nothing! Even learning, especially learning *per se,* is considered as a time-filler rather than an activity. For want of results we are impatient in the learning. We'll settle for mediocre artistic productions, for instant art, rather than spend the time to be proficient.

Here the psychiatrist may fail his patient in his treatment of him. Since the psychiatrist is a member of our society, he has incorporated the "doing" orientation and may apply this judgment to the aging. He may push for activity, achievement, and action, when the stressing of a "being in becoming" orientation may be of greater service to all concerned. What is true of the psychiatrist may be true of all of us in the behavioral sciences.

Another cultural grouping vital to the human condition which has a tendency to fail the aging is the family, of which I have already made mention. The family, being a universal institution, has definite duties to perform. One of its primary functions is the introduction of new members into society. This is an important part of reproduction for the preservation of the species. The introduction of new members into society in an orderly fashion and the assigning to each one of the individuals born into it the role he will play is a function of the family. Through the family as the mechanism, every society prescribes a place of a rank and order, a destiny, to each child at the moment of birth. The child is assigned an order of birth, a sex, a color, a class, and a culture when born. The family gives the child a place to begin and presents him with a range of roles for selection of his future place in the culture into which he is introduced. Within the mutual love of a family the child best learns the behavior required for his social role and the techniques for adjusting to the situations he will meet as an adult. These are learned through imitation and identification. The family provides the child with a fertile field of object relationships. If these relationships are varied and rich in emotional content, they will most certainly provide the individual with a repertoire of roles that he can enact.

In later life, maladaptive situations may arise from improper role playing because of failure to adapt to, or recognize, a change in status. This is particularly apparent when a parent's dependency on a child in all financial matters, his living space, etc., is complete. In this reversal of the roles they had played earlier, the parent has become the child and the child the parent. Neither is quite prepared for this state of affairs and paradoxically enough, the more well-intentioned each is, the more difficult to carry out the new role properly. The child, accustomed to a set of expectations from his parents, may recognize the parent's inability to perform in the manner the child had learned to expect. Yet, the child, now the man, may be emotionally unable to accept any other relationship with his parent than the one he had established in childhood. He may resent the change and feel a hostility toward him because of the parent's increasing inability to measure up to that standard. Hurts and resentments may appear in either member of this relationship. The child may unconsciously act out on his parents the real or imagined angers which he believes were once perpetrated by them on himself. The parent on the other hand may be totally unable to give up his previous stand and position, or he may realize that he no longer fits his earlier conception of himself. This frustration may push him into inappropriate behavior which is likely to be misunderstood. All sorts of subtle, and not so subtle, situations may arise which help to disrupt the lines of communication that previously existed between the parent and child.

What I am saying is, of course, apparent. In the discussion of the human being versus the man, I have tried to bring into sharper focus the problems of emotional health. In pointing out some of our cultural values, communal-familial attitudes, and some of man's inner struggles I have tried to indicate the magnitude of the human being's job at adaptation. However, the very magnitude bespeaks for a rich and varied spectrum of ways out. The health of our society, and this can be measured by the way it treats its aged, is dependent upon a realistic approach to all of man's ills. It calls for a cessation of debate and the mouthing of clichés and a start of action on the part of the individual and the society that he lives in. We must find a way to answer man's biological needs so that he can be a human being.

I could do much worse, certainly not nobler, than to quote from the faultless prose of Faulkner's Nobel Prize speech: "I believe that man will not merely endure; he will prevail. He is *immortal, not* because he alone among creatures has an inexhaustible voice, but because he has a soul, a spirit capable of compassion and sacrifice and endurance. The poet's, the writer's duty is to write about these things. It is his privilege to help man endure by lifting his heart, by reminding him of the courage and honor and hope and pride and compassion and pity and sacrifice which have been the glory of his past. The poet's voice need not merely be the record of man, it can be one of the props, the pillars to help him endure and prevail."

NOTES

[1] Eugene Ionesco, "Dans les armes da la ville," *Cahiers de la Compagnie Madilua Renaud-Lea-Louis Barrault* (Paris), No. 20 (October, 1957).

[2] Ethel Shanas, *Family Relationships of Older People,* Research Series 20 (New York: Health Information Foundation, 1961), p. iii.

[3] Samuel Beckett, *Proust* (New York: Grove Press, n.d.), p. 57.

INDEX